AN ASSASSIN IN UTOPIA

AN
ASSASSIN
IN
UTOPIA

THE TRUE STORY OF A NINETEENTH-CENTURY
SEX CULT AND A PRESIDENT'S MURDER

SUSAN WELS

PEGASUS BOOKS

NEW YORK LONDON

AN ASSASSIN IN UTOPIA

Pegasus Books, Ltd.
148 West 37th Street, 13th Floor
New York, NY 10018

Copyright © 2023 by Susan Wels

First Pegasus Books cloth edition February 2023

Interior design by Maria Fernandez

Library of Congress Cataloging-in-Publication Data is available.

ISBN: 978-1-63936-312-4

10 9 8 7 6 5 4 3 2 1

Printed in the United States of America
Distributed by Simon & Schuster
www.pegasusbooks.com

For David,

my partner in life and adventure

CONTENTS

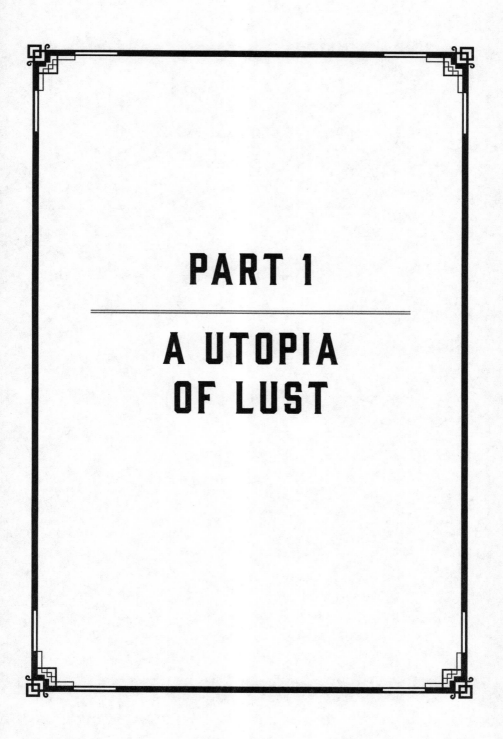

PART 1

A UTOPIA OF LUST

1

THE SECRET HISTORY

ONEIDA, NEW YORK
1869

It was heaven on earth—and, some whispered, the devil's garden. Thousands came by trains and carriages to see this infernal Eden, carved from hundreds of acres of wild woodland. They marveled at orchards bursting with fruit, thick herds of Ayrshire cattle and Cotswold sheep, whizzing mills, and outlandish machinery. They picnicked on spreading lawns, drowsy from plates piled with strawberries and cream and the sweet, soothing voices of singing children.

And they gaped at the people who lived in this place—especially the women, with their queer cropped hair and shamelessly short skirts. The men and women of this strange outpost worked and slept together—without sin, they claimed.

Dozens of committees ran their farms, stables, silk and trap works, childcare, and education. Their babies were raised in a communal Children's House until they were adolescents. Special bonds—between parents and children and men and women—were banned. Every man was married to every woman, and sex, in the Oneida Community, was a holy practice, the key to spiritual perfection.

The tourists, in broad bustles and derby hats, had heard hushed rumors about these exotic customs. They were eager to see this eccentric society for themselves. In an era so prudish that underclothes were "inexpressibles," more than fifty thousand visitors swarmed the Oneida Community in the 1860s, from church groups and journalists to social reformer Susan B. Anthony and President Abraham Lincoln's secretary of state, William Seward.

The residents greeted sightseers with genteel decorum. Friendly and proper in the public eye, they were seen by locals as generous, industrious, and honest neighbors. Nathan Meeker, a writer for the *New York Tribune*, spent three days in the compound, reporting on its "riches, adornment and every comfort." When he questioned residents about their sexual secrets, they were surprisingly frank and free in their responses. "They seemed pleased that I was shocked," he wrote, "or that the world would be." Oneidans flaunted their practices in newspapers they sent to subscribers across the country. Their aim was to convert the world, they said, through the explosive power of the press, and their founder, John Humphrey Noyes, documented every detail of his sexual theories.

Tall and bearded with a halo of red hair, Noyes was the center of this strange universe. He was a magnetic leader—"a born prophet, a missionary in the bone," writer Aldous Huxley later observed. He claimed divine authority over disciples—deciding who would bear children, with whom they would mate, and how. Lovemaking in

Oneida was a refined skill that would take its place among the fine arts, he predicted, ranking above music, painting, and sculpture. Like every art, sexual mastery required training. At Oneida, it was the duty of the oldest, most trusted members to teach the youngest. Men as old as sixty instructed the young girls, and boys were intimately tutored by women past menopause.

Sex, according to Noyes, was a sacrament, the most exquisite method of communing with God and Christ. Group marriage, he preached, was commanded by Jesus and the apostles. It was a radical theology. Many called it depraved, but Noyes, with his charisma and sexual power, fostered, for more than three decades, the most successful utopian experiment in American history.

Still, Oneida's erotic attractions drove hundreds of rogues and misfits to apply for membership. Decades later, some claimed that it planted the seeds of a crime that shook the country to its foundations.

2

A REVOLUTION OF THE SENSES

J ohn Humphrey Noyes, in his youth, was so painfully shy that
he could barely endure the company of women. "I could face a
battery of cannon with less trepidation," he wrote in his diary, than
"a room full of ladies with whom I was unacquainted." Born in 1811
on the Vermont frontier, he was the fourth of nine children of John
Noyes Sr., a former congressman, and flame-haired Polly Hayes,
whose nephew—the feeble, emaciated Rutherford B. Hayes—would
grow up to become the nation's nineteenth president.

John Humphrey was a precocious student, and he enrolled in
Dartmouth College at fifteen. He went on to study law, but his shyness was so paralyzing that he stammered and stuttered through his
first court appearance. Crushingly self-conscious, he felt daunted by
life's uncertainties—until the fall of 1831.

Religious revivals were inflaming New England that year.
Farmers, backwoodsmen, and frontier families flocked to these frenzied emotional festivals—wailing, jumping, barking, and speaking
in tongues in ecstatic expressions of salvation. John Humphrey had
little interest in these displays, but after attending a four-day meeting,
he felt transformed. Dedicating himself to God, he left the law and

entered the Andover Theological Seminary in Massachusetts. He soon found it too hidebound for his religious zeal, so he transferred to Yale Divinity School. A liberal theologian there, Nathaniel Taylor, urged him to seek his own truth, even "if it carries you over Niagara Falls."

Through study and revelation, Noyes found and announced his truth—that he was a perfect human, incapable of sin. God, he said, gave him special protection. But his fellow students declared him crazy, and Yale nearly expelled him. He was stripped of his license to preach, but Noyes began traveling to promote his gospel. In the winter of 1835, the twenty-three-year-old set out to win converts in Massachusetts. When he arrived in Brimfield with a fellow preacher named Simon Lovett, the free-thinking, religiously inflamed towns-people welcomed them with rare enthusiasm. One young woman, inspired by Noyes's shining gray eyes and expressive manner, kissed him seductively when he said goodnight. Panicked by her advances, Noyes, still blushingly shy, fled Brimfield that night, telling no one, and trudged sixty miles, through snow and temperatures below zero, to his family's homestead in Putney, Vermont.

Lovett, meanwhile, remained in Brimfield. One night, two young townswomen—Mary Lincoln and Maria Brown—slipped into that preacher's bed to test the power of their faith. They aimed to prove their religious zeal by showing that the spirit could always win out over physical passion. Predictably, however, Noyes later recounted, "flesh triumphed over spirit." The sexual scandal that resulted—infamously known as the "Brimfield Bundling"—was so explosive that Mary Lincoln fled to a mountainside, stripped off her clothes, and pleaded with God not to set Brimfield afire. The whole sordid episode was blamed on Noyes, although he had no part in it, having fled the town.

But Noyes chose to embrace that notoriety and soothed his own sexual jealousy over the next two years by professing a maverick theology. After a young woman he loved married another, Noyes—filled with anguish and envy—declared that, when God's will was done, marriage and sexual exclusiveness, guilt, and jealousy would no longer exist on earth. "In a holy community," he wrote to a friend, "there is no more reason why sexual intercourse shall be restrained by law than why eating and drinking should be, and there is as little occasion for shame in the one case as in the other." His declaration was published in 1837, to widespread outrage, but Noyes threatened to shout his new theology from the rooftops. "I cared nothing for reputation," he said, and vowed never to join any religion again "unless I was the acknowledged leader."

He was only twenty-six and still a bashful virgin. But in 1838, he married a practical, plain disciple named Harriet Holton. Their marriage, he told her, would be open and unsentimental. They would each be entirely free to love other people. But Harriet, an heiress, would be able to finance his passion for publishing his religious doctrines. The newlyweds spent their honeymoon in Albany, New York, purchasing a printing press.

Newspapers were a thriving business in the 1830s. There were twice as many of them in America as there had been in 1810. Alexis de Tocqueville, a French aristocrat who traveled the young country in 1831, was amazed at the number of periodicals. Every village, he reported, had a newspaper, and the power of the press was impressive. Noyes—God's self-anointed messenger—planned to launch a religious newspaper that would serve as the pulpit of the world.

As early as 1834, he had published a monthly in New Haven called *The Perfectionist*. It quickly attracted more than five hundred subscribers. Three years later, he launched a new paper, *The Witness*, in upstate New York, but he distributed only a few issues. Now, back in Putney, he and Harriet planned to ignite a new religious revival through the printed word. Noyes recruited three of his eight siblings to help with the publication and attracted a small coterie. Within five years, he had more than thirty disciples, who drafted and signed a "Statement of Principles": "John H. Noyes," they pledged, "is the father and overseer whom the Holy Ghost has set over the family thus constituted. To John H. Noyes . . . we submit ourselves in all things"—including carnal relations.

Two followers, Mary and George Cragin, agreed to join John and Harriet Noyes in a group marriage. Other converts soon followed their lead. Although the arrangements were an open secret, townspeople in Putney were outraged after Mary Cragin gave birth to Noyes's twins—Victor and Victoria—and authorities learned about the group's conjugal customs. In October 1847, Noyes was arrested and charged with adultery and fornication. Fearing mob violence, he fled the village.

Weeks later, he found refuge in central New York, with a follower named Jonathan Burt. The owner of a sawmill on Oneida Creek, Burt had read about and passionately embraced Noyes's theology. He invited the Putney group to settle on land adjoining his forty acres of fields and woodland. The property, once owned by the Oneida Tribe, had a barn and a primitive cabin on twenty-three rolling acres. Noyes purchased the land for five hundred dollars and summoned his devoted band.

On an icy March day in 1848, his wife, Harriet, and Mary and George Cragin arrived by train at the Oneida depot. Blasted by the biting wind, the three disciples gazed out at a bleak landscape of barren snowdrifts and bare trees. Soon, bundled into open sleighs, they made their way across frozen fields, where they would transplant the seeds of their new religion.

They were not the first to find fertile prospects in upstate New York. It was a hotbed of eccentric theology. In 1776, an Englishwoman named Ann Lee had settled near Albany with a few followers. She claimed she was the female embodiment of a bisexual God, and her disciples committed to complete celibacy. The sect, known as the Shakers, grew from nine original members to six thousand by the 1840s.

In 1823, in Palmyra, New York, a teenage treasure hunter named Joseph Smith claimed he had found golden plates inscribed with the true gospel. He later alleged that he had translated their hieroglyphics into *The Book of Mormon* and founded a new religion based on local New York legends about a pre-Indian race and the radical practice of polygamy.

Rochester, New York, was the hub of a massive movement founded by William Miller. In 1831, Miller, a Baptist preacher, declared that the world would end in 1843, a prediction widely promoted in a newspaper called *Signs of the Times*. Thanks to an aggressive publicity campaign, as many as a million Americans were waiting for the ecstatic moment when the wicked would burn up and God's children would fly into the sky to meet the Lord. Believers were said to abandon their crops, shut their businesses, and wait for the rapture in white ascension robes. The frenzy of anticipation was so great that the *New York Tribune* published a special issue refuting Miller's predictions. *The American Journal of Insanity* warned that thousands of American citizens had become deranged.

After 1843 came and went without the rapture, Miller revised his calculations and declared that the world would end, instead, on October 22, 1844. On October 21, disciples climbed trees and hills to be closer to heaven, but they were still earthbound on the twenty-third. The celestial flop, known as "The Great Disappointment," was reported in papers around the country. Believers had been "up a few nights watching and making noises like serenading tom cats," wrote the Cleveland *Plain Dealer*, before they gloomily gave up and went to bed.

The region was so aflame with religious fever that it was later called the Burned-Over District. But social and religious experiments had bloomed across the country after the War for Independence. The revolution had shattered institutions and traditions. Charismatic leaders filled the void with new, imaginative social structures. In America's new democracy, any man could do pretty much as he pleased, declared the *New York Tribune*'s founder, Horace Greeley. The individual was the world, said philosopher Ralph Waldo Emerson, and almost every reading man had "a draft of a new community" in his pocket. Inspired by faith in freedom and divine revelation, Americans launched more than seventy utopian experiments between 1800 and 1860.

Some, like New Harmony, Indiana, were secular communities. Founded by a Welshman named Robert Owen in 1825, New Harmony was formed "to promote the happiness of the world" through communal benefits and cooperation. In its first weeks, eight hundred people joined the community, but by 1828, New Harmony was divided into fighting factions and dissolved in discord. Other utopias, like the Kingdom of Matthias, promised disciples divine salvation. Its founder, Matthias, was a carpenter named Robert Matthews. In the early 1830s, he announced that he was God the Father and Jesus Christ. He strolled Manhattan in a coat embroidered with silver stars, carrying a great key to the gates of paradise. Matthias soon moved into a follower's mansion in Westchester, New York, where he attracted a community of devoted converts. In a ritual called the "Fountain of Eden," members of his kingdom would surround him, naked, in a circle while Matthias sluiced them with a sponge and declared them virgins.

The spirit of the age was singularity. As Emerson urged, "A man must be a nonconformist." Life in America in the early nineteenth century was a grand experiment in which every man, he wrote, could build his own world.

In 1848, John Noyes's world on Oneida Creek was bleak and frigid. After they arrived by sled at his crude homestead, Harriet and the Cragins moved into the log hut, with its single room, but soon built shelters for families who followed from New York, Vermont, and Massachusetts. By the end of the year, there were eighty-seven men, women, and children in the new community. Together, they constructed a three-story mansion, with sleeping quarters for a hundred people. The bedrooms were still unfinished in December, so the whole community moved into a thirty-by-thirty-five-foot room on the second floor. They divided the space into twelve compartments, flimsily separated by hanging sheets.

Neighbors whispered about the group sleeping chamber, and scandalous tales multiplied when Noyes published his *First Annual Report*. The document chronicled the assets, members, and history of the Oneida Community. As a branch of the Kingdom of Heaven, Noyes wrote, the society banned private property, monogamy, and sexual shame. Physical union, he maintained, was as holy as the Garden of Eden and God in heaven. And perfecting it as a form of worship, Noyes insisted, required what he called "male continence"—the suppression of ejaculation. Members mastered this technique through careful practice. As Noyes explained, a boatman, approaching a waterfall, would reach "a point on the verge of the fall where he has no control over his course." But if he was willing to learn, "experience will teach him" how to remain, devoutly, in "the region of easy rowing."

Noyes was eager to send his report to a wide audience, including the governor of New York and Horace Greeley at the *Tribune*. He was sure that Oneida's publications would draw legions of new followers. From his printing office at Oneida, he mailed his weekly newspaper, *The Free Church Circular*, to everyone who wanted it, with no charge. He was certain of the power of religious journalism and aimed to create a theocratic daily modeled on Greeley's popular *New York Tribune*.

So when a fire destroyed his press in early 1849, Noyes seized the opportunity to move his publishing office to New York City, where he could reach people of importance and influence. By April of that year, he had set up a satellite branch of the Oneida Community in Brooklyn, on Willow Place—with a brand-new printing press, a staff of reporters, and easy access to railroads, telegraphs, and steamboats. He soon managed to give copies of his *First Annual Report* to Greeley and to Henry James—an eccentric intellectual who was the father of Henry James, the novelist, and William James, the psychologist and philosopher. The senior James was a frequent visitor at Willow Place and encouraged Noyes to share his ideas and theology as widely as possible.

Upstate, too, the Oneida Community won many friends, despite their exotic practices. Members considered themselves a family, and its head was indisputably John Noyes. His power over his followers was so complete that even his own mother called him "teacher and father." He controlled his subjects through a process called "mutual criticism," in which members appeared before a committee that frequently humiliated them with brutal critiques of their personalities and actions. Noyes alone was exempt from criticism—but a challenge soon came from Oneida County's district attorney.

In 1850, New York's governor had appointed a pompous twenty-year-old named Roscoe Conkling to the post. A towering presence at six-foot-three, with cold blue eyes and strawberry blond hair, Conkling had just passed the bar and was still, by a year, too young to vote, but he brilliantly prosecuted cases with great success. Although Conkling lost the next election, his successor, Samuel Garvin, was equally forceful. When he learned of Oneida's sexual habits in 1851, he summoned nine of its members to testify before the grand jury and answer salacious questions. The Community defended itself with a petition signed by many of its neighbors:

> . . . we, the undersigned, citizens of the towns of Vernon and Lenox, are well acquainted with the general character of the Oneida Community, and . . . regard them as honorable businessmen, good neighbors, and quiet, peaceable citizens. We believe them to be lovers of justice and good order, men who mind their own business, and in no way interfere with the rights of their neighbors. We regard them, so far as we know, as persons of good moral character, and we have no sympathy with the recent attempts to disturb their peace.

The *New York Observer*, however, soon attacked the Community for a theology "so loathsome in its details, so shocking to all the sensibilities even of the coarsest of decent people that we cannot defile . . . our paper with their recital." Inflamed by this public denunciation, Garvin launched an aggressive new prosecution. But when leading citizens attested to the value of Oneida's industry, he again relented.

By September 1852, Noyes no longer faced legal threat. Now, with local support, he had complete license to pursue his vision. He coined a revolutionary new term—"free love"—and announced that it was an essential principle of the Oneida Community. Noyes's concept of free love, however, was hardly free—as he explained in a talk he gave that month to Oneida members:

1. The Sexes should sleep apart. Their coming together should not be to sleep but to edify and enjoy. . . .

2. Proposals for love interviews are best made . . . through a third party. . . . It allows of refusals without embarrassment. . . . The third party will also be helpful in arrangements. This method . . . makes love a Community affair.

3. . . . Lovers should come together for an hour or two, and should separate to sleep. If they part before over-excitement, they will think of each other with pleasure afterwards. It is an excellent rule to leave the table while the appetite is still good.

4. [Do not] spend much time in talk. . . . I imagine that the impotence, which some men complain of, may be connected with over-activity of the tongue.

The third parties in Oneida lovemaking were Noyes and his closest confidantes. They held spiritual, and often physical, power over other members of the Community. Oneidans were encouraged to have sexual relations with their superiors, who were often much older than they were. And men and women in the top tier of the fellowship had the unique privilege of initiating young members at puberty. This structured practice of free love reflected the balance between order and ardor, work and play, that energized Oneida.

Men and women worked in groups—on agriculture, manufacturing, housekeeping, and other tasks that changed frequently. And individuals rotated through different jobs, enabling them to discover special talents and sources of inspiration. Each morning at precisely ten, a bell would ring, summoning members for morning coffee, gingerbread, and ten minutes of dancing to fiddle music before returning to their assigned tasks. Noyes—strong and lanky, with a broad, pale forehead and steely eyes—often labored beside them as a blacksmith, mason, tanner, cook, printer, and silk-winder, saying that the devil knew where to find people who fell into ruts.

And he encouraged followers to exploit their unique skills. In 1849, a local hunter and trapper named Sewell Newhouse had joined the Oneida Community. Newhouse was already famous in the region for inventing a superior animal trap. In 1854, Noyes encouraged him to develop trap-making into a mainstay of Oneida's business—first in a small trap shop, then in a large factory fitted with inventive machines. Oneida shipped thousands of Newhouse traps each year, at considerable profit.

By 1861, the Community was so prosperous that it started construction of a new brick Mansion House. It was also drawing hordes of visitors, especially in strawberry season, when members graciously dished out berries and cream to hundreds of drop-in guests. On the Fourth of July that year, nearly a thousand tourists arrived to stroll the grounds, enjoy musical concerts, and feast on copious helpings of strawberries, ice cream, beer, and lemonade. Oneida became such a popular public destination that it was forced to post rules banning graffiti, snooping in private rooms, trampling the flowers, and stealing fruit.

It was also receiving hundreds of requests from people who wanted to become members. Most, Oneidans complained, were "infidels, spiritualists, irresponsible free lovers," and assorted riffraff. Many of them, like William Mills, were attracted by the fantasy of a willing harem at their disposal. Mills joined the Community in the early 1860s with his wife and their three children. After all of Oneida's women rejected his advances, he soon set his sights on its young girls, luring them to his room with candies, sugarplums, wine, and perfume. Community leaders finally had enough of his antics and, one winter night, abruptly heaved Mills and his belongings out an open window of the Mansion House into a snowbank.

With some success, the Community tried to screen candidates by insisting that they show, through active correspondence, their readiness for the labors of communal life. In 1860, Oneidans received a series of letters from a nineteen-year-old applicant named Charles Julius Guiteau. His father, Luther Guiteau, hailed from Utica, New York, and was an ardent admirer of John Noyes. He had moved his family to the Midwest, but he still dreamed of someday joining the Oneida Community. Now his son, Charles—unhappy and failing at his studies in Ann Arbor, Michigan—claimed he was attracted to Oneida "by an irresistible power."

In February 1860, he declared to a Community member, rather arrogantly, his desire to be a medium "by which the truths that have been revealed to me by God, through Mr. Noyes, may be known to all the world." Four months later, after further correspondence, the slight, pale, ginger-haired disciple left Ann Arbor and joined the Oneida Community.

Life under Noyes, however, proved harsher and more taxing than Guiteau expected. While working in the trap shop and kitchen, he startled some co-workers with his odd behavior—he was excitable, with a quick temper, and would mutter mysteriously and gesture wildly when he was angry. Sometimes, he would sit in a corner for hours, alone and silent. Guiteau objected to labor on the grounds that it was degrading and stressful. "Why do you put business responsibilities on me when you know it oppresses me?" he complained to Noyes. He protested that he "felt like a slave . . . bound hand and foot."

Most frustrating to Guiteau was his rejection by Oneida's women, who referred to him, mockingly, as "Git Out." And he felt "crucified" when subjected to mutual criticism. There was much to criticize, according to Noyes—Guiteau, he remarked, was "moody, self-conceited, unmanageable," and "addicted to self-abuse." But Guiteau was sure he was destined for great things. One co-worker heard him say that he "aspired to the position of Mr. Noyes and the other leaders, by gradual promotion." He also had political ambitions. "I should be President of the United States," he declared. He esteemed "Mr. Lincoln and Mr. Greeley," and like them, Guiteau was certain, he was going to be "famous in this world."

By 1863, he had increasing doubts about his commitment to the Community. His real vocation, he suspected, was to become a great newspaper editor like Horace Greeley—although "I have scarcely written an article thus far," he conceded, because "Oneida . . . [was] very uncongenial to my literary ambitions and paralyzing to my brain." In 1865, Guiteau finally announced his plan to leave the Community. "They wanted to make a hard-working businessman of me," he said, "but I could not consent to that, and therefore deemed it expedient to withdraw." Oneidans were only too happy to help him out the door with generous presents of books and a new wardrobe.

Guiteau announced his intention to live thriftily in New York City—on dried beef, carrots, crackers, and lemonade—while he founded a daily religious newspaper called *The Theocrat*. The paper would be, he predicted, "the organ of the deity in this world," supplanting "churches and Christian associations." He had a grand opportunity, he declared, "to do a big thing" for God, humanity, and himself. Although John Humphrey Noyes had been aiming to publish a religious daily for at least a decade, there was room for more than one great theocratic paper, Guiteau reckoned.

He was destined to succeed, he announced, because "I am in the employ of Jesus Christ & Co.: the very ablest and strongest firm in the universe." He was only twenty-three, with no experience whatsoever as a writer or editor, but "under the power of God's inspiration," he reasoned, he might be able to successfully publish a daily paper. Since others had done it, "why may not I?" After all, he noted, "over thirty years ago, Horace Greeley arrived in New York homeless, friendless, and destitute; but now consider his influence on this nation."

Convinced of his fine prospects, Guiteau left the Community on April 3, stealing away after dark to escape another blistering session of criticism. He left a farewell note, hoping that the world would quietly let him follow his inspiration—although a man with such big ideas, he conceded, is "usually deemed insane."

PART 2

THE EDITOR AND
THE ASSASSIN

3

H. GREELEY & CO.

NEW YORK CITY

U nder a bleak gray sky, on the raw, icy morning of April 10, 1841, thirty-year-old Horace Greeley hunched at his desk over columns of type as the first copies of his new daily newspaper, the *New York Tribune*, thundered off the press. With his pallid skin, ivory hair, and old white coat, he looked like a rumpled ghost in the dawn light of his attic office at 30 Ann Street.

Greeley was nearly bankrupt, but he had staked everything—his meager capital and a thousand dollars from a friend—on the launch of a "new morning journal of politics, literature, and general intelligence." Hawked by newsboys for a penny a copy, it debuted, unhappily, on the same day as New York's funeral parade for America's ninth president, William Henry Harrison, who had died, suddenly, just six days earlier.

The dyspeptic sixty-eight-year-old Harrison had been president for just a month. On March 26, only three weeks after his inauguration, he had come down with a bad cold. Despite heroic treatments—including opium, heated suction cups, and a Native American cure using live snakes—Harrison expired on April 4, exactly thirty days after he was sworn in. He was the first American president to die in office. His body was interred in Washington's Congressional Cemetery. And now, in New York City, flags flapped at half mast and a solemn funeral parade made its way down Broadway to City Hall, to the grim tolling of church and fire bells on a cold, wet, wintry day.

The inaugural issue of the *New York Tribune*, mournfully bordered in black, attracted few buyers. Greeley had to give away thousands of copies, at a painful loss. But by the end of that week, he had two thousand paid subscribers, and ten thousand within a year.

It was an enterprise that Greeley was born for. From early childhood, he had adored newspapers and could read any book, even when it was upside down or sideways. Born in 1811 in the backwoods of New Hampshire, he was the third child of Zaccheus and Mary Greeley, impoverished farmers who barely scratched a living from the stony soil. Their first two children had died as infants. Horace himself was a feeble youngster but an expert speller, with a formidable memory. Those talents had little use on his family's farm, where he would wake at dawn to plow corn, potatoes, and hops in thin clothing and bare feet. When their home was impounded for debts, his destitute family moved to Westhaven, Vermont, to a farm on Flea Knoll, with poor land and poisonous water. Greeley fled the farm when he was fifteen, walking some twenty miles to the town of East Poultney to apply for a printing job. The editor of the village newspaper, *The Northern Spectator*, saw his intelligence and took him on, teaching him the art and mechanics of the printing trade.

Greeley read almost every book in the town library and was soon known as a local encyclopedia. He was a champion debater, too, in spite of his high-pitched voice and awkward appearance. Nearly six feet tall and spindly, with a shuffling gait, he wore short pants that flapped around his thin, bare legs and a bucket-shaped cap on a head that seemed too big for his body. But Greeley was a natural at printing and setting type, and he published some issues almost single-handedly.

But in 1830, *The Northern Spectator* failed financially and shut down. After rejoining his family—now living in a crude log cabin in Pennsylvania—he decided, with only ten dollars to his name and the clothes he was wearing, to make his way east to New York City.

On August 18, 1831, Greeley stepped off the boat onto a Manhattan dock. The sun was just coming up over the small metropolis. With two hundred thousand residents, New York was already the nation's financial capital, but it was squalid and filthy. Wild hogs rooted freely in the heaps of garbage and manure that lined the streets. The stench of tanneries, slaughterhouses, glue works, and bone boilers added to the miasma, made even more noxious by the lack of city sewers and indoor plumbing.

Still, New York was teeming with opportunity and newcomers from rural villages and overseas. Jobs were plentiful, if you had connections. Greeley, however, had no friends or letters of introduction. So he found a cheap bed in a boardinghouse for $2.50 a week and went door to door, looking for work. After two days, he got a job setting type for new versions of the Book of Genesis and the New Testament. His co-workers called him "The Ghost," because of his pallor and white hair. But he was the best hand in the office—until its business fell off in late fall, and he lost his job.

Greeley scrambled for work the next year, through the hellish "cholera summer" of 1832. "The season was sultry," he remembered, "the city filthy," and the water was pestilential. New York, he wrote, had "worse water than any other city of its size on earth." Every day, privies dropped a hundred tons of human waste into its sandy soil. It seeped into the water table and poisoned the city's wells. By early July, thousands of New Yorkers were fleeing a cholera outbreak. Roads were clogged, according to a reporter, with "stage coaches, livery coaches, private vehicles and equestrians, all panic struck, fleeing from the city," while "oceans of pedestrians trudged outward with packs on backs" and steamboats carried refugees up the Hudson. Only half the city's population remained, and of those, thirty-five hundred perished. There were more corpses than coffins, and bodies lay unburied in the streets.

Trade was dead, too, Greeley wrote, "and industry languished during that fatal summer." But inventive New Yorkers were soon back in business. One of them, a young medical student named Horatio Sheppard, wanted to invest in publishing. He had inherited money and intended to launch, for the first time, a daily newspaper that was cheap enough for ordinary consumers. At the time, only prosperous New Yorkers could afford dailies, at ten dollars for a year's subscription to dry shipping, financial, and political news. But mass literacy was on the rise, and it was time, Sheppard reckoned, for a paper as cheap as the oranges, apples, and oysters that street vendors peddled for a penny a piece.

That fall, Greeley and another young printer named Francis Story decided to start their own company and publish Sheppard's daily newspaper. Called *The Morning Post*, it would be hawked on the streets, like candy, by a pioneering new sales force—a cheeky band of children called "newsboys"—for two cents a copy. The first issue was published on New Year's Day 1833. It was a disastrous start. A furious blizzard froze the city and the army of shivering newsboys, who made few sales. Greeley and Story then dropped their price to a penny, but the venture failed. So they stopped the presses, ending the brief run of America's first penny paper, and Sheppard returned to the practice of medicine.

There was more bad news that year. Story went boating in the East River and drowned. But their printing business carried on, now called H. Greeley & Co. Twenty-two-year-old Greeley had big ambitions. American journalism was changing fast. *The Morning Post* had lasted just a month, but in September, another young printer named Benjamin Day launched America's second penny newspaper, called *The New York Sun*. It was a huge success. *The Sun*'s colorful news and slogan—"It Shines for All"—captivated the general public. *The Sun* covered ordinary New Yorkers, divorces, suicides, amusements, and grisly murders. Within a year, it had more readers than any daily newspaper in the world.

So Greeley decided to launch his own popular weekly publication. Unlike *The Sun*, he took pains to point out, it would not be "the Largest Paper Ever Published" or the "Cheapest Periodical in the World." Instead, Greeley's weekly, called *The New Yorker*, would feature in-depth political news, literary articles, and essays he would write on subjects from farming to capital punishment. Greeley printed the first issue in March 1834. It sold only a hundred copies, but readership jumped to twenty-five hundred in six months. It was "incomparably," an observer judged, "the best newspaper of its kind that had ever been published in this country."

Greeley was its busy editor and scribbler in chief, penning a torrent of essays, editorials, and poetry above the initials "H.G." One typesetter found him "sitting at a small table at one side of the little composing room, writing furiously," with "barely time to look up." Greeley had little time or talent for business, either, and the magazine never became profitable.

So he took other jobs. He had been passionate about politics since he was a child and supported the anti-Jacksonian Whig Party, which rejected slavery and supported many social reforms. Scores of newspapers at the time were published by political campaigns, and Greeley wrote for a daily Whig journal in New York State. The Whig Party was an upstart, formed in 1834 to oppose President Andrew Jackson's policies. As America's seventh president, elected in 1829, Jackson, a Democrat, supported slavery and the displacement of Native Americans. He also defied the elites and sought to strengthen popular democracy. He had served as a governor, general, and member of Congress and was a national hero after the 1815 Battle of New Orleans. Gaunt and scarred by sword and bullet wounds, Jackson, called "Old Hickory," was worshipped by his Democratic supporters. But opponents hated him so much for expanding presidential power that they called him King Andrew I. One demented critic fired two pistols at him, point-blank. Jackson survived only because the guns misfired, in the first attempt to assassinate a US president.

In 1832, Jackson won a second term. His vice president, Martin Van Buren, was a diminutive dandy known as the "Little Magician" and "Sly Fox" for his mastery of political intrigue. Van Buren, the son of a tavern keeper, had served as senator and secretary of state. He was a cunning tactician and a smooth operator. With his bright blond hair, orange cravat, and yellow gloves, he cut a dashing figure in the capital and soon became the president's right-hand man.

When Jackson was reaching the end of his second term, he chose Van Buren as his successor. The Little Magician was elected president in 1836 and inaugurated in March 1837, promising to follow in Jackson's colossal footsteps. He expected to be as popular as his predecessor. But thirteen days later, America's economy collapsed.

After two years of economic expansion, the price of cotton fell sharply, due to increased supply and falling demand. Cotton sales at the time were a cornerstone of America's economy, and the cascading effects of the cotton crash led to a financial panic. Factories shut down, ships idled in port, banks and companies failed, and a third of all workers in eastern cities were unemployed. "The country was in a wretched condition," Greeley reported, and that winter, New York City was the capital of beggary and destitution. Families huddled in cellars and stables. "I saw three widows," he wrote, "with as many children, living in an attic on the profits of an apple-stand." They earned less than three dollars a week, and the landlord pocketed a third of that. Poverty was "a hard master anywhere," he added, but nowhere else saw such suffering and desperation.

It was a "year of ruin," and Greeley barely kept his company afloat. But his prospects were salvaged by a power broker named Thurlow Weed. Affable and energetic, Weed was an Albany editor and shrewd politico who was plotting to expand the power and reach of the Whig Party. The depression had turned the tide against Van Buren's Democrats, who refused to support government relief. For the first time, voters in New York City, enraged by economic conditions, elected a Whig mayor. To build on that success, Weed asked Greeley to edit a new campaign weekly to help elect Whig candidates statewide. The paper was called *The Jeffersonian*, since Whigs claimed to be true followers of Thomas Jefferson's ideals.

At twenty-seven, Greeley was already stooping and nearsighted, but he took on the backbreaking challenge of editing two different weeklies in two locations—*The Jeffersonian* in Albany and *The New Yorker* in New York City. In 1838, there were no trains to connect the towns, nearly 150 miles apart, so Greeley shuttled between them by sleigh, carriage, and overnight steamboat. He spent Saturday nights battling bedbugs on the Albany boat, printed *The Jeffersonian* on Tuesday, then steamed back to Manhattan and printed *The New Yorker* on Friday. The next night, he steamed for Albany again. It was a frantic schedule. But *The Jeffersonian* was successful, with a circulation of fifteen thousand, and it helped elect William Seward as the first Whig governor of New York.

Whig officials were so pleased that, after the election, they asked Greeley to edit a new weekly for the 1840 presidential campaign. Van Buren was running for a second term and expected to win handily, despite continuing hard times. At fifty-seven years old, he was secretive, shrewd, and impeccably dressed. The Whigs scoffed that he was an effeminate dandy cinched up in corsets, but the Whig candidate, William Henry Harrison, had his own flaws.

Former president John Adams called Harrison indiscreet and vain, with a shallow mind. He was long past his greatest days, but he had a distinguished background. His father was a signer of the Declaration of Independence, and Harrison was raised on a grand Virginia plantation. He joined the army in 1791 and won fame in 1811 at the Battle of Tippecanoe. As governor of the Indiana Territory, Harrison had built a twenty-six-room mansion on three hundred acres. But in 1812, when President James Madison named him brigadier general and commander of the Army of the Northwest—a territory that included parts of today's Ohio, Indiana, Illinois, Michigan, Wisconsin, and Minnesota—Harrison moved to Ohio, where he owned a farm that had a mansion as well as a log cabin. He went on to serve as a congressman and diplomat before retiring from public life. After years of living in high style, Harrison had accumulated many debts, so he took a job as the clerk of courts for Hamilton County, Ohio. He was hardly a pauper, though. His county clerkship earned him six thousand dollars a year—more than the salary of America's vice president. In 1836, he had run, unsuccessfully, as one of four Whig candidates for president against Van Buren.

This time, in Harrison's second race for the White House, Van Buren's campaign mocked him as a demented granny who would be happy with a barrel of hard cider in his log cabin. It was a harsh attack, but the Whigs turned it to their own advantage. Harrison may have been the plainest of men, with no great or shining talents, but he was modest, retiring, and a man of the people. Whigs lashed Van Buren, by contrast, as a man who ate with a golden spoon at the expense of taxpayers. Many voters feared that the country would be controlled by a ruling class if Van Buren won a second term, and the Whigs played on that anxiety. They promoted Harrison as the people's candidate, proudly symbolized by the image of a log cabin and a barrel of hard cider.

Greeley's new campaign weekly, called the *Log Cabin*, debuted in May 1840. At two cents a copy, it was an instant hit, with a national distribution of nearly fifty thousand subscribers. By July, it had sixty thousand, and it reached a peak of nearly ninety thousand before the election. Its publisher—H. Greeley & Co.—could barely keep up with demand as it fueled one of the great political insurgencies in American history.

In 1840, more Americans than ever were entitled to cast a ballot. For the first time, nearly all white men were eligible to vote, as long as they paid their taxes or served in the militia. Property ownership requirements had been abolished. As a result, thousands of new, lower-income voters swelled the rolls. To win them over, Greeley helped launch the nation's first grassroots political campaign.

Before 1840, campaigns were restrained affairs aimed at elite voters. But the Whigs set out to orchestrate massive political events in communities across the country, funded, in part, by wealthy merchants connected to Thurlow Weed. Supporters erected log cabins in hundreds of towns and cities, including a mammoth structure in Manhattan that could hold nearly five hundred people. They also created huge balls made of paper and tin—some of them more than ten feet wide, covered with political slogans—and rolled them from town to town, symbolizing Harrison's growing momentum and adding the phrase "keep the ball rolling" to the American idiom. In Maryland, a hundred thousand people packed a Harrison rally, and in upstate New York, a nine-mile-long Harrison parade featured a hundred men on horseback and more than four hundred wagons. Floats, flags, banners, bonfires, barbecues, live bears, and human curiosities like Big Jim Porter—who, at seven foot eight, was known as the world's tallest man—attracted enormous crowds, who were thrilled by the spectacle and gargantuan quantities of free food. In Wheeling, then located in Virginia, one rally dished out three hundred hams, fifteen hundred pounds of beef, a thousand pounds of cheese, and more than four thousand pies. Drink flowed freely, too, at many events, with hard cider and whiskey supplied by a distiller named E. G. Booz.

Almost every town in the country had a Harrison glee club, singing songs that Greeley wrote and published on the back page of the *Log Cabin*. Harrison's running mate was former Virginia governor John Tyler, and "Tippecanoe and Tyler Too!" was one of the hit tunes of the campaign. Greeley, in awkward excitement, often led crowds in singing Harrison anthems—his white coat flapping, his white hat pushed back on his pale head, and both arms and one leg beating time in a clumsy musical display. The Harrison/Tyler campaign also pioneered political swag, giving away Tippecanoe soap, flags, medals, tobacco, handkerchiefs, ribbons, and neckties.

More voters turned out in 1840 than for any previous election. Harrison won with 53 percent of the popular vote and over three-quarters of the electoral college. More than any other campaigner, Greeley helped the Whigs capture the presidency and control of Congress—although "I doubt," he noted, that "Harrison ever heard my name." Still, his success with the *Log Cabin* and the election gave Greeley national fame and his own platform as a powerful writer, editor, publisher, and politico.

With the campaign papers behind him, Greeley was poised for his next venture. Newspaper readership in America had tripled since 1830. Penny papers were now published across the country, turning ordinary Americans into avid consumers of national and local news. In New York, a journalist noted, almost every driver and porter had a newspaper in his hands when he wasn't working. Newsboys were everywhere in the city, now the fastest-growing metropolis, with more than three hundred thousand residents. Newspapers competed aggressively for their attention, but the *New York Herald* dwarfed them all, with fifty-five thousand readers. Launched in 1835 by a spirited Scotsman named James Gordon Bennett, the *Herald* targeted "the great masses of the community—the merchant, mechanic . . . the private family as well as the public hotel—the journeyman and his employer." The *Herald* attracted readers of every class and station with shocking stories, police reports, and gossip about the doings of the social set. But none of the New York papers, Greeley observed, sought to elevate readers with thoughtful opinion and quality, independent reporting of national news.

So, on April 3, 1841, he announced his plan for a sophisticated new daily, the *New York Tribune*, promoting the public's moral, social, and political well-being. Only one day later, Harrison was dead, and John Tyler, "His Accidency," became president. It was a shattering blow to Greeley, who had toiled to put Harrison in the White House. The president's sudden death, he despaired, cast a gloom over the whole country. But the *New York Tribune* survived, and a weekly version, mailed to subscribers across America, was an instant hit. "Fame is a vapor," Greeley reflected, but his own renown was spreading fast across the nation.

His workload was punishing. It was usually midnight before Greeley left his office and walked a few blocks to the house he shared with his wife of five years, Mary Cheney. She was a teacher from Connecticut, and they had met in 1834. Both were living, at the time, in a New York boardinghouse devoted to the principles of Sylvester Graham. A Presbyterian minister, Graham counseled his followers to abandon coffee, tea, tobacco, meat, alcohol, condiments, and spices. Known as the "prophet of bran bread and pumpkins," Graham inspired the graham cracker and prescribed an austere diet of fruits, vegetables, cold water, and coarse bread. Such dietary discipline, combined with hard mattresses and cold showers, he preached, would inhibit sexual urges and their hideous effects, including dangerous inflammation of the viscera and sudden death. Married people, he advised, should have sex just once a month, and self-abuse, he warned, was the most deadly form of gratification, leading to insanity, bad breath, and a broken body covered with blisters and running sores.

Twenty-year-old Mary Cheney, according to a friend, was "crazy for knowledge" and a devoted follower. Greeley, too, was strangely attracted to Graham's regimen. He had long avoided coffee, tea, and alcohol, but he never gave up meat, and his appetite was famously excessive. Greeley "ate furiously, and fast, and much," according to observers, devouring everything in front of him. One evening, a hostess handed him a big platter of doughnuts, and Greeley absent-mindedly ate every one of them instead of passing them to the other guests. Still, he was drawn to Graham's theories and in love with Mary Cheney. When she moved to North Carolina to teach in 1836, he followed her there and married her that July.

The Greeleys immediately went back to Manhattan, where Mary taught and kept a Graham table, with spartan meals of beans, potatoes, boiled rice, and bread and butter. The couple dined frequently with a young preacher named Thomas Sawyer, whose Universalist congregation supported reason, social reform, and communal good. Greeley, a Universalist, attended Sawyer's Bible class and went to church on Sundays, although he often slept through the entire sermon.

In 1841, he met another devoted Universalist—a young man, one year older, named Phineas Taylor Barnum. Born in Connecticut, Barnum had been named for his grandfather, a practical joker, and he had published a Universalist newspaper in his home state. In 1832, Barnum had been convicted of libeling a deacon in his editorial screeds, and he spent two months in the Danbury jail. He soon moved to New York City, where he sold Bibles, ran a grocery store, managed a boardinghouse, and wrote advertising copy. Emphatic and energetic, with brown curls framing his cherubic features, P. T. Barnum became close friends with Greeley, whom he described as a "gangling, wispy-haired, pasty-cheeked man with the face of somebody's favorite grandmother."

In 1841, however, Barnum was facing hard times. "My recent enterprises," he confessed, "had not . . . been productive." It was time for him to make a decisive move. So he purchased a collection of curiosities housed in a five-story building, a stone's throw from Greeley's office. The huge edifice, at the corner of Ann Street and Broadway, exhibited stuffed birds and reptiles, wax figures, a live sloth, and a card-playing dog named Apollo. The musty museum had been losing money, but Barnum applied his prodigious marketing talents.

He changed the attraction's name to "Barnum's American Museum" and added mechanical figures, automatons, jugglers, ventriloquists, living statuary, tableaux, dioramas, panoramas, knitting machines, glassblowers, and live snakes, primates, and grizzly bears. He even had a taxidermy shop, where customers could drop off their dead pets and pick them up, a few hours later, stuffed and mounted. His museum opened on New Year's Day 1842, and one of his first major exhibits was a "Great Model of Niagara Falls, with Real Water!" Hundreds of honeymooners and others who could not afford to travel to Niagara flocked to the attraction, only to discover that the model was just eighteen inches tall. "I felt considerably sheepish about it," Barnum admitted, but "they had the whole museum to fall back on for twenty-five cents."

His patrons could also ogle unusual human beings, such as Charles Stratton, a four-year-old prodigy who had only grown one inch since he was six months old. Stratton was just over two feet tall and weighed fifteen pounds, and Barnum first introduced him—as "General Tom Thumb"—on Thanksgiving Day 1842. He menda-ciously said that the tot was eleven years old, and the tiny, precocious performer charmed customers with his singing, acting, and comic timing. He was so small that Barnum could easily hold him in the palm of his hand or hide him in his coat pocket. "It was a great act," Stratton later recalled, and the crowds loved it.

Barnum was a master at capturing public attention. He draped the museum with billowing banners and stationed powerful floodlights on the roof. On a third-floor balcony, overlooking the street, he seated a brass band—the worst musicians he could find—to raucously ser-enade the crowds and drive them, out of earshot, into the building. Inside, they would enter a great hall filled with grotesque creatures and relics, including moldy panoramas and small, dilapidated models of the world's great cities. When they reached the roof, which Barnum advertised as a restful garden, they would find a couple of stunted cedar trees and some wilted flowers.

Barnum was the first to admit that he was a con man, a prince of trickery and deceit, but the public applauded his shameless hoaxes. The novelist Henry James and thousands of other New Yorkers loved losing themselves for hours on end in his garish, bewitching "dusty halls of humbug."

In 1842, Greeley also crossed paths with Ralph Waldo Emerson, an essayist, philosopher, and Boston intellectual. Emerson was famous as a "startlingly original thinker," with "a thunderstorm" of eloquent ideas. Tall, blue-eyed, and romantically handsome, he was eight years older than Greeley, but they shared a strong commitment to reforming and reinventing society. The awful winter of 1837—when impoverished New Yorkers starved or froze to death—had made a haunting impression on Greeley. Was suffering like that inevitable? he wondered. Was there a remedy? He believed there was. The answer, Greeley decided, was social reorganization—cooperative ownership, collective labor, and communal living.

Emerson's cousin—a Unitarian minister named George Ripley—was also deeply affected by the hellish winter of 1837. A social reformer like Greeley, he took action in 1841 by forming a collective utopian community in West Roxbury, Massachusetts. Called Brook Farm, it embodied bold visions of work, education, and leisure, combining "the thinker and the worker, as far as possible," in each individual. The rural retreat attracted a small group of intellectual and artistic residents. It was, Emerson noted, one of "numberless projects of social reform" and new radical communities around the country. But Brook Farm, John Humphrey Noyes later judged, was the model and "chief of all the experiments." Its founders, he wrote, were "bewitched with the idea . . . that it is possible to combine many families into one great home. . . . The nucleus was small in number and well knit together by mutual acquaintance and spiritual sympathy."

Its residents, visitors, and supporters included Emerson, Ripley, Henry David Thoreau, Nathaniel Hawthorne, and the pioneering feminist Margaret Fuller—possessed of a "rich and brilliant genius," according to Emerson. They joined an assorted "knot of dreamers" composed of Harvard graduates, poets, musicians, philosophers, and reformers. Together, they all farmed and shared meals, lectures, and leisure hours filled with games, readings, costume parties, sledding, skating, and theatricals. Each resident bought a lifelong share in the community for five hundred dollars or equivalent labor. After that, a member explained, "the Greek and Latin, the aesthetic philosophy" and "the singing and dancing were thrown in."

Life at Brook Farm, Emerson wrote, was a constant picnic and miniature French Revolution. Greeley followed its progress very closely. Each week, he sent the residents copies of the *New York Tribune*, and in July 1842, he wrote to Ripley, asking if his wife, Mary, could spend some time in the community. In six years of marriage, she had lost two children and suffered two painful miscarriages, including a "cruel surgical delivery" that had left her bedridden for six months. Now, Mary was anxious, angry, depressed, and losing her sight. She was recuperating in Watertown, near Boston, where she was "quite solitary" and lonesome. A few weeks at Brook Farm, he was certain, would give her the companionship and mental stimulation she needed for the "sure and rapid" recovery of her health and vision.

Soon, Greeley himself paid a visit to Brook Farm, where he gave a lecture. He looked like a phantom, one resident said—with hair "so light that it was almost white" and a face that "was entirely colorless, even the eyes." Greeley was grateful to Brook Farmers for hosting Mary, and he admired their idealistic experiment. But he worried about the community's future. Brook Farm's utopia "is adapted," Greeley wrote, "only to angelic natures," and the "entrance of one serpent," he feared, might be fatal.

4
MUGGLETONIANS AND MYSTICS

Margaret Fuller clutched her spectacles and scanned the room, her crooked spine jutting her neck forward like a bird of prey. Pale and plain, with brown ringlets and nearsighted gray eyes, she draped a colored shawl over her black dress and sloping shoulders. It was a Wednesday morning, and the room was filled with women waiting to be animated by her kinetic mind. Fuller's intellect, one listener said, "was like the sun shining on plants," her glance as penetrating as an electric shock.

Thirty women that day had paid the princely price of ten dollars to attend this lecture and a series of other elevating "Conversations" with Fuller. In 1842, when educated Boston women had little to engage them beyond religion and domestic duties, Fuller aimed to expand and cultivate their minds through enlightening discussions about literature, mythology, art, and Eastern religions. In the presence of her opulent and fertile mind, Emerson enthused, "You stretch your limbs and dilate to your utmost size."

She was the best-read woman in America. Fuller had studied Greek and Latin since she was six years old, and her intellect had dazzled educators and peers. Still, as a woman, she was barred from attending

Harvard, but she was a member of the well-known Transcendental Club, a brilliant group of Cambridge intellectuals. Her fellow Transcendentalists—including Thoreau and Emerson—rejected organized religion and turned to nature for inspiration. Fuller edited their journal, called *The Dial*. She also visited Brook Farm—loosely based on Transcendentalist principles—where she read her latest essays to reverent acolytes and slept in a special room that was reserved for her.

Brook Farmers were leading a bohemian, romantic life—building a model, they hoped, for a new society. Bearded young men in belted tunics and young women with calico dresses and loose hair shared the same rights and responsibilities—from scrubbing floors and shelling peas to voting on community issues. In 1843, there were seventy members and scores of applicants, but the farm's financial picture was alarming. Its deficit exceeded a thousand dollars, its acreage yielded few products to sell, and many members lacked the capital to buy shares in the community.

Horace Greeley offered a solution. He was enchanted with the utopian theories of a Frenchman named Charles Fourier. A traveling salesman and amateur sociologist, Fourier argued that human beings have twelve common passions and exactly 810 character traits. He dreamed of organizing labor—and sexual love—according to his new taxonomy. If workers did a variety of jobs for which they were uniquely suited, he believed, they would find pleasure in their duties. And, by consulting special card files to find sexual partners with matching predilections—from homosexuality to orgies and incest—their liberated passions would boost their productivity and joy. People should work, live, and love together, he wrote, in four-story buildings called phalansteries, each with ideally 1,620 residents. Their children would be raised communally, and men and women would have equal rights in self-contained societies that he called "phalanxes."

Five years before he died, in 1832, Fourier met a young American philosophy student in Paris. The young man's name was Albert Brisbane, and he soon became a fierce disciple and evangelist of Fourier's theories. In 1840, Brisbane published a book about Fourier's grand vision—strategically leaving out the Frenchman's amorous ideas and his head-scratching predictions that the oceans would turn into lemonade and every woman would have four simultaneous husbands. The book, entitled *The Social Destiny of Man*, attracted wide readership in America. Greeley published articles in *The New Yorker* on Fourier's theories. He also printed Brisbane's magazine, called *The Future*, and featured his frequent columns in the *Tribune*.

Fourier's ideas soon "swept the nation," according to John Humphrey Noyes, who used some of the Frenchman's theories to plan the Oneida Community. With Greeley's encouragement, Brook Farmers began taking note. In late 1843, their library carried Brisbane's newspaper, called *The Phalanx*. The next spring, they officially transformed their bucolic community into the Brook Farm Phalanx. Its goal, according to a member named Charles Dana, was "nothing less than Heaven on Earth" and the conversion of the world.

They soon expanded their membership to disciples of Fourier, including shoemakers, carpenters, and other tradesmen. Some of the old guard left the community, mourning their elite paradise lost. One newcomer, seventeen-year-old John Codman, mocked these dissenters as "extinct volcanoes of Transcendental nonsense and humbuggery" who refused to live and work with people who had never studied Latin and Greek.

The new members managed to improve the farm's agriculture and commercial industry. Residents still played, painted, and picnicked in their rustic paradise, but they also held weekly Fourier meetings and classes on his social structure. Soon, they started building a phalanstery. The three-story complex, ringed by porches and piazzas, would include libraries, a chapel, a massive kitchen, and a dining hall that could seat four hundred utopians.

It was almost finished in 1846. On a cold evening that March, they held a noisy party to celebrate when suddenly, amid the dancing and merrymaking, someone screamed that the phalanstery was on fire. By time they raced through snowy fields and formed a bucket brigade, flames, ignited by a basement stove, were shooting out of its upper windows, and the edifice soon collapsed into a heap of embers. It was the cataclysmic ending of Brook Farm. Burned out and bankrupt, the community broke up. "It was not discord," Codman reflected. "It was music stopped." Charles Dana soon found a job at the *New York Tribune*. Ripley, too, found a perch with Greeley, writing editorials for the paper and publishing a Fourier journal from the *Tribune* building.

Greeley remained devoted to Fourier. He invested thousands of dollars in other social experiments, including the North American Phalanx in New Jersey. It prospered for more than a decade by producing and selling dried fruits and the first boxed cereal in the United States. But another community he launched, in the mountains of Pennsylvania, failed quickly. The Sylvania Association was meant to be a working-class paradise, but its soil was poor, winters were brutal, and its members were incompetent slackers. These projects, Greeley had to admit, attracted "the conceited, the crotchety, the selfish, the headstrong, the pugnacious, the unappreciated, the played-out, the idle, and the good-for-nothing. . . . They are sure to jump into any new movement," he grumbled, "as if they had been born . . . to direct it." But by 1849, America's Fourier fever had led to the creation of thirty-four phalanxes, and John Humphrey Noyes—inspired by Fourier, Brook Farm, and Christian theology—was building his own heaven on earth in rural Oneida, New York.

Margaret Fuller had a skeptical view of these experiments. "Utopia is impossible to build up," she wrote, and whenever she heard the name of a new community, "all my quills," she recoiled, "rise and sharpen." Brook Farm's romantic charms enticed her for occasional visits, but what really attracted her was the gritty, freewheeling chaos of New York City. In 1844, Greeley invited her to join his paper's staff as literary editor, penning front-page columns in the *New York Tribune* on any subjects she chose, from French novels to voting rights and female prison reform.

Greeley extended another, more personal invitation for Fuller to move into the sprawling, ramshackle new home he shared with his wife, Mary, in Turtle Bay. Mary had met Fuller in Boston and admired her knowledge and intellect. It was her idea that Fuller should join Greeley's staff and live with them and their baby son, Pickie, in the farmhouse they had recently rented. The creaky old property—which Greeley called "Castle Doleful"—was secluded and thoroughly rundown. It was close to the bustling center of town but could only be reached by a dark, narrow, private lane. With eight acres of fruit and shade trees, on the banks of the East River, it was "entirely charming," Fuller said—"completely in the country," with the busy, rushing world around it.

She loved the tranquility of the place and happily accepted their invitation. Life with the Greeleys, however, was far from peaceful. It was unappetizing to share meals with people who only ate beans, plain puddings, and boiled potatoes. She and Greeley barely knew each other, and the two of them bickered almost every day. Fuller liked comfort and luxury, while he exulted in "bare walls and rugged fare." When he criticized her for drinking strong tea and coffee, she sharply warned him never to lecture her, and he dropped the subject.

But over time, their antagonism turned into affection, and they all loved little blue-eyed Pickie. He was the Greeleys' third child, but only the first to live past infancy. He was eight months old when Fuller moved in—healthy and playful, with hair that was "the color of sunshine." She was soon his favorite companion—teaching him, telling him stories, and swinging with him on a hammock as they looked out over a dappled lawn lapped by the river. She was his "teacher, playmate, and monitor," and Pickie adored her. Greeley, moved by her warmth, soon embraced Fuller as a "great-souled friend," and she conceded that Greeley, despite his clownish and slovenly manners, had the heart of "a nobleman."

He believed in her abilities "to a surprising extent," she said, and they became "true friends." Fuller was the only woman on the *Tribune*'s staff, with a desk in the newsroom, and Greeley paid her well for her popular, provocative essays. She lived with the Greeleys for more than a year. And then, when a wealthy family offered to take her to Europe with them, she jumped at the chance. Greeley said he would pay her for any articles that she wrote abroad. So Fuller sailed, in August 1846, as America's first female foreign correspondent—reporting from a continent that was smoldering with discontent, on the brink of bloody revolutions.

———

By 1848, immigrants were pouring into New York City, escaping starving Ireland and violent uprisings in Europe to win democratic reforms. Living in crowded tenements, on streets piled with filth and garbage, the newcomers were vulnerable to contagion. That year, after a ship arrived with passengers who had been exposed to cholera, the deadly disease raced through the city's wards and ravaged the Eastern Seaboard over the next two years.

The epidemic was so widespread that, in August 1849, America's twelfth president, Zachary Taylor, called for a national day of fasting and prayer to stanch the outbreak. Ironically, almost a year later, Taylor celebrated a steamy Fourth of July with cooling servings of cherries and ice milk. Over the next few days, the sixty-five-year-old former general was plagued with terrible nausea and diarrhea. Opium, bleeding, and blistering had no effect, and he died on July 9, a year and three months after he was sworn in. Taylor was the second American president to die in office. Although his doctors had diagnosed him with cholera morbus—not the Asiatic cholera that was sweeping the country—many in Washington believed that he had succumbed to the epidemic. His sudden demise stunned the country, and cholera panic swept the capital.

In New York City, the epidemic killed more than five thousand—including, in 1849, little Pickie Greeley. His parents had lost three other children, but "we were never utterly desolate till now," his father grieved. Greeley poured out his anguish in a letter to Fuller, who wept "rivers of tears" when she learned the news. She had secretly born a child herself one year earlier, fathered by a penniless Roman count named Giovanni Ossoli. He was ten years younger than Fuller and active in a revolution to unite Italy, which was then split into states governed by Spain, Austria, and the pope. Fuller reported on and supported the revolution, and she grew close to Ossoli during her time in Rome. In December 1847, in her late thirties, she discovered she was carrying his child. Two years later, the revolution collapsed, and the couple, afraid for their lives, decided to flee to America in 1850 with their two-year-old son, Nino.

When the family boarded the freighter *Elizabeth* that May, Fuller felt "absurdly fearful," with vague expectations of crisis. But the first days at sea were calm and beautiful. Fuller celebrated her fortieth birthday, and all was well—until the captain suddenly died of smallpox and the first mate, Mr. Bangs, assumed command. They were barely past Gibraltar when little Nino, too, became gravely ill with smallpox, but he survived.

Finally, on July 18, they sighted the New Jersey coast. Bangs said they would be in New York Harbor the next morning. But the wind picked up, and at midnight, powerful gales began slamming the wooden brig. The *Elizabeth*, with its heavy cargo of Italian marble, struck a sandbar near Fire Island. The impact tossed passengers out of their bunks, and the marble tore a hole in the ship's hull. Waves crashed over the freighter, toppling its masts and carrying away life-boats. By morning, the crew and passengers could see the shoreline two hundred yards away. Some tried to swim to safety, but Fuller refused to be separated from her little boy. Finally, as the brig was breaking up, a sailor grabbed the child from her and plunged into the heavy seas. Fuller was last seen on deck, sitting in a white night-gown, as a giant wave broke over the splintering ship and swept her out into the ocean. Nino's dead body washed up on shore, but Fuller and Ossoli were never found.

In that season of grief, mourning the deaths of his child and his friend in a savage year, Greeley turned to strange sources of consolation. Mary, agonizing over Pickie's death, was drawn to the prospect of supernatural contact with her dead son. Greeley, too, was attracted to the promise of an unseen world. Forever curious, he believed in the "superusual"—events that he had no ability to explain.

That year, two young sisters in Hydesville, New York—sixty-four miles west of Syracuse—had caused a sensation by talking with spirits of the dead. They had first made contact two years earlier, according to witnesses, when they heard knocking noises in their bedroom. After hearing the sounds for many nights, twelve-year-old

Kate, as a joke, made a similar noise by snapping her fingers. She was shocked when the snaps were answered by raps that exactly repeated the sounds she made and stopped when she did. Her fifteen-year-old sister, Maggie, had the same experience. Their mother, Margaret Fox, then asked the invisible knocker to rap ten times, and it did so. She asked it to rap out the ages of her children, and it did, precisely.

Frightened, the family asked their next-door neighbor, Mary Redfield, to witness the strange occurrence. She agreed, thinking it was all a joke. "Mrs. Fox met me at the bedroom door," she recalled, "and she and the girls appeared to be much agitated. They looked very pale." Margaret Fox then asked her to sit next to her on the bed and began speaking to the walls around her. "Count five," she instructed, and Mary Redfield heard five knocks. "Count fifteen," she continued, and there were fifteen raps. Mrs. Fox then asked the invisible knocker "to rap my age," the neighbor swore, "and it rapped thirty-three times"—her age exactly. Margaret Fox then asked the rapper, "If you are an injured spirit, manifest it by three raps," and they heard three knocks.

Word spread that the Foxes could speak to the dead, and scores of locals came to see for themselves. They all asked the same questions and got the same knocks in response, time after time. Soon, hundreds of people lined up to witness the rappings. Committees gathered in different parts of the house to make sure that there was no deception. "The questions were put in every shape," the girls' brother, David Fox, testified, "and there was no contradiction at any time." By reciting the alphabet and hearing raps in response to certain letters, witnesses were eventually able to receive messages, apparently from several spirits. The spectral knockers then informed them, after a few months, that their communication should be made public.

So, in November 1849, the Fox sisters appeared at Corinthian Hall, the newest, grandest theater in Rochester. During three days of extraordinary demonstrations, citizens' committees inspected the hall for any indications of trickery. The sisters were taken to a private home and tested for signs of ventriloquism or manipulation. Witnesses found nothing that accounted for the strange thumpings. Finally, a ladies' committee took the sisters into a private room, undressed them, and examined their bodies thoroughly for any devices that could produce the noises. They found nothing at all.

The girls' notoriety spread so widely that in June 1850 they traveled to New York City and held lucrative private séances for paying customers, three times a day, at their hotel and in private homes. All their visitors, Greeley wrote, were astonished by the experience. He, too, attended a séance with Kate and Maggie Fox, now fourteen and eighteen years old. The dark-haired sisters were quiet and refined, he recounted, with skin "of a transparent paleness." They were seated on a sofa, with a plain table in front of them. "We had scarcely taken seats on the opposite side," he wrote, "before a succession of raps was heard, some on the table and some on the floor," originating from different sources. Some of the thumps were so strong, Greeley said, that they jarred the floorboards and shook the tabletop.

At the sisters' request, he took a seat next to them on the couch. He swore that they made no attempt to touch the table and that there were no devices of any kind that could have produced the loud and frequent knocks they heard beneath it. One of the spirits, Greeley added, correctly indicated personal details about an obscure relative of his. "All this sounds . . . ridiculous and amazing," he acknowledged, but those who witnessed the event were "men of high intelligence and respectability, who are not likely to be deluded by their . . . imaginations." The sisters told him, with some annoyance, that the knocks had followed them everywhere—in trains, steamboats, hotels, and carriages—for the past two years. The subject, he concluded, "is curious, to say the least."

The Fox sisters were so famous that summer that they inspired a showtune and souvenirs touting the remarkable "Rochester Knockings." Greeley said he had no desire for a second sitting, but his wife attended two or three séances with the girls. She was so enthralled by the sisters that she invited them to spend nearly two weeks with them at their home. The girls came, and, during séances there, Mary was sure that she received messages from little Pickie. Both of the Greeleys became especially fond of young Kate Fox and invited her to stay with them that fall, so that she could benefit from some excellent schooling in New York City. The Foxes agreed, and Kate stayed on with the Greeleys, taking classes six days a week. She liked her teachers, but she detested Mary and the horrible meals she endured in the Greeley household. She was lonely and isolated and gratefully went back to Hydesville at the end of autumn.

Greeley's experience with the sisters left him changed, with an expanded sense of possibilities. He often criticized the gullibility of the public, but when it came to the Fox sisters, he had few misgivings. His good friend P. T. Barnum, the prince of humbuggery, was certain that the rappings were a fraud. The girls, he believed, had learned that movements of their anatomy could produce the noises and that their knockings could be a profitable business. But Greeley was sure that the spirit rappings had "something in them."

The world, he acknowledged, was far too familiar with false prophets, counterfeit clairvoyants, and shamming religionists, from Jumpers and Sandemanians, he wrote, to Muggletonians and mystics. Spiritualism, he realized, might be rife with "frauds and impostures," but he sensed that there was more to the rappings than "knee joint rattling" and "toe-cracking." Greeley was sure that he had witnessed "real and momentous communications from the unseen world" and that it was unaccountably possible to pierce the veil between human existence and the afterlife.

Shortly after Kate Fox departed, the Greeleys abandoned Castle Doleful and purchased a two-and-a-half-story townhouse on East Nineteenth Street. The editor's white coat hung on a peg in its narrow foyer, near his fraying top hat stuffed with crumpled newspapers. Since Pickie's birth, he and Mary had had two other children, but only one, Ida, had survived infancy. When Greeley arrived home at the end of a busy day, he would rush up the stairs to play with his two-year-old daughter before he warmed his feet, in tattered stockings, by a hole in the floor where hot air rushed up from the furnace.

It was a spartan and demanding life, with few diversions. Greeley hardly ever attended parties and took only two flavorless meals a day. But in early 1851, he decided to rest and refresh himself on a trip to London to see the spectacular Crystal Palace Exhibition, the first World's Fair. An immense glass building, almost two thousand feet long, housed wonders of international industry, from steam engines, reapers, and surgical instruments to steel-making machinery and electric typewriters.

Greeley was scheduled to sail on April 16 aboard the *Baltic*. John Humphrey Noyes was then residing at the community's branch in Brooklyn, while his followers upstate struggled to keep the Oneida enterprise financially stable. Noyes secretly learned about Greeley's plans and booked a cabin aboard the same ship. The long voyage, he predicted, would give him "a natural and favorable opportunity" to meet Greeley—whose publishing success, influence, and support for social experiments he deeply admired—since they would be shut up together on the steamship for two weeks.

It was a cold, bleak Wednesday morning when Noyes, Greeley, and some two hundred other passengers boarded the *Baltic*. Storm clouds loomed on the horizon as Greeley—dressed, as usual, in his white coat—took off his top hat and waved it to friends seeing him off on the Canal Street wharf, as the ship belched black smoke and steamed out into the Atlantic. The *Baltic* was not a luxury liner. When Noyes took a turn out on deck, he was quickly covered in soot and ashes. It was a bit more agreeable below, in a heated sitting room near his cabin, and he happily managed to persuade Greeley to join him there for some spirited conversation about religion and travel. Noyes was delighted to learn that Greeley was familiar with his radical theories, since the editor had read Oneida's first and second annual reports and regularly perused its newspaper. But they had few opportunities to meet. Greeley spent most of the trip green, gagging, and so horribly seasick that he believed, and hoped desperately, that he would die. The twelve-day voyage, he reported, was "absolute torture," as bad as two months' hard labor in prison. Traveling east across the Atlantic, he said, was a violent misery. Americans should stay on their own continent, he warned, and go west instead, traveling overland.

5

GARFIELD'S CRUCIBLE

After midnight, in a cold and muddy army camp near Columbus, Ohio, Colonel James Garfield nuzzled his two horses, rubbing his cheeks against their velvet noses as they pretended to nibble his brown beard. He had never felt such a crushing need for love and affection. At twenty-nine, he was chronically tormented by self-doubt, depression, and debilitating diarrhea. A former schoolteacher and state legislator, he had no military experience. Now, in October 1861—six months after the first shots in the Civil War—he was training raw recruits in a rainy, ramshackle army complex at Camp Chase.

In mid-April, after Fort Sumter fell, President Lincoln had called on every state to defend the Union. Ohio had a quota of thirteen regiments, but it had no infrastructure to equip, organize, or train them. The governor tapped Garfield to lead a regiment, the 42nd Ohio Volunteer Infantry, but when he reported to Camp Chase in August, he had no training or any soldiers to command. Inside his tent, swarming with flies, he huddled under a few yards of pink mosquito netting, read books on military strategy, carved blocks of maple wood into troops, and marched them across his desk to practice commands.

To recruit a real-life regiment that summer, Garfield turned to the students he had taught at the Western Reserve Eclectic Institute—a school founded by a Christian group called the Disciples in the small town of Hiram, Ohio. Garfield had studied at the Eclectic in his early twenties, and his classmates idolized him as a school hero. Tall, beefy, athletic, and serious, he was known for his charm, scholarship, and speaking ability. Garfield went on to Williams College in Massachusetts, graduating in 1856. He then returned to the Eclectic to teach Latin and Greek and was appointed its principal the next year. Garfield was only twenty-six, but his leadership was drawing notice, and his students adored him—although he was often away from campus after 1859, when he was nominated and elected as the Ohio State Senate's youngest member.

In 1861, after Fort Sumter, his students, too, were distracted by the world outside the institute. The young men, dreaming of glory, drilled every day under the tutelage of an ancient veteran of the War of 1812. After Garfield's commission, they hoped to enlist together, under the leadership of their beloved principal. So, at the end of August, when Garfield gave a recruiting speech in a Hiram church, sixty boys immediately signed up. He had a full company within a week, and his young recruits reported to Camp Chase. By early October, he had more than six companies to command and took on "the immense work of organizing a thousand men, getting them properly outfitted, armed, and equipped . . . together with the usual routine of drill and discipline." Garfield's leadership skills were competent, but he often doubted them. His nature seesawed from ambitious self-confidence to gloomy insecurity. But after three months of intensive training, the 42nd Ohio Regiment was ready to march. On December 14, 1861, they were ordered to meet the rebel army in eastern Kentucky.

Their destination was the Sandy Valley, a remote wilderness drained by the Big Sandy River. Confederates were advancing on the region, and Garfield's task was to repel them. He had never had any experience in battle, and the desolate, six-thousand-square-mile terrain depleted his confidence. "The work will be positively enormous," he wrote. "It is a horrible country." But if he controlled the river, Garfield knew that he could supply his troops. He had no artillery, but the winter weather was a weapon. As the rebel army marched over the mountains from Virginia, the cold, drenching December rain nearly drowned them in a sea of mud. Poorly trained and ill-equipped—many of them barefoot, without blankets or coats—the Confederates were starving, "ragged, greasy, and dirty," fighting one another over loaves of bread and falling sick with measles, mumps, and other contagions. In early January, the rebels retreated. Garfield had won without firing a shot, but, he reported, "Our forces were very much exhausted and our sick list large. . . . The deepest, worst mud I ever saw was under foot, and a cold fog hung around us" while his troops routed the retreating rebels in the Battle of Middle Creek.

His victory broke a string of dispiriting losses. An instant hero, Garfield was lauded as "the bold lion" of the Union Army, commended for his perseverance and strength. But disaster lay ahead. Garfield and his troops remained in the Sandy Valley, where he was charged with administering the region and maintaining order. On February 22, while his men bivouacked along the Big Sandy River in drenching rain, the water rose twelve feet in just an hour, and then sixty feet overnight. It surrounded the camp, and his troops barely had any time to stow their guns and ammunition and escape the flood. In a shelter surrounded by the wild river, Garfield watched houses, "stacks of wheat and hay, gigantic trees, saw-logs, fences, and all things that float . . . careening by with fearful velocity." The receding flood polluted water supplies, destroyed their stores, and left a wake of dysentery and other diseases. "I tremble," he wrote, "for the sickness and suffering that must follow." Garfield himself had been flat on his back with dysentery two weeks earlier. He had lost nearly twenty pounds and was "more depressed," he admitted, "than at any time since I entered the service." By March 10, more than four hundred of his soldiers were so gravely ill that nearly fifty of them perished, including some of his young Hiram volunteers. "This fighting with disease," Garfield despaired, in snow, rain, and hellish mud, "is infinitely more horrible than battle." In the midst of this suffering, he was promoted to brigadier general, but the news only deepened his misery. "The thought . . . of taking command of nearly four thousand men who had never been tried in battle, who were strangers to me," he wrote, ". . . made the future a gloomy one."

In April, Garfield decamped for Tennessee. Over the next four months—as he led a brigade through fierce fighting, followed by frustrating inaction, in the Shiloh and Corinth campaigns—his health and melancholy hit bottom. In the first weeks of his command, he was recovering from bloody dysentery, and his hemorrhoids made it agony to ride a horse. "I never suffered such acute and crushing pain in my life," he recounted, "as I did for 40 hours during that attack." He was bedridden again in early June—so sick that he lost forty-three pounds in fewer than four weeks. Close to death, Garfield was finally granted a leave to return home.

In early August, his flesh sagging and sallow, he arrived back in Hiram, where he lived with his wife, Lucretia Rudolph. The handsome, dark-haired "Crete," as her friends called her, was serious, sympathetic, and shy. She had been one of the best Greek students at the coeducational Eclectic, and Garfield started courting her in 1852. But when she agreed to marry him three years later, Garfield, almost instantly, began doubting his choice. Dreading the exclusiveness and grim finality of wedlock—perhaps because his mother had had a difficult second marriage—he turned his attention to a charming, clever young woman named Rebecca Selleck. Her ardent letters to

Garfield inflamed his "wild, passionate heart," and he freely admitted their romantic affair to Crete. However, when a friend scolded him for his "unpardonable neglect" of his wife-to-be, he resolved to marry Crete, against his instincts. But Garfield was unable to suppress his doubts. After they wed in 1858, he announced to Crete that their marriage was a terrible mistake. As her husband, he declared, he felt as though he "died daily." But two years later, they had a daughter, and the iciness of their marriage began to melt.

Now, after nearly a year away in the Union Army, Garfield had returned home to his family. He had time to recuperate from his grave illness and reunite with Crete and their two-year-old daughter, Eliza. He also paid careful attention to Republican politics. The local nominating convention was coming up, and friends were urging him to run for Congress. Garfield hated the army and was attracted to the idea of serving in Washington—but only, he insisted, if he was nominated by a show of overwhelming public support, without making any effort on his own behalf. He was fearful that his name "should go before a convention and be rejected."

Garfield's terror of political failure had also been an issue five years earlier, before he was elected to the state senate. He had refused to lift a finger for that nomination, but he campaigned vigorously after he secured it, making dozens of long speeches to win support. Now, behind the scenes, Garfield's friends worked energetically to push his name forward as a congressional candidate. In September 1862, he won the nomination on the eighth ballot as a "spontaneous act of the people," he boasted, rather disingenuously.

Garfield won the election the next month, but the new Congress was not scheduled to meet until December 1863. He could not take his seat in Congress for more than a year, and until then, he was still in the army. In late summer, Lincoln's secretary of war, Edwin

Stanton, summoned him to Washington for a new military assignment. In the capital, Garfield felt anxious and lonely as he waited for his new commission. The war was lasting longer than predicted, and, he observed, "There is a settled gloom on nearly every face"; a great nation "groaning in an agony . . . to have something done. A people that have poured out . . . their life and treasure to save their Government" and who "are now beginning to feel that their confidence has been betrayed, their treasure squandered and the lives of their children sacrificed in unavailing slaughter."

Garfield's mood, too, was dark and restless as he approached his thirty-first birthday. In Washington, crossing paths with the country's military, political, and business elite, he felt ashamed that he was born in poverty. His father had died when he was a toddler, and his mother, Eliza, raised him and his three siblings in a crude log cabin in the Ohio wilderness. Garfield despised manual labor and loved books. But when he finally started going to school at age seventeen, he felt embarrassed by his patched clothing and humiliated that he had to live for a while on bread, milk, and pudding because he was penniless. Although his fear of inadequacy made him moody and sensitive, he longed to live a grand, heroic life with "thunder in it" and make his mark on the world.

Waiting for his new military assignment, with a whole year ahead of him before he could serve in Congress, Garfield felt so useless that he shuffled and sulked in the cheap rooms he had rented over a grocery. He started stooping so badly that he had to wear shoulder braces to improve his posture. His head ached, he wrote, and his mood was fouled by the smell of rotten potatoes wafting up from the shop downstairs. He was also uneasy about his marriage. He had been away from Crete for many weeks and confessed that he had gone to see his former love interest, Rebecca Selleck. Fidelity, he admitted, did not come easily or naturally to him; it was only sheer brute force and a sense of duty that could prevent his lapses. "I know fully and sadly," he told his wife, "how many faults I have that need to be forgiven."

But happily, the opening of Congress on December 1 brought notables to town, and on January 1, he was invited to the White House. It was a lively custom, on New Year's Day, for all army and navy officers in Washington to visit the president. "We met at the War Department," Garfield recounted, "and proceeded in a body with General Halleck at the head to call on His Excellency. There were not less than eight hundred officers of the army and navy there. The foreign ministers were there in . . . gaudy court dresses, the judges of the Supreme Court, the leading senators and representatives, and the heads of the cabinet departments."

Finally, in mid-January 1863, Garfield received his commission and was ordered to report to the Army of the Cumberland, one of the main Union armies in the Western Theater. After Garfield arrived at the headquarters in Tennessee, he quickly developed a close rapport with the army's commander, Major General William Rosecrans. Energetic and intense, Rosecrans had a volcanic temper and a foul mouth. He was also deeply religious and philosophical, and he engaged Garfield in seemingly endless spiritual and military discussions, often keeping his subordinate awake until the early morning. Garfield was sleep-deprived, and Rosecrans, some whispered, "had a screw . . . loose in him somewhere," but the two grew devoted to each other. Their connection, Garfield said, was "not a mere official or even social acquaintance, but a meeting and mingling of spirits." He had been hoping to secure a field command, but when Rosecrans offered to make him his chief of staff, Garfield accepted.

He served as liaison between the general and his army—running headquarters and field operations from a plain pine desk and a tall stool. He alone was permitted to call his commander "Rosy."

"Rosecrans shares all his counsels with me," Garfield reported, "and places a large share of the responsibility of the management of this army upon me, even more than I sometimes wish he did." Garfield respected the general, he said, for his "sharp, clear sense, ready, decisive judgment, and bold reliant action."

Word of Rosecrans's admirable qualities reached Washington. In May, Horace Greeley sent a journalist, James Gilmore, to Tennessee to write articles about the general and his forces. But Greeley secretly instructed Gilmore to ask Rosecrans if he would be willing to run against President Lincoln in the next election. Greeley had known Lincoln for fifteen years and supported his campaign for president. By May 1863, however, depressing military defeats had shaken Greeley's confidence in him. If Rosecrans ran against Lincoln and won, the editor believed, it might save the Union. But when Gilmore approached Rosecrans about the plan, the general refused to entangle himself in Greeley's scheme. The reporter's mission failed, but he came away impressed by Garfield, now physically fit and restored to his imposing presence. Gilmore described him as

> a tall, deep-chested, sinewy built man, with regular, massive features, a full, clear blue eye, slightly dashed with gray, and a high, broad forehead, rising into a ridge over the eyes as if it had been thrown up by a plough. . . . A rusty slouched hat large enough to have fitted Daniel Webster, lay on the desk before him, but a glance at that was not needed to convince me that his head held more than the common share of brains. Though he is yet young—not thirty-three—the reader has heard of him, and if he lives he will make his name long-remembered in our history.

Another reporter for the *New York Tribune*, Henry Villard, wrote that Garfield "presented a far more commanding and attractive appearance" than Rosecrans. The chief of staff was "very nearly, if not fully, six feet high, well formed, of erect carriage, with a big head of sandy hair, a strong-featured, broad and frank countenance, set in a full beard and lighted up by large blue eyes and a most pleasing smile. . . . I recognized also his general capacity and great store of information. A distinguished career," he wrote, "seemed certain for him."

But Garfield, by then, was impatient and exasperated with delays in moving against the rebels in Tennessee. He was sure that the only way to stop the Confederates was by "striking, striking and striking again, till we break them." As Rosecrans's chief of staff, he was gathering intelligence from spies and believed that the moment was right to attack and drive the rebels out of their central Tennessee headquarters in Tullahoma. He was certain that his troops were ready. But Rosecrans only delayed and dithered, week after week, despite the urgings of President Lincoln, Secretary of War Edwin Stanton, and General-in-Chief Henry Halleck. Garfield sank into a black mood of disgust and discouragement. He was sick again, too, and feeling lonely. "I have been married four years and five months," he wrote his mother, and had been away from home and female companionship for more than half that time.

Garfield needed feminine comfort, and he found it—with a cross-dressing actress and Union spy named Pauline Cushman. Her real name was Harriet Wood. But the tall, slender, dark-eyed performer had taken a stage name that linked her to a popular actress named Charlotte Cushman, who was famous for playing both male and female roles. Pauline Cushman, like her namesake, had the dramatic and comic ability to play roles ranging from young boys to Frenchmen, old ladies, and seductive vixens. That April, she had put her talents to use for the Union Army, gaining the confidence of Confederate sympathizers in Louisville and posing as a Southern gentleman to gather intelligence over brandy and billiards.

The next month, the head of Rosecrans's spy service had given her a special mission. She would pose as a Confederate woman who had been forced to flee Nashville without protection. Traveling alone, armed with a six-shooter, she would make her way to several Confederate headquarters, memorizing their artillery and defenses. But before she could return to Union territory, she was captured in Shelbyville, Tennessee, and scheduled to be executed for espionage. When Union forces took the town, they found her gravely ill and brought her back to safety in Nashville. Garfield arrived in the city on July 15. At his special request, Cushman was moved to a comfortable boardinghouse to recuperate, and he became, she recalled, one of her "most constant companions"—such a fervent supporter that he persuaded President Lincoln to give her the honorary title of "major" in the Union Army.

By the time Garfield left Nashville in late July, Rosecrans had finally attacked the Confederates in Tullahoma. His forces had captured central Tennessee, but they had failed to crush the retreating rebels. Now, once again, Rosecrans was idling his army from what Garfield considered an overabundance of caution. "I love every bone in his body," Garfield wrote, but he blamed the general for ignoring opportunities to strike. Finally, in August, Rosecrans sent his soldiers into battle in jagged, wooded terrain near Chattanooga. Garfield almost had to miss the action. He was once again so sick with dysentery that he had to be carried in his cot to watch the troops prepare. When he was finally well enough to ride, he suffered in the saddle again from hellish piles. But on September 20, as Rosecrans retreated his forces from the field, Garfield managed to advance alone, riding ahead through enemy positions, ravines, and swamps to bring intelligence to a commander who was able to hold off the rebels that day in the Battle of Chickamauga.

It was a brief reprieve. The Confederates prevailed in combat, with many thousands of casualties. It was Garfield's last military engagement. On October 15, he was ordered to Washington. On his way there, he stopped in Hiram, for the first time in ten months, to see Crete; their three-year-old, Eliza—who was nicknamed "Trot"—and their new baby boy, Harry Augustus. It was a quick visit, before he delivered the report on the Battle of Chickamauga to President Lincoln and General Halleck. But a few weeks later, he rushed back to Hiram after learning that Trot was very ill. By the end of November, he and Crete realized that there was no hope for their little girl. "We have been watching for twelve hours to see our darling die," he wrote a close friend on December 1. "She is still alive but cannot last till noon. . . . Our hearts are breaking." The toddler died at seven o'clock that evening.

Before they buried their daughter, the Garfields asked a photographer to take a memorial photograph with her lifeless body. They had few portraits of her alive, and they wanted an image to keep as a remembrance. So, as the photographer carefully positioned his tripod, Garfield, in his army uniform, cradled his little girl's dead body on his lap, gazing down at her small, ashen face. His grief was so crushing that he thought, for a while, that he could no longer live in Hiram. He was never the same, Crete acknowledged, after the death of Trot.

But he hurried back to Washington after her burial, for the opening of Congress on December 5. As he began his civilian duties as a congressman, he put away his general's uniform and moved into a C Street boardinghouse. He also plunged into a passionate affair with a very young widow named Lucia Gilbert Calhoun. She was only twenty years old and beginning a brilliant writing career with Greeley's *New York Tribune*. Garfield was infatuated with her, and by May, gossip about their illicit romance had reached Hiram. A friend confronted Garfield and urged him to end the affair. At first, Garfield denied it and called the rumors "wickedly and maliciously false." But in early June, he made a sudden trip home and felt moved to confess his "lawless passion" to Crete. It was a devastating revelation, only six months after their child's death, but Crete said she would forgive him if he agreed to end the liaison.

Soon after leaving Hiram, Garfield wrote her a regretful letter. He hoped, he said, that "when you think over my trip home and balance up the whole of my wayward self, you will still find . . . a small balance left on which you can base some respect and affection. . . . I ought to have a great deal more head, or a great deal less heart. Either would be better," he admitted, "than my present proportions." He and Crete had long struggled with his indecision, gloom, and passion for intelligent, free-spirited women. He wondered if he had the character or the strength to change.

While Garfield was attempting to make amends with his wife, Pauline Cushman was creating a sensation in New York City. As Major Cushman, "Union Scout and Spy of the Cumberland," she was captivating audiences at P. T. Barnum's American Museum, where she was as much a curiosity as his giants, midgets, and rare birds and beasts. Barnum proclaimed her

the greatest heroine of the age, the modern American model of the renowned "Joan of Arc," the pure and beautiful girl, revered and loved by all friends of American unity and liberty. MISS MAJOR PAULINE CUSHMAN, the Union Scout and Spy, who, under the orders of General Rosecrans, passed through the enemy's lines and accomplished such wonders for the Army of the Cumberland, while she was engaged in the secret service of the United States. . . . This high-souled, gallant girl, who, in her determination to serve her country, risked her inestimably precious life, and was rescued . . . from a rebel prison where . . . she lay wounded, and languishing with sickness, UNDER SENTENCE OF DEATH! Those who would avoid the crowd should bear in mind that the most pleasant time to hear this heroic lady recount, in her own fervid language, her adventures, is at ELEVEN O'CLOCK IN THE MORNING, on which occasion, the lecture room is thrown open without any extra charge.

Striding the stage before a packed audience of three thousand people, Cushman—who wore a military uniform and occasionally a fake mustache and beard—sang and recited her story. A Southern newspaper panned her performance as a mixture of patriotism, humbug, humanity, and mock heroics. But a *New York Times* reporter called her "charming and intelligent," and another journalist complimented her "magnificent physique; tall, commanding and graceful. . . . She in no wise disappoints." Cushman was such a success that Barnum paraded her onstage in June and July 1864—twice every day, with his giants, albinos, diminutive dwarfs, and a seal who could play the hand organ.

6
DREAMS AND DISASTERS

On the sultry afternoon of July 13, 1865, at 12:35 P.M., the engine room of Barnum's American Museum was suddenly engulfed in flames. Within minutes, the derelict structure was a blazing tinderbox. Patrons and performers stumbled, gasping, out of the building, while animals trapped inside shrieked as fire torched the dusty, crowded halls.

Huge anacondas and pythons escaped and slithered down the museum's stairwells. Two panicked lions broke free but died, bellowing, in the smoke. A tiger leaped from the second story to the street and was butchered by a fireman's ax. Soon, tongues of flame were shooting from the windows, and the roof fell in a volcanic mass of fiery debris. A crowd of forty thousand New Yorkers watched the Ann Street wall of the building buckle and collapse with a thundering blast, while eagles, parrots, and cockatoos soared above their heads to safety. No humans died in the inferno, but the museum's menagerie of monkeys, alligators, porcupines, cats, dogs, and a kangaroo perished in the conflagration.

So did two beluga whales that were boiled alive in a giant tank. The pair—a male and female—were the last of eight belugas that

Barnum had procured for display. In 1861, inspired by the novel *Moby-Dick*, he had hired dozens of French Canadian fisherman to capture two white whales and send them down to New York City by train. The huge creatures traveled in a crate filled with seaweed and salt water, attended by a keeper who kept swabbing their mouths and blowholes with a sponge. The pair died after just two days in the brick-and-concrete tank that Barnum had erected in the basement, filled with fresh, tepid water that was artificially salted. Barnum soon replaced them with two more belugas, installed in a new glass seawater tank on the second floor. Those animals died quickly, too, but Barnum was set on replacing his profitable "monsters." So he hired fishermen to send him another pair of white whales two weeks before the blaze. When the fire broke out, they were floating sullenly in their murky tank as the seawater began to boil. Frantic firemen broke open the glass walls of the enclosure to release the salty flood, hoping to quench the flames, and the giant mammals flopped out onto the burning floor. When the side of the building collapsed, they plunged to the sidewalk, where their giant carcasses lay steaming, and then rotting, for days.

It was the cataclysmic ending to a decade of disaster for Barnum. His grand-scale dreams and schemes had gone up in smoke—including his huge minareted palace in Bridgeport, Connecticut. The extravagant Moorish mansion, which he called Iranistan, was topped by a great dome and housed a Chinese library and astronomical observatory. Inside, its walls were lavishly adorned with murals, orange satin, and the atrocious oil paintings he loved to collect. The estate, with its seventeen-acre elk park, was vast enough to entertain a thousand guests. But in December 1857, a workman left his smoldering pipe on a cushion in the house, and by the night of December 16, the whole Byzantine palace was ablaze. There was nothing left of it the next morning, except a few scattered pieces of furniture.

The loss was devastating to Barnum, who had gone bankrupt two years earlier in a land development deal. But by 1860, he had recovered financially—thanks to a profitable tour of Europe with his tiny star performer, Charles Stratton. He even built a new residence, called Lindencroft, and refurbished his American Museum. But now, the incineration of that showplace was a brutal blow. It was, he declared, "a national loss" in a grim season of nationwide shock and sorrow.

Three months earlier—on April 15, 1865—President Lincoln had died from an assassin's bullet. The nation had plunged into sudden grief. "When the head of thirty millions of people is hurried into eternity by the hand of a murderer," Horace Greeley wrote, words fail. Lincoln was not a man "of transcendent genius, of rare insight" or force of character, he believed, but he was eminently fitted to soothe and heal a nation just lapsing into peace after years of devastating civil war.

Ohio congressman James Garfield, too, had reservations about Lincoln. But he sensed that, in spite of "all his awkward homeliness, there is a . . . transparent, genuine goodness which at once reaches your heart, and makes you trust and love him." Garfield's own heart, he wrote his wife, was "so broken with our great national loss that I can hardly think or write or speak." He blamed America's intense individualism for the crime, but, he insisted, "I do not believe it is in the American character to become assassins."

—⁓—

Eleven days before John Wilkes Booth fired the shot that killed President Lincoln, Charles Julius Guiteau fled the Oneida Community and traveled south to New York City. His mission, he declared, was to establish a great daily theocratic newspaper. He was sure, he said, that he could be as famous and successful as Horace Greeley. With a hundred dollars in his pocket, he rented a cheap room in Hoboken, New Jersey—across the Hudson from Manhattan—and attempted to enlist the help of editors, printers, and reporters. "They all laughed at the idea," he conceded. The concept, he believed, was tremendous, but the twenty-three-year-old had no money, no friends, and no experience. After three months of failure, he admitted, he might have overestimated his prospects. Lonely, disappointed, and broke, he pleaded with the Oneida Community to readmit him—even though, he complained, the women there all laughed at his advances. Despite his strange behavior and maniacally inflated ego, Community leaders agreed to take him back in August, on a trial basis.

They put Guiteau to work in their manufacturing plant, about a mile away from the Community. He was assigned to the silk works—with its winding, spinning, twisting, and spooling machines—and the trap factory, which made thousands of profitable bear, beaver, otter, fox, and mink traps every year. Guiteau worked as the shipping agent, dispatching traps to buyers from Manhattan to Saint Paul, Minnesota. He also carried water and wrung mops in the communal kitchen.

The workload, he complained, was a nightmare. He especially despised his celibacy in a community, he grumbled, that encouraged "promiscuous intercourse." Noyes, he noted, was about the only man who was allowed to practice it. Sexual frustration, in fact, was the main cause of Guiteau's misery. When he whined about his lack of access to Oneida's women, leaders scolded him that he had to earn those privileges. "We took you in out of charity," they berated him. "You are now, and always have been," they declared, "a dead weight."

By the fall of 1866, Guiteau was feeling tortured by the Community's restrictions. So, one evening in November, after shipping traps all day, he returned to the Mansion House, quietly packed his trunk, hired a stable hand to cart his luggage to the station, and boarded a train for New York City. He left without a word to anybody. The next morning, Oneida's daily paper reported that "one of the trap-packers shipped himself last night" and left a farewell note explaining that he planned to find a job with a New York bank. But for an entire year after leaving Oneida, Guiteau, in fact, made no efforts to find employment. His father had sent him a little money, so he rented a room in Brooklyn and spent the whole winter and spring wandering around the city. In the summer, he had a brief ambition to study law, but by November 1867, he was dreaming again about a career in newspapers.

So Guiteau decided to ask Horace Greeley for a job. One winter day, he headed to the *Tribune* offices, now on Printing House Square, at the junction of Nassau Street, Park Row, and Spruce Street. Across from City Hall, the grimy five-story building was widely known as the Old Rookery. Newsboys crowded its steps in the early morning, waiting for the basement presses to ink the day's edition, while other boys folded newspapers for the early mail. By noon, the *Tribune*'s next issue was in the works. Busy editors hunched over their desks, and teams of compositors—divided by Greeley into four "phalanxes"— labored at long tables of copper-faced type.

Guiteau, uninvited, entered the building and climbed the dingy staircase to the editorial rooms, lined with dusty bookshelves and heaps of paper. He found his way to Greeley's sanctum, where the editor—rapidly scrawling editorials with stained fingers—had to endure frequent interruptions by strangers who evaded all his gatekeepers and claimed his attention to express their political or religious views, beg him for a loan, demonstrate bizarre inventions, or announce their passion to be published in the *New York Tribune*. That day, however, Greeley was out of the office, and his managing editor informed Guiteau that he had no chance in the world of being hired. But the twenty-six-year-old had unshakable faith in his potential. "Where there was a will," he insisted, "there was a way," and he was destined, he knew, to do great things. Like "Mr. Lincoln and Mr. Greeley," he reckoned, "I have had a hard time, a hard road to travel," but the time was coming, he said, when he would be "just as famous as they are."

—–⁗—–

Although Horace Greeley was an editorial icon, newspapers were changing. For nearly twenty-five years, he had personally embodied the *New York Tribune.* But by 1867, he had a staff of younger editors, and competition for readers was fiercer than ever. New York City had about a hundred fifty newspapers, and individual journalists had less power to shape public opinion. People were now buying newspapers "to learn what they want to know," Greeley complained, instead of "what they ought to know."

But the *Tribune* was still a forum for new, vigorous ideas and voices. After the drowning death of Margaret Fuller, his friend and foreign correspondent, Greeley published articles by a destitute German writer named Karl Marx. Living in a squalid London flat with his wife and six children—three of whom died from the lack of medicine and food—the burly, black-haired Marx mailed dispatches to the *Tribune* on conditions in Germany. Although he always sent the pieces under his own byline, he rarely wrote them. The irascible German had never learned to write in English, so he persuaded a fellow exile, Friedrich Engels, to ghostwrite the dispatches for him.

"You must," he implored his friend, ". . . come to my aid" and write "a series of articles on Germany since 1848." Engels agreed, so Marx would send the newspaper columns to Greeley and keep all the *Tribune*'s payments for himself. But it was hardly enough money to make a difference. His wife was sick, he confided to Engels one day, and so was his little daughter, but "I . . . can't call the doctor," he wrote, "because I have no money for medicine." For eight to ten days, he added, his family had lived on nothing but bread and potatoes.

After begging the paper, unsuccessfully, to raise his pay, Marx called its managing editor "that ass," the *Tribune* "that lousy rag," and Horace Greeley "an ass with an angel's face." It was, he groused, "disgusting to . . . regard it as good fortune to be taken into the company of such a rag." After a decade, when the *Tribune* scaled back its foreign coverage, Marx ranted that those "damned lousy bums" now wanted "to toss him aside like a squeezed lemon." But the articles he sent to Greeley were not a waste. Most of that prose reappeared in his 1867 opus, *Das Kapital*.

That year, Greeley hired a new foreign correspondent—a thirty-two-year-old from Missouri named Samuel Clemens. He was heading to Europe and the Middle East on a five-month tour aboard a paddle-wheeler, the *Quaker City*, visiting Paris, Italy, Greece, the Crimea, and the Middle East. Clemens agreed to mail the *Tribune* two stories a week, and Greeley promised to pay him forty dollars for each column of type.

In November and December that year, Clemens mailed Greeley articles from Paris, Jerusalem, and Cairo—under the byline "Mark Twain"—and their publication in the *New York Tribune* helped raise his national profile as a writer. When he later published his travel articles as a book, *Innocents Abroad*, Twain achieved, he claimed, "my first notoriety"—due, in part, to Greeley's interest in writers with distinct, unconventional points of view.

In 1865, he hired a new agricultural editor. The fifty-two-year-old writer, Nathan Meeker, was a dedicated utopian. Born and raised in Ohio, he had published poems and stories and worked as a teacher. In 1844, he and his wife had joined the Ohio branch of a utopian community that Greeley had co-founded. Called the Trumbull

Phalanx, the colony, located in Braceville, Ohio, had more than five hundred acres and was, according to John Humphrey Noyes, "one of the three most notable experiments" of its time. By 1846, the enclave had a hundred fifty members who operated a wooden bowl factory, a wagon works, and a shoe shop. Meeker was the community's secretary, teacher, historian, librarian, and poet laureate. From that elevated position, he declared that "there is nothing so serious, hearty, and I might add, sublime, as the building up of a Phalanx." The Trumbull colony, however, disintegrated after four years. The land, it turned out, was swampy and prone to flooding. Several members fell sick with malaria. Many were slaggards, and some lived "huddled together like brutes" in derelict shelters, nearly starving and drinking coffee made out of burnt bread.

After the failure of this experiment, Meeker moved to the village of Hiram, Ohio, and opened a general store. The region was considered to be "healthful and free of distractions." He planned to help establish a new college there—the Western Reserve Eclectic Institute—until its leaders discovered that he was selling whiskey (only by prescription, Meeker insisted). One of the Eclectic's very first students was twenty-year-old James Garfield, who later became the head of the new school. Garfield's closest friend in Hiram recalled that one of the few places of interest there was "a small store, kept by a man named Meeker," who sold nearly everything that a man, woman, or child could want or imagine.

In 1857, Meeker sold the store, moved to Illinois, and started writing articles for the Cleveland *Plain Dealer*. His journalism attracted the attention of Horace Greeley, who hired him as a Civil War correspondent, then brought him on to the *Tribune's* staff—sending him, in 1866, to visit and report on the Oneida Community in an article that attracted wide readership and fueled Meeker's dreams of one day founding his own utopia.

Back in Hiram, a friend had told him about the glories of the Rocky Mountains. Intrigued by the west, Meeker traveled to Colorado in 1869 and thought that it was the perfect place to establish his own colony. When he got back to New York, he mentioned the idea to Horace Greeley. The editor was enthusiastic, saying it was sure to be a great success—"if I could," he exclaimed, "I would go myself"—and he offered the full support of the *New York Tribune*.

On December 14 that year, the newspaper published an announcement of Meeker's venture, along with Greeley's editorial endorsement. Meeker declared in his promotion that

> a location which I have seen is well watered with streams and springs, there are beautiful pine groves, the soil is rich, the climate healthful, grass will keep stock the year round, coal and stone are plentiful, and a well traveled road runs through the property. . . . The Rocky Mountain scenery is the grandest, and the most enchanting in America . . . the air is remarkably pure, summer is pleasant, the winter is mild, with little snow . . . tourists and visitors will find great attractions there during the summer. . . . Schools, refined society, and all the advantages . . . will be secured in a few years. . . . In the success of this colony a model will be presented for settling the remainder of the vast territory of our country.

Meeker advised interested readers to write him at the *New York Tribune*. Greeley predicted that he would hear from more than a thousand people, but before two months had passed, three thousand hopeful utopians had written to express their interest.

On the frosty night of December 23, hundreds of people overflowed a meeting room at Cooper Union, a Manhattan college, where Meeker and Greeley held an organizing session for the new colony. Meeker would serve as president, and Greeley as treasurer. The pair was seeking to recruit "farmers, nurserymen, florists, and almost all kinds of mechanics, as well as capitalists," noting that applicants must be sober and "ambitious to establish good society. . . . Those who are idle, immoral, intemperate or inefficient need not apply." Applicants should have some money, Meeker added, although Greeley warned that "no one who is doing well" should leave his business and go west, unless they were absolutely certain of success. During their first months in Colorado, Meeker cautioned, settlers would face privations while they built their houses, mills, and mechanic shops. But the crowd was excited. By the end of the meeting, chaired by Greeley, more than four hundred farmers, craftsmen, and small businesspeople had enrolled in the utopian project, and hundreds more signed up the following week.

The colony's financial launch, however, was less auspicious. Every member was asked to pay five dollars to join the project and one hundred fifty more to buy a lot, but only fifty applicants at the meeting paid the fee. Others promised to mail the funds to Greeley at the *Tribune*. Eventually, though, after Meeker invested his own money and borrowed more, the organizers had enough capital for a committee to set out in February to find the perfect location for the new community. They intended to call it Union Colony Number One, since Greeley hoped it would be the model for ten thousand settlements.

The committee traveled west by train to Cheyenne, Wyoming, then continued on to Colorado by rail and stagecoach. They explored Pikes Peak but found that available lots in the area were too small and dry for agriculture. But the Cache la Poudre Valley, where the high plains met the Rockies, fit the bill. The scenery, organizers gushed in the *Tribune*, was "grand, the soil fertile, and pure water abundant." It was the perfect place to build a new communitarian fellowship that, they said, would be like Arthur's Round Table—the beginning of a heroic legend.

The site, however, was not quite Camelot. Most of the available lots were on poor land and scattered along the Poudre River, a stream that was, residents joked, "three-fourths of a mile wide and three-fourths of an inch deep." But the committee plunged ahead, buying a hundred thousand acres for the project. The town that would arise there would be called "Greeley," they decided, and the editor himself bought a couple of lots. The town would have its own newspaper—the *Greeley Tribune*, edited by Nathan Meeker—and it would be stone sober. Drinking and gambling would be forbidden. There would be "no black-legs, grogsellers, nor any class which aims to get rich by speculating on the needs or pandering to the vices of others." There would be "no whiskey dens, no beer shops, no gambling halls nor billiard saloons; no rows; no street fights," and little profanity. People in Greeley, they expected, would "generally mind their own business."

The treeless plain, too, was dry as dust, but Meeker promised ample irrigation. Still, when colonists began arriving in the spring, conditions were far less pleasant than they expected. There were no shelters for them when they got there, and hardly any materials to build with. There were, Greeley admitted, some "soreheads and malcontents," but most settlers, he believed, were "sober, industrious, intelligent moral men." They would build a model community in the barren West, despite its "savage solitude and bleak desolation."

The colonists hoped that Greeley himself would visit on the Fourth of July, but the editor was ill with sciatica, rheumatism, and fever. Finally, however, in the fall of 1870, he traveled west to inspect the new utopia that bore his name. On October 12, hundreds of cheering colonists—nearly every citizen of the town—came out to welcome him when he arrived by train and escorted him to the office of the *Greeley Tribune*. On a makeshift stage outside the building,

Greeley addressed the settlers—praising their new irrigation ditch, which, he expected, would bring ten thousand acres into cultivation the next year.

That hope was almost comically optimistic. As one writer reported after visiting the town, the "Great Ditch" was a total failure, since there was no water to fill it with. The colony, he wrote, consisted of shanties on a bare desert plain. Wood, he added, was "a natural curiosity in Greeley." Colonists boasted that there was plenty of it in the Rockies "just back" of town, but the mountains were forty long miles away. The colony's only products, he wrote, were prairie dogs, cacti, weeping women, and squalling babies. "Greeley, Colorado," he declared, "is a graveyard."

It was hardly an exaggeration. As one pioneer recalled, it was almost impossible to grow shade and fruit trees in the desert soil, even "with the greatest care and . . . utmost attention."

> Thousands . . . of evergreens and larches have been set in this town and vicinity, and now we know of one larch that is alive, and which perhaps grows an inch a year; and there are not more than a dozen evergreens. . . . Chestnuts live about as well as bananas would. Of the vast number of apple trees obtained the first year, it is doubtful whether twenty are alive; and pears, cherries and plums have gone the same way. . . . What we can save from the winter . . . the grasshoppers seize; they eat out buds, and blossoms, cut off leaves, even gnaw bark, and do disgusting work.

According to another settler, "All the women tried to have lawns and no one succeeded. . . . The developer had not mentioned that the closest tree to the east was five hundred miles away." The river, which the colony depended upon, was "a mile wide and an inch deep;

too thin to plow and too thick to drink." Finances were murky, too. Although Horace Greeley was treasurer of the colony, he never produced a balance sheet that was anywhere near accurate.

———

Despite these disappointments, one investor was delighted with the new town. Horace Greeley's close friend P. T. Barnum became a charter member of the community and bought a total of eleven lots. Once again, he was awash in cash. Just weeks after the fire of 1865 torched his American Museum, Barnum had opened another, even bigger showplace on an entire block of Broadway, between Prince and Spring. The four-story building, on six lots, featured model steam engines, a shooting gallery, an aquarium, and the only lions, tigers, and giraffes in the whole country.

Barnum's prospects had been boosted by James Gordon Bennett, the founder and editor of the *New York Herald*. Bennett had bought out Barnum's lease on the burned-out museum property for two hundred thousand dollars and built a brand-new *Herald* building on the lot. Barnum, in the chips again, gave lectures on the "Art of Money-Getting" and bought a spacious brownstone on Thirty-Ninth Street. He gave Greeley his own set of keys to the Murray Hill house, and the editor—wearing his cowhide boots and a flowing dressing gown that Barnum lent him—was a regular guest.

The showman's fortunes seemed unsinkable—even after his new American Museum burned down in March 1868, during a snowstorm. When firemen tried to quench the flames, water from their hoses turned to icicles on the walls of the burning building. Few of its creatures and curiosities survived, and Barnum, at long last, decided to abandon the museum business—at a hefty profit. He sold the lots for nearly half a million dollars and built a huge new elaborate estate on Long Island Sound. The ornate Victorian mansion, which he called Waldemere, featured copious gingerbread, wide porches, and a comfortable guest chamber that he called "the Greeley Room."

Barnum was flush again, after a brush with disaster, and the Union Colony was a handy place to put some of his money. He constructed its largest, finest building—the two-story Barnum's Hotel. In a town made up of tents and shanties, the lodging offered the miraculous luxuries of Brussels carpet and bedsprings.

The colony's liquor ban was a key attraction for Barnum. Although he had once been known to guzzle an entire bottle of port or champagne with lunch, he had reformed and was a vocal, if occasionally lapsed, teetotaler. His investment in the community also had personal uses. He employed one of his cousins, a Mr. Nichols, to build his grand hotel, and he relocated some problematic relatives to the colony, including illegitimate offspring and a wayward daughter.

Barnum and his wife, Charity, were the parents of four girls—Caroline, Helen, Frances, and Pauline. Helen had married one of his employees. But in 1870, she abandoned her husband and children and ran away with a doctor from Indiana named William Buchtel. In 1871, after a sensational divorce, she married Buchtel, who was five years younger than she was. To quiet the scandal, Barnum installed the couple, far out of the way, in his new hotel in Greeley, Colorado. All was not well, however. Dr. Buchtel suffered from tuberculosis. He was also a secret, raging alcoholic—a delicate problem in the bone-dry town.

Soon after the newlyweds arrived in Greeley, the doctor began running the Colony Drugstore, located on Barnum's Main Street property. The deed banned liquor on the site, and the attitude of Greeley citizens toward booze sellers was extremely clear. According to one colonist:

Just across the border of Greeley, some enterprising soul had set up an outdoor saloon. . . . The men from Greeley took the butts off their guns and knocked out the tops of all the barrels, allowing the whisky and gin to run out into the field. True, the barrels were not in Greeley, but they were next to the fence, which was in Greeley. The man took his loss meekly and left. The next day . . . the cows, and there were quite a few, evidently liked the taste of the liquor and lapped up so much it made them extremely drunk. . . . They would stagger, fall, pick themselves up, stagger some more, until they finally fell down for good and dropped off to sleep.

Rumors began spreading that Buchtel, the "skillful apothecary," was selling liquor from his drugstore. So the good citizens of Greeley organized a sting. They dispatched a young man to the pharmacy, with the mission of buying some "good whiskey." The clerk obliged and sold him a half-pint for fifty cents. Greeleyites were aghast that the doctor was selling "doses of damnation," as well as a patent medicine that was 47 percent alcohol. Outraged at this assault on what Barnum called their paradise protected by "flaming swords of sobriety," residents threatened to "place our hands upon a long rope—the hands of 500 men of us, and . . . put an end . . . to whoever strikes at the foundation . . . of our Colony and town."

At this, the Buchtels finally packed up and departed Greeley for good. Barnum, who admitted that his son-in-law was a "shyster," soon partnered with him in a new sanitarium in Denver. Barnum also built Greeley's first auditorium, called Barnum Hall, and brought his traveling circus—called "The Great Moral Show"— to the prairie colony, with four hundred performers, packed into fifty-four railroad cars. It was a legendary success. His son-in-law Dr. Buchtel eventually sold the Greeley drugstore to his brother John, who was also run out of town for selling booze. Their other brother, Henry Buchtel, became governor of Colorado.

7

HORACE GREELEY FOR PRESIDENT

As the most famous newspaper editor in the country, Horace Greeley had the power to sway public opinion with a stroke of his pen. But his genius and influence were never enough for him. He craved the prestige of public office.

Between 1848 and 1871, Greeley ran, unsuccessfully, for governor, congressman, and senator multiple times. He also lobbied to be postmaster of New York and postmaster general of the United States. His lust for office was ignited in 1841, when he was appointed to fill a vacant congressional seat in Washington for three months. As a Whig representative from New York, he was known for his ludicrous legislation, such as changing the name of the United States to "Columbia." He quickly became, he admitted, "the most detested man who had ever sat in Congress."

Still, his brief time in Washington fueled his drive for elected office. As a Republican, he ran, unsuccessfully, for New York's US Senate nomination in 1860. Six years later, after the Civil War, he ran for Congress and was beaten badly, but the next year, he ran for the US Senate nomination again. This time, he faced two enormous obstacles. First, he had no political organization, and second, he had made an enemy: Roscoe Conkling, Oneida County's former district attorney. He had been named to that post, precociously, at the age of twenty. Now, at thirty-seven, Conkling was flexing his political powers as a brilliant bully. Tall and imposing, with fierce blue eyes and reddish hair circling his ruddy face, he was sarcastic, shrewd, and a gifted speaker, with an exceptional memory. He was also a crack shot with a pistol and a powerful boxer, unable "to forgive an enemy, or even to pass him without a kick." He was temperamental and aloof, compulsively neat, and hated to be touched, even in a friendly way. Still, Conkling's formidable skills had won him unusual success at an early age. At only twenty-eight, he was elected mayor of the city of Utica in Oneida County, and at twenty-nine, he was elected to Congress as Oneida's Republican representative. New Yorkers reelected him twice, but in 1866, when he was nominated again, Greeley's *New York Tribune* surprisingly refused to endorse him. Conkling never forgave Greeley for the snub.

He began enjoying his revenge the next year, when he ran against Greeley for the Republican Senate nomination. The editor's run quickly collapsed, while Conkling captured the nomination with such acclaim that his supporters carried him on their shoulders. With his bumptious self-importance, restless drive, and flamboyant sense of fashion, Conkling ascended to the US Senate, looking

> as if he had just stepped out of a band-box. His polka-dot tie was fastened together with a plain gold pin. A checked kerchief was visible in the upper pocket of his cutaway coat. He wore English gaiters and pointed shoes that had been freshly polished. On his head was a high white hat, and his whiskers had been trimmed with great care. In his hand he carried a sun umbrella. He walked along with the air of a Prince, unmindful of the attention he

attracted. His private secretary walked a few paces behind him, carrying a small satchel.

Arrogant, punctilious, and ambitious for political power, Conkling, known as "the giant of Oneida," seemed born to be worshipped on a pedestal.

His feud with Horace Greeley was just beginning. In 1868, when the editor sought the Republican nomination for governor, Conkling stage-managed the convention to win the nomination for a friend from upstate New York. Then, when Greeley ran again for governor in 1870, Conkling savagely sabotaged him. The senator teasingly supported Greeley on the first ballot—then abruptly switched his support to another candidate, who won the Republican nomination. He had pummeled the editor again, making it clear that he, not Greeley, was the political boss of New York State.

But the editor got his own revenge in ink. In a *Tribune* screed, he ridiculed Conkling for "the pose of [his] majestic figure," his "bolt-hurling arm, the cold and awful gleam of that senatorial eye." Nobody, he wrote, could approach the senator "without being conscious that there is something great about Conkling. Conkling himself is conscious of it. He walks in a nimbus of it." If Conkling had been Moses at Mount Sinai, and they "had asked him what he saw there," Greeley sneered, "he would promptly have replied, 'Conkling!'"

———

They were bitter enemies, despite their shared Republican allegiance and disgust for slavery. Greeley had backed the Civil War as a way to abolish the infernal practice. But he had doubts that the Union Army could beat the rebels, and he feared that Lincoln would be defeated in reelection by a pro-slavery Democrat. So the editor had actively searched for another Republican who could run and win in 1864. Ultimately, Greeley supported Lincoln and celebrated his reelection, but he advocated leniency for the South as a way to bring the nation together. On April 9, 1865, after Lee's surrender at Appomattox, Greeley called for a general amnesty for Southern rebels.

Less than one week later, Lincoln was assassinated, and Vice President Andrew Johnson, a Democrat from Tennessee, rose to the presidency. At first, Greeley endorsed his relaxation of Reconstruction, while insisting on full voting and civil rights for Black citizens. But when he saw that Johnson would ignore those protections, Greeley withdrew the support of his *New York Tribune*.

Conkling, too, detested Johnson—calling him an "angry man, dizzy with the elevation to which assassination has raised him, frenzied with power and ambition." While in Congress from 1865 to 1867, Conkling was a member of the Joint Committee on Reconstruction and helped fashion the Fourteenth Amendment to the Constitution, guaranteeing Black men the right to vote. He was determined, he said, "that slavery shall never range this continent" but would "wither and die." Despite his alignment with Greeley on these issues, their political views split sharply after Ulysses Grant was elected president in 1868.

General Grant had led the Union Army to victory in the Civil War, winning brutal battles and the rebels' surrender at Appomattox. Before Lincoln's reelection, Greeley had viewed Grant as a potential candidate, but the general refused to be considered. A military man, he insisted, should not engage in politics—although after the war, he hinted, he might run for mayor of his hometown in Ohio so that, if elected, he might have the sidewalk repaired from his house to the railroad station.

But in 1868, when Republicans nominated him unanimously for president, Grant dutifully accepted. Greeley supported the general's candidacy with "honor and esteem" for his wartime leadership. Grant, many believed, was the only man who could bring the country together after the savagery of civil war and the presidency of Johnson—a white supremacist and Southern sympathizer who avoided impeachment by a single vote. Grant, unlike his predecessor, was a shy, humble man—"as plain as an old shoe," according to an army doctor. Journalist Charles Dana, who traveled with Grant during the war, recounted that he was

> the most modest, the most disinterested, and the most honest man I ever knew, with a temper that nothing could disturb, and a judgment that was judicial in its comprehensiveness and wisdom. Not a great man, except morally; not an original or brilliant man, but sincere, thoughtful, deep, and gifted with courage that never faltered.

Although Grant earned a heroic place in US history, he was a slight man—five foot eight and a little stooped, with tawny hair, a square jaw, penetrating blue eyes, and small hands and feet. Quiet, good-natured, and careworn, he had risen to greatness after years of crippling defeats.

Born in Ohio in 1822, he graduated from West Point, where he was known for his exceptional skill with horses. After serving bravely in the Mexican-American War, Grant's soldiering took him to the West Coast during the gold rush. In 1854, he was assigned to a remote post at Fort Humboldt, California. Far away from his wife, Julia, and their two sons, he soon took to drink. As one officer recalled, "Liquor seemed a virulent poison to him, and yet he had a fierce desire for it. One glass would show on him, and two or three would make him stupid." Unable to conquer his depression and drinking, Grant, at thirty-two, resigned from the army and rejoined his wife and children in Missouri.

For the next seven years, he stumbled from one failure to another, unable to support his growing family as a farmer, clerk, or bill collector. One friend had never seen him so depressed; "He was shabbily dressed, his beard unshaven," and he seemed filled with a profound discouragement. Finally, in April 1860, Grant took a job at his father's leather goods shop in Galena, Ohio, but he had no aptitude for the work. As one local merchant recalled, he "would go behind the counter very reluctantly, and drag down whatever was wanted, but [he] hardly ever knew the price of it, and, in nine cases out of ten, he charged either too much or too little."

Still, Grant and his family found some threadbare stability for a year—until rebels attacked Fort Sumter on April 12, 1861. Within a week, Grant abandoned the store and rejoined the Union Army as colonel in the 21st Illinois Infantry. His appearance, however, inspired little confidence. Grant's "dress was seedy—he had only one suit . . . that he had worn all winter." With his short pipe, grizzled beard, and old slouch hat, he did not look like a promising candidate for a colonel—or even "if he knew enough to find cows if you gave him the hay," a soldier joked. But his troops soon realized that Grant "knew his business," for he did everything without hesitation. As one soldier later remarked, "So intelligent were his inquiries, so pertinent his suggestions, that he made a profound impression upon every one" by his quickness and knowledge of important details about the army.

Over the next three years, Grant rocketed from colonel to brigadier general, to major general, to lieutenant general in command of all of the Union armies. Only George Washington had previously held that exalted rank. But Grant, after years of failure and hardscrabble living, retained his "natural, severe simplicity in all things." Slightly stooped, good-natured, and courteous to all, everything about him seemed ordinary except the fierceness of his military brilliance. As one observer commented, he habitually wore "an expression as if he had determined to drive his head through a brick wall, and was about to do it."

As a candidate for president in 1868, Grant remained, for the most part, in Galena, while others stumped the country on his behalf. Senator Roscoe Conkling campaigned for him in New York—despite the fact that Conkling's own brother-in-law, Horatio Seymour, was the Democratic candidate for president. Thanks to Conkling's support, Grant carried Oneida County, although Seymour managed to win New York State. Still, Grant swept the national election by 310,000 votes and the electoral college 214 to 80.

At age forty-six, Grant was inaugurated on March 4, 1869. His political naivete was hardly a secret, and his homespun habits in the White House became common knowledge. He was particularly fond of rice pudding, cribbage, and horrendously strong cigars—although he cut back his smoking habit from twenty to ten a day. He called his wife "Mrs. G.," she called him "Ulys," and he enjoyed rolling bits of bread into balls at the dinner table and hurling them at their children.

He was so shy and quiet that senators and members of Congress attempted to translate his grunts. And like many presidents before him, he was flooded with requests for government jobs and faced a daily mob of office seekers in the White House. His appointments, however, began drawing fire for secrecy, patronage, nepotism, and personal favors, while his cabinet had a revolving door, with twenty-five different men in the seven posts during his presidency.

Whenever he faced criticism, however, Grant could always count on one stalwart defender: Senator Roscoe Conkling. The New Yorker quickly cultivated Grant's confidence, inviting the president to visit his home in Oneida County during his first summer in the White

House. Grant, who had few close friends, welcomed Conkling into his inner circle and regarded him "as the greatest mind . . . that has been in public life since the beginning of government." Conkling's canny advice, coupled with his lack of obsequiousness to a president who was used to having his orders obeyed, won him Grant's admiration and respect.

But they were complete opposites in many ways. Grant was humble, while the senator was high-handed and haughty. The president cared little about his appearance, while Conkling strutted in bright-colored, foppish butterfly bows. Grant was always smoking a cigar, while Conkling hated the smell of tobacco smoke. But the president realized that Conkling was a fighter with knife-sharp political skills, and he trusted that the senator would not betray him. According to Grant's son Jesse, "Conkling and my father loved each other. They were devoted." A journalist even remarked that Grant had a "romantic affection" for Conkling, who returned it "in a manner almost womanly," despite his imperious, high-toned, impetuous character.

Conkling, in fact, was never disloyal to Grant, and he benefited hugely from the president's confidence. Grant made Conkling the most powerful politician in New York State. The center of that power was the New York Custom House. With jurisdiction over all the state's seawaters and coastline, it collected about three-quarters of the nation's customs receipts, and its fifteen hundred jobs made it the greatest source of political patronage in the country. Its granite building on Wall Street, with a soaring dome and massive columns, housed the nation's largest federal office, and its halls were filled with job seekers and politicos hoping to reward supporters. Whoever controlled the custom house headed the biggest political machine in the United States—one rife with corruption since the 1820s. Presiding over it was the collector, whose pay—based on shares of all the fines that were collected—exceeded that of the president of the United States. In 1829, President Jackson had appointed Samuel Swartwout as New York collector. In that post, he embezzled about $1.2 million—more than $33 million in today's money.

Although the collector had official maritime, administrative, and commercial duties, his real job was to fire, hire, and dispense political spoils. The largely unqualified ranks of custom house workers owed their precarious livings to the party and the politicians who bestowed employment. In spite of their low pay, they were expected to hand over campaign cash to support their sponsors—making custom house employees a mighty political army that could be deployed at will.

Its power belonged to whoever controlled the collector. Under Grant, that kingpin was Roscoe Conkling. In July 1870, with Conkling's support, Grant nominated a corrupt hatmaker, Thomas Murphy, as the New York Customs Collector. He was, according to *The Nation*, "a hack politician, unfit for any trust." During the Civil War, he had sold shoddy hats to the Union Army, but he was devoted to Conkling and the Republican party. He was quickly confirmed. Murphy swindled importers and removed more than three hundred employees, replacing them with operatives who were loyal to Conkling. Murphy also supported the Oneida senator by collecting "voluntary" campaign contributions from his workers and dispatching delegations of them to support Conkling. While traveling around the state, Greeley reported, he "came upon hundreds of Senator Conkling's New York Custom House officials—supposed to be guarding the waterfront—far in the interior, traveling upon trains everywhere in connection with their party duties at local nomination conventions, committee meetings, and caucuses under the command of Conkling."

By autumn 1871, it was clear that the collector was "as rotten as his hats." Grant defended Murphy, but in November, public pressure was so great that the president accepted his resignation. It was all a charade, though, because Grant and Conkling allowed Murphy to name his own successor. He chose his closest colleague in corruption, Chester Arthur.

Gregarious and impeccably dressed, Arthur, a New York attorney, had lobbied for Murphy in Washington during the Civil War, defending him from complaints about his defective hats. They soon became intimate friends. Arthur spent almost every evening at Murphy's home, indulging in whiskey, cigars, and political plotting until early morning. Tall and portly, with a taste for backslapping and the good life, Arthur was Murphy's political tool and a loyal lieutenant of Senator Conkling. According to Horace Greeley, he was "Tom Murphy under another name," but much more skilled at running a political machine.

At the age of forty-two, Arthur took his place atop New York's empire of grift and graft. From the grand collector's office, he did favors for Republican office holders; collected campaign contributions from nearly a thousand employees; hired and fired workers for political leverage; and grossed fifty thousand dollars a year—more than a million in today's dollars. He almost always arrived late at the office, after marathon nights of smoking, drinking, feasting, and playing poker with politicos. He was also a regular at risqué restaurants, where waitresses in low necklines and short skirts were available for assignations.

Arthur was Murphy's "faithful shadow" in the collector's office, the *New York Tribune* thundered. He may have been "courteous and agreeable to all . . . genial and 'cultured' at the clubs and in social relations." But he was leading "as corrupt a band of varlets as ever robbed a public treasury," according to one observer, and the paper blasted Grant for blatant civil service corruption.

Although Greeley had supported Grant when he ran for president, the editor increasingly criticized the general and his appointments.

He had a growing distaste for Grant personally and had now come to believe that he was "too small a man for the presidency."

———

Despite Grant's tolerance for corruption, he had strongly supported Reconstruction and full civil rights for Black Americans. He also created the Justice Department to crush the Ku Klux Klan. But Greeley believed that the time for Reconstruction had passed. He now claimed that Southern whites were victims of prejudice and wanted full amnesty for former rebels. He even, shockingly, extended support to the Ku Klux Klan. These were dizzying positions for a Republican, and they caused outrage. His ties to the Republican party establishment began to disintegrate.

Although pro-Reconstruction Republicans controlled Congress, a third party—called the Liberal Republicans—emerged in 1871. The new party, which opposed Grant and Reconstruction, needed a candidate for the 1872 presidential election. Greeley threw his white hat in the ring. Many found his candidacy absurd. His former associate Thurlow Weed said that no one "outside of a lunatic asylum" would nominate Greeley. But in May 1872, when the Liberal Republicans held their national convention, the editor won the nomination—even though, according to one observer, hardly anyone was worse-equipped for the White House. Ohio congressman James Garfield was not a great fan of Grant, but he was sure that a Greeley presidency would be much worse. "Grant," he wrote, "is not fit to be nominated, and Greeley is not fit to be elected."

But in 1872, both Greeley and Grant were the candidates. Greeley shared the Liberal Republican ticket with Benjamin Gratz Brown, the party's nominee for vice president. An alcoholic Kentuckian and former governor of Missouri, "Boozy Brown" was well-known for his garbled speeches and bizarre behavior at public events, such as buttering a slice of watermelon that he drunkenly mistook for a piece of bread. At a bibulous speech he gave to former classmates at Yale, Brown declared that he never thought much of Greeley, but that people should vote for him because "he has the largest head in America."

More confounding was the fact that the Democrats also nominated Greeley and Brown. It was, according to the Democratic party's national chairman, "one of those stupendous mistakes which is difficult even to comprehend." But Greeley—the first presidential candidate to be nominated by two political parties—kicked off his campaign with blasting cannons in New York's City Hall Park. While Grant, who hated public speaking, stayed at home, Greeley resigned from the *Tribune* and set off on a whistle-stop tour around the country, giving thumping campaign speeches at every stop. In New England, Pennsylvania, Ohio, Indiana, and Kentucky, he sometimes gave twenty speeches a day. They were marvels of impromptu oratory, a supporter said, and moved thousands who had doubted the abilities of the eccentric editor. He was not, however, a gifted speaker. As a close friend of his wrote,

> He had a poor and somewhat squeaking voice; he knew nothing of gestures; and he could not take an orator's pose. . . . But . . . he invariably had *something to say*; and he said it in such clear and wholesome English, with such utter sincerity.

As his audiences swelled, the New York Tribune Association issued a collection of popular jokes and campaign songs celebrating the man in the white hat. One of them, called "The Dead-Beats' Funeral," took a swipe at Roscoe Conkling and his custom house machine:

From that grand and costly building,
Come moanings like a storm,
'Tis the death of fraud and stealing
Crushed by virtue and reform . . .
Through four long years of hard stealing
The wretches have grown fat,
When comes a man with square dealing,
Who wears an old white hat.

Although some critics considered the editor an "inspired idiot" and "illbred boor," he took no notice of their sniping. He had momentum, and Republicans were starting to worry. Rutherford B. Hayes, the former governor of Ohio, confided to his diary that he had "just now a feeling that Greeley will be elected!"

———

On the warm, windy night of October 8, 1871, a blaze broke out in a barn in southwest Chicago. Within hours, fierce gales had whipped the flames into hundred-foot-high fire tornadoes that torched more than seventeen thousand buildings. Hundreds died in the firestorm, and nearly a hundred thousand residents were homeless. Among the thousands who fled for their lives with just the clothes on their backs or a few possessions was thirty-year-old Charles Guiteau.

He had moved from New York to Chicago in the spring of 1868—after trying and failing to blackmail John Humphrey Noyes. Guiteau had demanded that Noyes pay him ten thousand dollars; otherwise, he said, he would announce to the public that "nightly, innocent *girls* and innocent young women are sacrificed to an experience easier imagined than described" and that "the founder of their 'delightful' system" mated with his own flesh and blood. Oneida's women, Guiteau threatened to disclose, "were forced to cohabit at such an early period that it dwarfed them."

When the Community's lawyer threatened to have him prosecuted for extortion, Guiteau dropped his blackmail attempts and fled New York for Chicago. His sister and her husband, a lawyer named George Scoville, resided there, and with Scoville's encouragement, Guiteau set his sights, once more, on studying law. After just a few months of apprenticeship in a Chicago firm, he was admitted to the bar of Illinois.

Guiteau, all of a sudden, began acting and looking like a legal professional, sporting jaunty side-whiskers and a mustache. At the YMCA, where he spent much of his time, he seemed like an "exemplary young man," according to the librarian there, a young woman from England named Annie Bunn. Guiteau had long hair, she said, and "was rather good-looking." He courted her, and they married in July 1869.

At first, his new bride recalled, there was nothing disturbing about Guiteau. "He was rather peculiar in his manners and dress," she said, "but nothing very remarkable." Soon, however, his behavior became alarming. He cheated his clients and "everybody that he came in contact with, great or small, in any way he possibly could." Guiteau, she added, was determined to live far beyond his means. He wanted "nothing but the best," and he was very particular about his appearance. He "wore the best of everything," buying expensive suits with some money down but never paying the balance. When he posed for photographs, "he would be very fastidious in his directions, saying . . . 'get the right expression of my face and eyes,'" but he objected to his profile, because he thought his nose was much too long. Their accommodations, too, had to be the best, but Guiteau never paid their boarding bills. So their baggage was detained, time and again.

After fleeing the Chicago fire, they moved to New York City, where it was the same story—until the summer of 1872. After Horace Greeley's nomination for president, Guiteau became obsessed with the idea that, by supporting the editor's campaign, he would be rewarded with a prestigious post in his administration. He decided to "get out of the law business and get into politics with Mr. Greeley," his wife recalled. He talked about Greeley constantly and "became infatuated with the idea of . . . doing everything he possibly could" for his election. He almost entirely neglected his law business, and they had no money. But Guiteau assured Annie that, after a while, he would have a grand position. "There is no doubt that Mr. Greeley will be elected," he promised, and as president, the editor would reward him generously for his campaign work. As compensation, Guiteau would ask for an appointment to a foreign mission. He knew the time was coming, she said, when he would be a "big man."

> He used to walk back and forth before the glass and pull down his coat and straighten back his shoulders, so as to give himself a conspicuous appearance. If there was any peculiarity in his style of dress or deportment in the street, it was in keeping with his desire to look like some of our noted men. He . . . asked me the question repeatedly: "Don't you think I would look like a good Foreign Minister?"

Guiteau, she added, wrote a campaign speech for Greeley. "He read it over and over again," she said; "sometimes he would sit up nearly all night . . . thoroughly revising it." He thought it was a "wonderful production," she said, and he actually won permission from the campaign to give it at some open-air events in New York City. On August 13, he was the first speaker at a Wednesday-evening rally for Greeley on Third Avenue and Fifty-Eighth Street. The crowd, illuminated by Chinese lanterns, fireworks, and blazing tar barrels, burst into laughter at Guiteau's speech. But he continued to work on the campaign for Greeley until the autumn, believing that he would be appointed to a foreign ministry.

He was confident but aggressively cautious. Guiteau carried a small black cane that was filled with lead. "If I were to be attacked by anybody," he explained, he would be able to "strike him and kill him," then disappear, so "no one would find it out."

In early September 1872, Horace Greeley still believed he might win the election, but his support was waning. Grant's campaign had much more money to spend, and his allies in the press attacked the editor without mercy. The sharpest barbs were delivered by his nemesis, Roscoe Conkling. At the Cooper Institute in New York, the Oneida senator blasted Greeley with an assassin's aim. The editor, he declared, was "peevish, eccentric, grotesque and harmless, a man of oddities, flattered by many, and most of all by himself," whose "brief career in Congress was a sad fiasco." More than once, Conkling charged, Greeley "voted without understanding the question" or mistakenly cast the wrong vote. He was "a poor judge of human nature," and "the worst men have stuck to him and used him." Greeley was stung by these words and wondered whether he was running for the presidency or the penitentiary. "Nobody," he conceded, "seems to deny that I would make a capital beaten candidate."

He was bruised and battered by the bitterness of the race and soon broken by the illness of his wife, Mary. Their devoted but difficult marriage had been a "domestic hell." He had met Mary when she was a bright, high-strung, and curious twenty-two-year-old. But a seemingly endless string of pregnancies, miscarriages, stillbirths, and childhood deaths had plunged her into an "almost insane melancholia." Feminist

Victoria Woodhull—who, as the country's first woman presidential candidate, ran against Greeley and Grant in 1872—accused the editor of "souring the temper, unstringing the nerves, and completely disorganizing the machinery of a delicate woman's organization."

The Greeleys, of course, were partners in domestic dysfunction. After their first two tots had died in infancy, Mary babied their son, Pickie, so much that she kept him in diapers until he was almost four. And she seemed to have no heart for another child. In 1847, when Pickie was three, she gave birth to a little girl who died from her complete neglect. Greeley confided in letters that Mary "often said she wished her dead on account of the labor and anxiety she caused." She would sit on a bare mattress in the dark, unable to take care of herself or the baby, who lay quietly starving in a basket, so weak that she could hardly cry. After the child came down with dysentery, no one picked her up for days at a time, and she lay staring in her basket, her eyes exaggerated by her wasting flesh. Pickie wanted his parents to give his sister away, since she competed for their attention and care, but the baby died on May 6, 1847. Greeley wrote, "I never saw a creature so patient under suffering and so grateful for kindness. . . . With proper treatment and care, I am sure my darling would have survived."

But he had done nothing to intervene. Instead, with Mary's encouragement, he stayed away from home as much as possible—sleeping in his office, taking rooms in a boardinghouse, traveling around the country or overseas, and spending weeks with P. T. Barnum and other friends. He coped with Mary's insanity, and worsened it, by deliberately avoiding his house of horrors. He told Margaret Fuller that, between mid-1846 and early 1848, he ate dinner at home only twice. When he did return home, Mary often became pregnant again, with little capacity to cope, and she ruled the home like a mad queen.

"Mother," as Greeley called her, could never keep servants more than a few days because of her shrewish behavior. There was no furniture in the house except for a few chairs and beds, and certain rooms, she decreed, had to be kept dark. When he was at home, Greeley lit the morning fire, cleaned the house, and milked the cow because of her "inability to accomplish anything." Mary would repeatedly scrub the same spot on the floor, hour after hour, until she fell asleep there from exhaustion. She would also wash the same garment repeatedly, then deliberately soil it with black soot.

After Greeley bought a farm in Chappaqua, New York, in 1853, Mary spent much of her time there and increasingly traveled around Europe and the West Indies in search of expensive health cures. In 1870—to care for her on her travels and keep her company—Mary took their two surviving children, twenty-two-year-old Ida and thirteen-year-old Gabrielle, on a two-year health pilgrimage to Europe. Ida, born in 1848—who had somehow survived malaria and cholera under Mary's care—had grown into a doting daughter. Her younger sister, however, hated waiting on their demanding mother—who was now crippled by rheumatism—and following her around the continent.

The trip ended abruptly in June 1872, when Gabrielle, stricken with typhoid, returned home. Two weeks later, when Mary and Ida docked in Hoboken, Greeley met them on the ship. He found his wife in her stateroom, practically toothless and looking ghostly and ancient. By October, she was sinking fast. Strangely devoted, he remained sleepless by her side. As she lay dying and the campaign ended, he wrote to a friend, "I wish she were to be laid in her grave next week, and I to follow her the week after."

Mary died in his arms on the morning of October 30. Only six days later, voters went to the polls in the presidential election. Greeley was crushed by Grant, who won more than 55 percent of the popular vote. The editor was, he said, the worst-beaten man who ever ran. In less than one week, he had lost his wife and the election, and he no longer even owned the *Tribune*, since he had sold nearly all his shares.

Bankrupt and "out of his head" with insomnia and delirium, Greeley shockingly died in an asylum only three weeks later—before the electoral college had even voted. With his reputation "seriously shattered and his usefulness nearly destroyed," Garfield reflected, the editor's sudden death, on November 29, was "pathetically tragic." His body, dressed in black, lay in state in New York's City Hall, across from the *Tribune* building. More than fifty thousand people came to pay their respects to "Uncle Horace," standing in lines that stretched more than four blocks long from morning until late at night. On the cold, gray morning of his burial, buildings throughout the city were draped in black; flags flew at half-mast; crowds of mourners lined the streets; and church bells rang as a massive funeral procession made up of one hundred twenty-five carriages moved slowly down Fifth Avenue to Greenwood Cemetery in Brooklyn. President Grant rode in the first carriage of the cortege, followed by the governors of New York, New Jersey, and Connecticut; the mayor of the City of New York; and hundreds of other dignitaries. The US Senate had recessed so its members could attend. Above Greeley's grave, the printers of America erected a bust of the great editor, fashioned from melted newspaper type.

Charles Guiteau had staked his future on Greeley's election. He was stunned by his loss at the polls and his sudden death. His expectations for a high political office were crushed—at least for the moment. But there were other paths to fame, Guiteau told an acquaintance. "If I cannot get notoriety for good," he explained, "I will get it for evil." When asked what he meant, Guiteau replied, without hesitation, "I will shoot some of our public men."

PART 3

KINGDOM COME

8

THE MASTER OF LOVE

Tirzah Miller was just a child, entering adolescence, when her uncle, John Humphrey Noyes, had sex with her for the first time. In truth, he was like her father. She had been a baby when her birth father, John Miller, died, and her uncle, she said, was "the only father I have known since childhood." Now, Noyes was also her "first husband" and, she declared, "the one man on earth in whom I absolutely trust."

Love, in the Oneida Community, was a family affair. When Tirzah was twenty-seven, she bore a child by another of her uncles, George Washington Noyes. Serious and intelligent, with dark hair and a gift for music, Tirzah was deeply attractive to many of Oneida's men. Her uncle John Humphrey Noyes also wanted to have a child by her. "He said he believed it to be his duty," she wrote in her diary, "and he had considerable curiosity to see what kind of a child we should produce. He said to combine with me would be intensifying the Noyes blood more than anything else he could do." They never did produce a child together, but Noyes successfully sired a baby with her sister, Helen.

He believed in "breeding in and in" to increase the moral perfection of Oneida offspring. And he had no qualms about shattering the taboo of incest. In overthrowing it, he wrote, "I am conquering the devil's last stronghold." To found a new race, he announced, "the fellowship of brothers and sisters is fundamental. . . . It is concentration" and "approaches nearest to the fashion of God himself."

Noyes was so eager to smash moral and sexual conventions that he even planned to have couples mate onstage, before the whole Community. "We shall never have heaven till we can conquer shame," he said, "and make a beautiful exhibition on the stage." According to Tirzah,

> he would have a man and woman go up upon the stage . . .
> disrobe themselves and dance or perform other evolutions
> until a man is prepared. . . . "It is a sight," he said, "which
> would purify the whole Community." It would give plea-
> sure to a great many of the older people who now have
> nothing to do with the matter. There is no reason why it
> should not be done in public as much as music and dancing.

Oneidans practiced "regulated promiscuity," controlled by Noyes. Godlike and generous—so long as his dominance was never threatened—he determined every aspect of Oneida's culture. Although he considered women inferior to men, he allowed them to take part in community life on a relatively equal footing. Tirzah became editor of the colony's newspaper, and her sister served as a bookkeeper for the Community. Male continence spared Oneida's women from unwanted pregnancies, and they were as free to select their work assignments as men. Even their dress was designed to make them appear more like a "female man," according to Noyes. He complained that women's long skirts made them look "something like a churn, standing on castors." At Oneida, he instructed, men and women should wear more similar clothing.

So Oneida's women took off their corsets, cut their billowing skirts to the knee, and made matching trousers, or "pantalettes," to wear beneath them. They also bobbed their hair to spare the time and effort of arranging it. "Perhaps we don't look as well as your city belle who is puffed and padded and painted," declared one Community woman, "but we are *genuine*," she said, "from head to toe."

Liberated from traditional marriage, women were free to accept or decline sexual invitations—unless they were solicited by a Community leader. Young women especially were pressured to mate with men between the ages of fifty and seventy. And men controlled the frequency, length, and enjoyment of their choreographed coupling. They prided themselves on their virtuosity. Holding a woman like a cello, her back to him, a man, after entering her, would use his fingers to orchestrate her climax, while denying himself that satisfaction. This was, Noyes said, a sublime spiritual act, and women, as the instrument of this connection, brought different tones and responses to the performance and discipline of the men. "There is as much difference between women in respect to ability to make social music as there is between a grand piano and a tenpenny whistle!" he told his niece Tirzah while lying in bed with her one night. Sex, he believed, was an act of human and celestial discovery. "As a man is said to know a woman in sexual intercourse," he remarked, "why may we not speak of the telescope with which he penetrates her heavens, and seeks the star of her heart?"

Those communions would last all night in the early years, but it was too exhausting. So special rooms were made available at night for brief sexual "interviews," between the hours of ten and twelve. Eventually, men visited women in their bedrooms for encounters, returning to their own rooms afterward. Little time was to be spent in conversation. "Talk less, love more!" Noyes instructed Tirzah—that was God's message, he said, although he frequently spent hours talking when he was in her arms. Tirzah held a special place in his heart—"You are a true daughter to me," he told her—and he was "bewitched" by her.

As the Community's father, Noyes led an experiment that was as notable for its success as for its practices. By early 1874, the Community had 283 members—131 males and 152 females. They happily rotated through household departments, including the laundry, the kitchen, the fruit cellar, the bakery, the dairy, the dining room, the icehouse, and the tailor shop. "They even had a Turkish bath in the basement," one Oneidan remembered. "Small groups of people worked side by side in most of these places, and they were able to talk with each other as they worked," so "no matter how menial the job was . . . time always flew."

They also rotated through a range of farming and industrial jobs. In addition to the lucrative trap business, Oneidans made mop handles, hoes, brooms, traveling bags, palm-leaf hats, embroidered slippers, and rustic outdoor furniture. They produced jams and jellies from homegrown fruit and made silk thread with water-powered spinning and winding equipment. Business was so brisk by the 1860s that the Community started hiring outside workers. During the Civil War, in fact, demand was so high for its products that in 1864 the Community's net worth soared by over a third. Because of a bureaucratic mistake, Oneida's young men were never told to register for the draft, so the war years produced wealth without sacrifice.

By 1870, more than two hundred outside workers helped run the farm, factories, laundry, and kitchen. The Community offered good wages, housing, free transportation, and even classes for its employees. With plenty of outside help, Oneidans began spending less time working and more time in pleasurable pursuits, from ice-skating and swimming to fishing and baseball. They adored music—Noyes played the violin, badly—and the Community orchestra, which rehearsed in the dairy house, gave free concerts to packed audiences of Oneidans and appreciative neighbors. They staged dramatic readings, theatrical performances, and tableaux, and they studied, too, pursuing subjects such as algebra, astronomy, trigonometry, geography, chemistry, physics, rhetoric, Latin, Greek, and Hebrew. Oneida was an energized social and intellectual hub, with daily lectures, activities, and entertainments. "I was a child in the old Community," recalled one member, "and I can tell you that they were a happy group. They used to meet nightly in the Big Hall to socialize, discuss problems, etc. The outside world had their get-togethers on Saturday night. We had ours every night, and it was something to look forward to."

And the outside world flocked to Oneida. The Community attracted so many tourists, including families and church groups, that in 1870, the Midland Railroad built a line running right through the property. At a station called "Community," visitors would debark almost every pleasant Sunday for strawberry shortcake, band concerts, and tours of its factories and farm. "All with whom I had occasion to speak," one visitor reported, praised the Oneidans for their "honesty, fair dealing . . . peaceable disposition, and great business capacity."

With the success of his social experiment, Noyes started another radical project. In 1865, six years after Charles Darwin published his book *On the Origin of Species*, Francis Galton suggested the notion of selectively breeding humans to improve their physical and mental qualities. More than a decade before Galton invented the term "eugenics," Noyes decided to test its possibilities on his thriving utopian community. He chose the term "stirpiculture" to describe his endeavor—from the Latin word "stirps," meaning root or stock. "We believe the time will come," Noyes declared, "when involuntary and random propagation will cease, and when scientific combination will be applied to human generation as freely and successfully as it is to that of other animals." His program of human breeding was the first eugenics experiment in US history.

To select the couples who would breed, the Community, in 1875, appointed a formal Stirpiculture Committee. In most cases, fathers were a dozen years older than mothers, and nearly half of the children were fathered by only ten men. Noyes himself sired nine of the children, who were called "stirpicults." Oneida's leading elders, in fact, fathered an inordinate number of babies—a practice that Noyes justified. "It is very probable," he wrote,

> that the feudal custom which gave barons the first privilege of every marriage among their retainers, base and oppressive though it was, actually improved the blood of the lower classes.

The children, Noyes declared, belonged to the Community and God, and they were saluted with a bit of royal pageantry. At a ceremony called "Weighing the Babies," the "stirps" were paraded into the Big Hall and weighed, in order of their birth, to the sounds of kettle drums and a musical fanfare.

"Sticky" parental affections were banned. The stirps were raised in a Children's House from the age of fifteen months until adolescence, when they became regular members of the Community. The Oneidans who ran the Children's House provided food, clothing, health care, and education. They did a fine job, according to the records, and "all the children seemed happy enough," one graduate recalled.

> Everybody was good to us. You know you were loved because it was like a big family. Also, there were so many

activities for the youngsters, so many things to do . . .
believe me—we were happy children.

—⁓—

By 1871, though, when John Humphrey Noyes reached the age of
sixty, his social and sexual charisma was starting to fade. He had
always been enormously attractive to women, who were drawn to
his intellect, intensity, and force of will. But now his vigor was
being sapped by headaches, back pains, deafness, and a terrible
burning in his throat that crippled his ability to speak. As each year
passed, his sexual powers diminished, along with his command
over younger members of the Community. His anxiety about his
frailty was obvious one winter day, when he stood at the edge of
a frozen pond with a group of young Oneidans. To prove to them
that he was still powerful and virile, he stripped off his clothes, dove
naked into its icy water, and swam across it, daring the young men
to follow him. They did. But they increasingly resisted his rule and
religious principles.

A secular spirit was spreading among younger Oneidans. The
Community had sent twelve of its young men—including Noyes's
eldest son, Theodore—to study at Yale University. Immersed in
new scientific theories and discoveries, they began placing reason
and science above theology. Some now especially chafed at Oneida's
discipline of male continence—and the fact that its older men
reserved the privilege of coupling with the young women. Noyes
himself—although he was aging and increasingly infirm—had the
nearly exclusive right to initiate girls as young as twelve. In 1874,
Noyes boasted to Tirzah that he was having an "exquisite little
romance" with a thirteen-year-old child. He defended the practice,
writing that

I have never made free with girls, as they have come to the natural development of sexual feelings, and I have not felt bound to inquire their age, or whether they were past puberty. . . . I cannot swear that I have never had sexual intercourse with persons of less than the legal age, because . . . I have not referred to age as the rule to go by; but I swear that I have never had sexual intercourse with anyone who did not give what I considered evident tokens of a mature state of passional and physical development.

He allowed his son Theodore to initiate another thirteen-year-old, and his son, too, defended the practice. "The seduction of a young girl," Theodore claimed,

entails fearful consequences in ordinary society. . . . But in our society, the consequences of the first sexual experience . . . eliminated the whole mass of sentiment and passion which, in the world, revolves around the question of virginity. . . . Moderate association with men is normal to any healthy women beyond the age of puberty, and she is better for it in every way, if social conditions are honorable and attractive. . . . To quite a late period father filled this situation perfectly. . . . The circle of young women he trained when he was between forty and fifty years of age, were by a large majority his devoted friends. . . .

According to Theodore, the power of regulating the sexual relations of Community members was, in fact, the most effective way of governing. It was his father's source of power in the Community, and "for many years," he noted, "there was very little dissatisfaction and no envy" of his father's prerogative.

But now, that power was declining. To lead Oneida into the future, Noyes looked to Theodore to succeed him. With a medical degree from Yale, his son was intelligent, educated, good-natured, and attractive, although he tended toward corpulence and was "inclined to apoplexy." He had always been popular with Oneida's women. Theodore had had a torrid affair with his first cousin Tirzah Miller, and he fathered four children with other women in the Community.

He also had a keen eye for business. In 1867, when Oneida had taken on heavy debt to expand its enterprises, Noyes placed Theodore in charge of its commercial activities. The twenty-six-year-old had no business experience, but in less than a year, he had cleared up the Community's debts, created a cash reserve, and led an ambitious expansion—even erecting a dam to supply more power for its busy printing and silk-spinning workshops. Theodore ran Oneida's businesses successfully and profitably—until Community members complained that he was too much of an autocrat, neglecting to involve other Oneidans in his decisions.

So in early 1872, his father seized back control of the enterprises, and Theodore had a nervous breakdown. Noyes dispatched him to a sanitarium in Dansville, New York—a huge, fortress-like facility known as "Our Home on the Hillside." It was run by Dr. James Caleb Jackson—the inventor of granola, which he called "granula." The largest health resort in the country, it drew thousands to its water cures and vibrating machinery, and its famous patients included nurse Clara Barton, who founded the first chapter of the American Red Cross in Dansville.

After four months of intensive treatment, Theodore returned to the Community—as its doctor instead of its business manager. But he was ill-suited to heal its festering problems. Some of his closest young relatives abandoned the colony. His half-brother Victor departed, and so did his cousin Joseph, who rejected the notion that Noyes was God's earthly messenger. Theodore admitted to his father that he shared his cousin's skepticism and even doubted the existence of God. He, too, then decided to leave Oneida. With fifty dollars in his pocket, he boarded a train for New York City "to conquer his doubts," his father explained to the Community. But Oneida was the only real home he had ever known, and within a week, Theodore was back, asking for readmission. He had not resolved his spiritual doubts, he conceded, but he believed in the social principles of the Community.

So Noyes came up with a plan to restore his son's faith in a higher power. Since the Fox sisters had first amazed the country with their demonstrations of spectral rappings, Noyes and the Community had flirted with the idea of spiritual communion with the dead. They believed that communication was possible but doubted that the spirits were reliable. In 1851, Noyes declared that "those who are swallowing the 'rapping' oracles" were "monstrously deluded"—not because the mediums were fakes, but because the ghosts they summoned were "lying spirits" who were not credentialed by Jesus Christ. Still, Noyes believed that it was possible that God could be sending messages through spectral communication.

By 1858, the Community had become more open to the power and possibility of spirit contact, acknowledging in its newspaper that it was

> simply absurd to attempt to ignore Spiritualism by calling
> it a humbug, a delusion, &c. The facts in this case are
> too well authenticated for any reflecting mind to doubt
> their reality.

Now, in 1873, Noyes asked Theodore to undertake a deep investigation of the spirit world. He hoped it would excite the Community's young people and ignite their belief in an afterlife. From there, he believed, it would reawaken their faith in God and Christ.

Theodore welcomed the challenge, filling the Community's library with books on mediums, spirits, and immortality. He also cultivated Oneidans who showed some ability as mediums—holding séances every day in a dark room in the attic of the Mansion House. During those sessions, one participant recalled, "we sat around a table and people *shook*." Noyes, too, participated in the gatherings and even rebuked the spirits of dead Oneidans in ghostly sessions of mutual criticism.

His cure had the planned effect. By March 1875, Theodore was convinced that there was "conclusive evidence of the existence of a spiritual world, inhabited by spiritual beings. I think it extremely probable," he wrote, "that these beings have lived as men and women in this world." There was, he claimed, "an invisible, intelligent force which can affect matter . . . which we do not yet fully understand."

His conversion was driven by firsthand experience. In the course of his investigations, he and a companion traveled around New York and New England to witness the powers of well-known mediums. His research, he specifically noted, took him to Vermont, where, in 1874, two nearly illiterate brothers, William and Horatio Eddy, were startling neighbors and visitors on their rundown farm near the town of Chittenden. In October that year, a New York newspaper published a letter that described William Eddy as "the greatest medium in history." The author of the letter was no crank, but a highly regarded attorney, Henry Steel Olcott, who specialized in fraud. Olcott had been a farm correspondent for Horace Greeley's *New York Tribune*, as well as a special commissioner charged with exposing corruption in the US Navy. He was also one of three panelists who officially probed the assassination of President Lincoln. In September 1874, Olcott traveled to the Eddy farm, seven miles north of Rutland, to investigate rumors of psychic phenomena orchestrated by the brutish brothers. He was commissioned to report on his findings to both the *New York Sun* and the *Daily Graphic*. If he discovered fraud, he planned to expose the brothers publicly as hoaxsters.

Olcott arrived at the farm on September 17, in the middle of a violent rainstorm. In rugged country surrounded by the Green Mountains, the two-story homestead had crude accommodations for visitors in a single large room with walls of peeling plaster. Olcott paid the low fee for bed and board and found the two middle-aged brothers to be "sensitive, distant and curt with strangers." They looked

> more like hard-working rough farmers than prophets or priests of a new dispensation, have dark complexions, black hair and eyes, stiff joints, a clumsy carriage, shrink from advances, and make newcomers feel ill at ease and unwelcome. They are at feud with some of their neighbors and, as a rule, not liked.

The Eddys had shown powerful psychic abilities since childhood, falling into trances and summoning strange apparitions. Their father, Zephaniah Eddy, tried to break these disturbing habits by beating them, scalding them with boiling water, and even using a red-hot coal to try to burn the devilish spirits out of them. When nothing stopped their trances, Zephaniah hired the boys out to a traveling freak show that exhibited them across America, Europe, and Canada. Audiences had a free hand in attempting to challenge their psychic powers by hitting them, locking them in boxes, and even pouring molten wax into their mouths to stop them from producing "spirit voices." Mobbed, chased, stoned, and shot at, they were finally able to return to the family farm when their father died. There, with their sister Mary and their mother, Julia, they began taking in guests and staging regular séances, with no admission fee.

On his first night at the Eddy farm, Olcott attended one of these ghostly gatherings. Twenty-five guests assembled in what the brothers called the "circle room" on the second floor. Sitting on wooden benches, they watched William Eddy enter a tiny space behind a door. There, he was tied to a chair and fell into a trance. Guests were instructed to hold hands as they listened to some unartful vocal and instrumental music. After a short intermission, the spirits began to appear—among them several Native American women; a man named Santum, who stood six-foot-three; and the spirits of other dead, including a baby and a child of twelve or thirteen.

Every night, except Sunday, at similar séances over the next ten weeks, Olcott saw three or four hundred materialized spirits of both sexes, of all shapes and sizes, in "every imaginable variety of costume." He also saw disembodied hands and musical instruments soaring over his head. The virtuosity of the music they played, according to the testimony of a Connecticut musician in the audience, was extraordinary. At a séance he attended, he recounted, the musician heard

> various solos, duos, trios, and concerted pieces . . . played by some mysterious performers. The solos were upon the violin, guitar, flute, piccolo, concertina, and mouth harmonicon. The two most surprising features of the performance were: 1) the playing on a guitar as it floated from one side of the room to the other, through the air, a distance of at least fifteen feet (this was not a mere strumming of the strings, but a delicate and artistic playing of a popular air in pianissimo); and 2) the execution of the air of "Home Sweet Home" on the concertina. The invisible performer managed to get more power, and at

the same time preserve as good expression as any person I have ever heard handle the instrument. I noticed the same striking feature as with the guitar playing . . . that the musical sound was prolonged and the swells maintained through a much greater space laterally than any mortal performer could cover and at the same time sustain the same quality of tone.

According to Olcott, the Eddy brothers performed other spectral displays, including the levitation of bodies and writing of messages by disembodied hands.

To detect any signs of fraud, Olcott scrupulously examined and measured the circle room, looking for secret doors, panels, and passages. He even brought in engineers and carpenters to scrutinize the premises, but they found nothing at all out of the ordinary. Olcott was familiar with the tricks of fake mediums and theatrical staging techniques but found evidence of none, making it even more bizarre that he observed hundreds of different materialized spirits. If fraudulent, those manifestations would have required the impoverished Eddy family to pay for troupes of actors and many trunks of costumes.

The spirits conversed in six languages known to members of the audience. Their multicultural materializations multiplied when a Russian woman, fluent in several tongues, joined Olcott at the Eddy farm. During one séance they both attended, they saw apparitions including a man dressed in a Georgian jacket with loose sleeves, leggings of yellow leather, baggy trousers, and a white fez with a tassel. The next night, another spirit appeared wearing a long yellowish coat, Turkish trousers, a vest, a black Astrakhan cap, and a traditional Cossack hood with its long tasseled ends thrown over his shoulders. He was followed by a spirit dressed, in the most exacting detail, like a Kurdish warrior the woman had known well at an

Armenian summer resort near Mount Ararat, when her husband, she related, was vice-governor of the provincial capital. The warrior first appeared empty-handed—then suddenly, an immense twelve-foot spear materialized in his hand, a ring of ostrich plumes circling the base of its steel tip. The weapon, she explained to Olcott, was always carried by Kurdish horseman, who were known for handling it with astonishing dexterity.

———

Communing with the dead had come a long way since crude knocking noises had first been orchestrated by the famous Fox sisters. Still, Maggie and Kate Fox continued to draw clients to their spirited séances. Both sisters, unfortunately, also developed an acute fondness for distilled spirits. In 1871, Kate Fox, then a thirty-four-year-old alcoholic, moved to London on the advice of the ghost of Benjamin Franklin, who encouraged her to make a new start there. Small, thin, straightforward, and highly intelligent, Kate enchanted British spiritualists with her ability to summon raps by placing her hand on any substance. The noises were so thunderous they could be heard three rooms away. As the well-known chemist and physicist William Crookes reported,

> I have heard [the sounds] in a living tree—on a sheet of glass—on a stretched iron wire—on a stretched membrane—a tambourine—on the roof of a cab—and on the floor of a theater. I have had these sounds, proceeding from the floor, walls &c, when the medium's hands and feet were held—when she was standing on a chair—when she was suspended in a swing from the ceiling—when she was enclosed in a wire cage—and

when she had fallen fainting on a sofa. I have heard them on a glass harmonicon—I have felt them on my own shoulder and under my own hands. I have heard them on a sheet of paper, held between the fingers by a piece of thread passed through one corner.

A friend of Crookes, Henry Dietrich Jencken, had met Kate at a reception when she first arrived in London. A barrister, he was tall and fair and a scholar of Roman law. In 1872, he asked Kate to marry him, and she agreed. At their wedding breakfast, it was reported, loud, approving raps were heard all over the room, and the table holding their wedding cake joyfully jumped into the air.

Charles Guiteau, meanwhile, was sinking into destitution and delusion. After the death of Greeley and his high hopes of political office, the thirty-two-year-old, his wife said, was often "intensely high-tempered" and angry. Many times, Annie Bunn recalled, "he took hold of me suddenly (he had great strength in his arms and hands), opened the door . . . wherever we might be boarding, and kicked me right out into the hall." Sometimes he would lock Annie up all night in a freezing closet. He also started sleeping with other women and contracted syphilis. In the summer of 1873, his wife had to nurse him through a bout of the infection that almost killed him. In September, she filed for a divorce. It was finalized the next year.

Guiteau acknowledged that he was "very much reduced in circumstances." Out of business, out of money, and out of friends, he was thrown in jail for his failure to pay debts. It was, he conceded, "the unhappiest streak I ever struck in my life." After thirty-five days, his sister and brother-in-law paid his bail and took him to live with them in Wisconsin, but they threw him out after he threatened his sister with an ax. A doctor said they should commit Guiteau to a hospital for the insane, but he managed to escape across the state line to Illinois. He briefly opened another law office in Chicago, then abandoned it and traveled to his father's house. But Luther Guiteau had no hope for his son's redemption. Charles, he had come to see, was wicked, lecherous, deranged, and "a fit subject for a lunatic asylum." Someday, he conceded, he would not be surprised to learn that his son had "committed a fearful crime."

9

PRIZES OF POWER

When John Humphrey Noyes was a young boy in Vermont, his father, the elder John Noyes, had a successful mercantile business called Noyes & Hayes. His partner in the company was his brother-in-law, Rutherford "Ruddy" Hayes. Their business was one of the first chain stores in America.

In 1817, they decided to sell their shares, and thirty-year-old Ruddy and his wife, Sophia Birchard, traveled west to Ohio in covered wagons. They settled in the town of Delaware, where Hayes built a brick house and bought a fruit farm. But five years later, typhoid killed him—only ten weeks before the birth of his second son. The infant—Rutherford Birchard Hayes, called "Rud"—was so tiny and weak that a neighbor said, "It would be a mercy if the child would die." As he grew older, he was so emaciated that his family worried he would be an invalid, and he was seven before he could roughhouse with other children. Rud was "timid as a girl"—but, over time, he grew into a sturdy, steady, studious young man.

In 1861, with a law degree from Harvard and a successful legal practice in Ohio, Rud enlisted as a major in the Union Army. He was the definition of a happy warrior. He enjoyed the fighting as though on "a pleasure tour," he claimed, even though he was wounded five times. He loved his life as a soldier, he declared, "as much as a boy does the Fourth of July." By war's end, he was a major general. His transformation was stunning to Sergeant William McKinley, who would one day become a US president. "From the sunny, agreeable, the kind, the generous, the gentle gentleman," Hayes was, in the heat of battle, "intense and ferocious."

After the war, he turned to politics. In 1867, after winning two terms as a congressman, Hayes was elected governor of Ohio. He was reelected in 1869 and had reached, he believed, the pinnacle of his career. At the age of fifty, he was physically strong and successful, with a reputation for honesty, moderation, loyalty, and quiet competence. He was a happy family man, too, with his wife, Lucy, and their four children. He had no contact with his notorious first cousin, John Humphrey Noyes, but he had grown close to another Noyes relative in Ohio, Edward Follansbee Noyes. The two of them had served together in the military, where Noyes, a brigadier general, had lost his leg. When Hayes finished his second term as governor, Noyes won the election to succeed him. Although he lost reelection in 1873, Noyes stepped into a new role as a commissioner of the 1876 Centennial Exposition in Philadelphia.

It was America's hundredth birthday party and its very first World's Fair. Nearly nine million people—about a fifth of the population—showed up to marvel at its many wonders, from George Washington's false teeth to Alexander Graham Bell's telephone and the huge right arm of the Statue of Liberty. Never had so many Americans flocked to a patriotic event. But just over a decade after the end of the Civil War, its unifying effect masked dark divisions that still threatened the fragile democracy.

Although Black people had won freedom and rights in the wake of the Civil War, white paramilitary groups in the South were now waging viciously effective campaigns against Black citizens, Republicans, and Reconstruction. Groups including the Ku Klux Klan, the Knights of the White Camelia, the Red Shirts, and the White Brotherhood attacked and murdered thousands in their efforts to restore white supremacy in the region. Meanwhile, federal troops maintained martial law in three of the Southern states—Florida, South Carolina, and Louisiana. And the country was reeling through a financial panic that had crushed eighteen thousand businesses and thrown more than three million people out of work. In 1876, a hundred years after its founding, America was wounded and still painfully fractured.

It was also the year of a presidential election. Grant, after two terms, would not seek a third, and Republicans were jockeying for position. Hayes—who had recently won a third term as Ohio's governor—was rumored to be in the running. Although he "discouraged rather than encouraged" the chatter, he was intrigued. As he wrote in his diary on March 21, "It seems to me that good purposes, and the judgment, experience and firmness I possess would enable me to execute the duties of the office well. I do not feel the least fear that I should fail. This all looks egotistical," he conceded, "but it is sincere."

Eight days later, at the Ohio Republican Convention, every delegate voted to support his candidacy. But Hayes was unknown on the national level. The leading Republican candidates included Grant's stalwart ally Roscoe Conkling, the powerful senator from New York. To win the Republican nomination, Conkling had to defeat political foes, including his greatest enemy, Senator James Blaine of Maine. Ambitious and powerfully built, Blaine relished political battle. He and Conkling had hated each other since 1866, when they first served together in the House. In a battle over legislation, Blaine had made fun of Conkling's "cheap swagger" and "turkey-gobbler strut." From then on, the two men never spoke a single word to each other, and their breach became more bitter over time.

Blaine was the Republican front-runner in the spring, supported by a band of fans called Blainiacs. With his deep voice and theatrical style, he always commanded attention on the floor of Congress. Blaine was a splendid orator, with such apparent warmth and frankness that he was known as "the magnetic man." Although that charm was calculated, it had great effect. "Had he been a woman," one admirer said, "people would have rushed off to send [him] expensive flowers." Blaine, though, had come under suspicion for shady financial dealings, which darkened his prospects for the nomination. Conkling, too, for all his foppish arrogance, faced difficult odds; even President Grant, his political ally, privately preferred another candidate.

It was a stroke of luck for Governor Hayes when the Republican National Committee chose Cincinnati for its convention. Although Conkling brought fifteen hundred workers to the city—many of them, no doubt, public servants—and Blaine filled seventeen train carloads with supporters, Hayes enjoyed the home-field advantage, and his campaign badges and banners filled the echoing Exposition Hall when the convention opened on June 14.

He was considered a winning choice for the vice presidency because of his unimpeachable character and electoral record. Conkling was so convinced of his appeal that he hired a Vaudeville team to write a catchy campaign song touting Conkling and Hayes as "the Ticket That Pays." But Hayes was aiming for the top spot. Thanks to the able work of his cousin and campaign manager, Edward Noyes, Hayes took the lead on the seventh ballot and clinched the presidential nomination. Although some critics called him "a plaster saint" and "a third-rate nonentity," others praised him as a "neutral man . . . without flaw or spot"—competent, affable, and offensive to no one—who was fit to lead America into its second century.

His Democratic opponent for president was Samuel Jones Tilden, the governor of New York. Pale and slight, with no personal charisma, the sixty-two-year-old was a quiet bachelor who had suffered a stroke and had a drooping eyelid. Although Tilden was an unlikely politician, he was a brilliant strategist and political organizer who had battled corruption in New York's Democratic machine. And he had the electoral advantage. After eight years under President Grant, the country was mired in a depression and exhausted by Reconstruction. To make matters worse, Grant's secretary of war, William Belknap, was being impeached by the Senate for admitted graft. The country seemed eager for political change.

With two colorless candidates, the presidential contest was "flat and tame," according to the *New York Herald*. But it was a nerve-rackingly close race—so close, in fact, that on the morning after the November 7 election, the *New York Times* announced that Hayes was elected president, while the *New York Sun* declared Tilden the winner. While most newspapers put Tilden ahead, returns were still coming in. The Democrat, sporting a cheery red carnation on his lapel, enjoyed a day of glad-handing and congratulations, while Hayes, calm and unflappable, went about his usual routine.

The race was excruciatingly neck and neck. Tilden, it became clear, had won the popular election by a margin of more than 250,000, but he fell short—by one vote—of winning the electoral college. He had swept seventeen states, with 184 of the 185 he needed. Hayes had just 166 electoral votes. But three crucial states were still in play—Florida, South Carolina, and Louisiana. If those three Southern states went for Tilden, he would run away with the election. But if they went for Hayes, their combined electoral votes would put the Ohio governor over the top, with 185—exactly the number he needed to win. Over the next four months, the ferocious battle over vote counting in Florida, South Carolina, and Louisiana triggered an explosive constitutional crisis that rocked America's democracy on its hundredth birthday and foreshadowed perilous election disputes more than a century later, in the years 2000 and 2020.

Most rebel states, by 1876, had successfully thrown off the yoke of Reconstruction. But Florida, South Carolina, and Louisiana remained under federal control, with Republican governors protected by US troops. The election in all three states hung by a razor's edge. In Florida, Tilden seemed to have won by less than a hundred votes. In both South Carolina and Louisiana, the electoral margins were also exceedingly thin, with Hayes winning, apparently, in South Carolina and Tilden in Louisiana. But widespread reports of fraud and electoral violence—mostly targeting Black voters and Republicans—threw the counts of all three states into dispute.

In South Carolina, where Black men had a large voting majority, armed white rifle clubs had roamed the state to suppress their participation at the polls. In September, more than five hundred armed whites had threatened to kill or whip Black citizens in the town of Ellenton if they voted Republican. As many as a hundred were massacred in the resulting riot.

The mayhem was even worse in Louisiana. At the instigation of the state's central Democratic committee, masked and heavily armed bands of white supremacist night riders terrorized Black communities—attacking, murdering, and mutilating men, women, and children. Three days before the election, armed and organized whites staged a brutal and bloody attack on Black Republicans, including a sixty-year-old man named Abram Williams.

He was taken from his house, stripped, and severely whipped. They visited the house of Willis Frazier, took him also from his bed and brutally whipped him. They visited the house of a son of Abram Williams. He had taken the precaution to spend the night in the cotton-field. Not finding him at home, they whipped his wife, and committed another outrage upon her person. Merrimon Rhodes, on that night, was killed. A few days later, his body, disemboweled, was found in the bayou and was buried. They visited the house of Randall Driver. They took him from his bed and from his house and brutally whipped him. They visited the house of Henry Pinkston. He was taken from his bed, from his house, and shot to death. His infant child was killed. His wife was cut in different places; she was shot and nearly slain.

Beyond these hellish cruelties, blatant corruption threatened the election. The state canvassing board in Louisiana was said to have offered to certify the election for Tilden for a bribe of a million dollars.

President Grant was so worried by these reports that he sent federal troops to all three states to maintain civic order until returns were certified. He also deployed troops to secure Washington's bridges and the federal arsenal. There were rumors that a Democratic militia planned to attack the capital and install Samuel Tilden as president. Meanwhile, prominent Republicans, led by Edward Noyes, hurried to Florida to monitor the official count of the state canvassing board. And Grant asked Congressman James Garfield to go to New Orleans and stay there until Louisiana's votes were officially tallied. Garfield hesitated, but the president pleaded with him to go—"to calm the public agitation and witness the canvass of the Electoral votes." So, on November 11, Garfield left for New Orleans.

He and other official observers watched closely as the Republican-controlled state canvassing board counted the votes and rejected ballots from districts where Democrats had perpetrated fraud or intimidation. When their tally ended, Louisiana went for Hayes. So did Florida and South Carolina, with their Republican-controlled boards. With all three of the states now in the Republican column, it looked like Hayes had precisely the 185 electoral votes that he needed to win the presidency—by a one-vote margin—when the electors would formally send their election certificates to Congress on December 6.

But that constitutional process erupted in chaos. Democrats in Florida, South Carolina, and Louisiana claimed that their Republican-dominated returns boards had committed fraud, and in all three states they submitted to Congress a second certified slate of electors, claiming that Tilden had won the election instead of Hayes.

Many Americans had a renewed sense of dread. As former *New York Times* editor John Bigelow wrote in his diary, "Another civil war may be the consequence of this state of things, and we may enter upon the next century under a different form of government." There were rumors of a coup d'état. In early January 1877, a Democratic congressman called for a hundred thousand partisans to rally in Washington for the inauguration of Tilden. Joseph Pulitzer, publisher of the *New York World*, urged them to come to the capital "fully armed and ready for business." In Chicago, a former general supposedly recruited veterans to steal weapons from federal arsenals. The White House was even warned that Tilden supporters in Missouri were planning to seize seven hundred cannons and "fixed ammunition, enough to supply an army of sixty thousand men" from the federal arsenal in St. Louis. Democrats, meanwhile, feared that President Grant would use the military to install Hayes. Faced with these poisonous tensions, Tilden urged his supporters to stay calm. "It will not do to fight," he said.

We have just emerged from one Civil War, and it will never do to engage in another; it would end in the destruction of free government. We cannot back down. We can, therefore, only arbitrate.

To resolve the crisis, at the end of January, Congress created an independent electoral commission to rule on the competing certificates. The bipartisan, fifteen-member body would be "a tribunal whose authority none can question and whose decision all will accept as final." Garfield was named to the commission, which included five congressmen, five senators, and five justices of the Supreme Court. On February 9, after long deliberations that lasted far into the night, they decided the Florida case in favor of Hayes. One week later, after another marathon session—"a day of the most nervous strain and anxiety I have ever passed since Chickamauga," Garfield recalled—they decided Louisiana for Hayes, too, on a party-line vote. The South Carolina decision still hung in the balance.

The atmosphere in Washington crackled with political peril. Congressmen were carrying pistols on the House floor for protection. And Garfield heard whispers that he might be the target of a murderously partisan assassin. In the midst of this perilous crisis, a group of Republicans and Southern Democrats gathered at a capital hotel to try to work out an electoral compromise.

———

Lafayette Square, across the park from the White House, was the most prominent location in the nation's capital, and just one block away stood the city's most elegant, expensive, and sought-after spot for lodging, dining, and political dealing—the unparalleled Wormley's Hotel. With its large, sumptuous reception, guest, smoking, dining, and wine rooms, the five-story hotel on Fifteenth and H Streets was especially famous for its exquisite restaurant, specializing in terrapin—the small, diamond-back Chesapeake turtle coveted for its sweet meat.

The owner of the hotel was James Wormley, a respected, successful Black entrepreneur. Born in Washington in 1819, he was the ninth child of a freeborn couple, Mary and Lynch Wormley. Lynch had built a good business driving a hackney cab around the capital. With the profits he made, he bought so much property on I Street that a lane behind it, Wormley Alley, was named for him.

His son James had the benefit of excellent schooling. By the time he was seventeen, he was driving a hackney carriage for his father. In 1841, when he was twenty-two, he married Anna Elizabeth Thompson, and the pair displayed enormous entrepreneurial energy as they raised their young, growing family. In addition to taking care of their four children, Anna had a confectionary shop on I Street, while James worked as a racehorse jockey, a riverboat steward on the Mississippi, and a gold prospector in California. Then, in the 1850s, he launched a catering business next door to his wife's confectionary—preparing and delivering daily breakfasts and dinners, in tin boxes, to the many senators, congressmen, and clerks who chose to dine in their rooms while living in the city's hotels and boardinghouses. The business was so prosperous that James was able to purchase and run four successful boardinghouses of his own between Fifteenth and Sixteenth on I Street, attracting prominent guests including the English writer Anthony Trollope. While running these properties, he also catered private parties and was the steward for Washington's Metropolitan Club. James was so well thought of that he was asked to accompany a new US minister to England across the Atlantic as his personal chef, along with a delicate cargo of live terrapins.

When James opened his grand hotel in 1870, with a bank loan and backing from a Republican congressman, it quickly became the favorite of the city's elite. Wormley's had the highest prices and best food of any of the capital's hotels, including the Willard and the Metropolitan. It was so favored by Europeans that its residents included the German and Dutch foreign service delegations. Since Wormley's was profitable from the beginning, James continued to expand his business and land holdings. In addition to maintaining his I Street enterprises, he bought property in the free Black community of Tenleytown, where he raised fresh vegetables for his hotel; built stables, a racetrack, and three homes for his family; and opened a popular roadhouse.

It was his reputation for discretion, above all, that won him the patronage of powerful politicos. So at Wormley's, on the night of February 26, 1877, amid a festering constitutional crisis, a group of Republicans and Southern Democrats gathered to confirm an agreement. Earlier that day, the electoral commission had examined South Carolina's competing certificates and awarded its electors to Hayes. He would win the presidency, when Congress finished counting the votes. But Democrats threatened to delay that conclusion by staging a filibuster in the House. If the delay lasted longer than March 4— when President Grant's term officially ended—the country, for the first time, would have no president at all.

To avoid that disaster, those who gathered at Wormley's that evening endorsed a deal. Democrats would accept Hayes if he agreed to end Reconstruction. He would withdraw federal troops from Florida, Louisiana, and South Carolina—leaving their Black populations defenseless in the face of new Jim Crow laws that would strip them of their voting and civil rights. Although most of the agreements had been worked out before the meeting, they came to be known as the "Wormley Compromise"—ironically reached at a property owned by a Black businessman. Three days later, on March 1, the Democrats dropped their filibuster, and on March 2, at 4:10 in the morning—after an incendiary eighteen-hour session in which congressmen yelled, drew their pistols, and almost pummeled one another with fists—the final electoral counts were announced: 184 for Tilden and 185 for Hayes.

———

The president-elect heard the news that morning, just after dawn. He, his wife, and three of their children—Scott, Fanny, and Webb—had traveled by train from Ohio before the vote counting had ended. Their journey was kept quiet because of a real fear of assassination. Weeks earlier in Columbus, they had dodged a bullet that was fired through their parlor window. Now, after spending the night near Harrisburg, Pennsylvania, they pulled into Washington at nine o'clock in the morning. Despite their plans for a stealthy arrival, they were greeted by thousands of cheering supporters. The following evening, on March 4—Grant's last night in office—they were the guests of honor at a White House dinner. And there, in the Red Room of the Executive Mansion, the chief justice administered the oath of office to Rutherford Hayes, secretly swearing him in as president two days before the official inauguration.

That event, too, was unusually hushed, with little fanfare. As the carriage carrying Hayes and former president Grant made its way to the Capitol, it was surrounded by Secret Service agents, on high alert for assassination attempts. "There were many indications of relief and joy," Garfield wrote in his diary, "that no accident . . . occurred on the route." Hayes survived his elevation to the presidency, but for half the population, he had no right to be there. He was, to them, "His Fraudulency," "Rutherfraud B. Hayes," and "The Great Usurper."

He promised to serve for only a single term, focused on reforming the civil service. Presidents had long had to put up with "the endless whine of office-seekers," as Horace Greeley described it. Even on the day after Hayes's inauguration, his supporter James Garfield said his home was besieged, from morning till night, by crowds seeking his help to secure positions. But political patronage was not only an annoyance, Hayes believed—it promoted and protected the unworthy and degraded government. The entire spoils system, he declared, should be completely and radically abolished.

His predecessor, Ulysses Grant, had made some gestures toward reforming it. In 1870, he had told Congress,

> There is no duty which so much embarrasses [the] Executive, and head of departments, as that of appointments; nor is there [any such] arduous and thankless labor imposed on Senators and representatives as that of finding places for constituents.

Grant had established the first Civil Service Commission, but Congress mainly ignored its recommendations. And his allegiance to Roscoe Conkling, America's most powerful party boss, undermined any reform ambitions he might have had.

But Hayes assumed a tougher stance, with Conkling in his sights. In early April, barely a month after his inauguration, he made plans to investigate the New York Custom House. His motive was partly personal. Conkling had snubbed him during the campaign. As a result, Hayes had lost New York, and there were rumors that Conkling would have preferred Tilden. But there were also suggestions of bribery, salary padding, and other misconduct at the custom house—leading the *New York Times* to call it "the most complete and offensive example" of the need for civil service reform. In June, Hayes issued an order that forbade party "assessments" of federal office holders—prohibiting their forced "contributions"—and barring them from participating "in the management of political organizations, caucuses, conventions, or electoral campaigns." Then, in September, he asked Conkling's lieutenant, New York collector Chester Arthur, to resign his post. Arthur refused, triggering a vicious political battle between Hayes and Conkling, who, Hayes remarked, was driven by "a desire to rule or ruin."

Over the next two years, Conkling, as chairman of the Senate Commerce Committee, made sure that all the president's nominees for New York collector were rejected. Finally, during a congressional recess, Hayes successfully removed Arthur from his post and replaced him with a civil service reformer named Edwin Merritt, who was confirmed by the Senate in 1879. "Granny Hayes," as Conkling called the president, had finally dealt the New York senator a bitter defeat.

Conkling's swaggering arrogance took another blow that summer. He had long been estranged from his wife, Julia, who lived with their daughter, Bessie, in a stately stone mansion in Utica, New York. Conkling, with his majestic height, broad shoulders, and carefully coiffed whiskers, was reputed, in Washington, to be a Casanova—"the Pet of the Petticoats," as Greeley called him. Most of his adventures were discreet, until he started an affair, in the mid-1870s, with Kate Chase, a woman who was the toast of Washington.

She was the daughter of Salmon P. Chase—the chief justice of the Supreme Court and former senator and secretary of the treasury. Kate—who was tall, vivacious, and politically canny—was his hostess and the queenly confidante and counselor of many of Washington's most powerful men. In 1863, she had married Rhode Island governor William Sprague, a rich and irascible alcoholic who later became a senator. It was a miserable marriage, and by the late 1870s, she and Conkling were a couple. She came and went from the apartment he had taken at Wormley's and traveled with him around Europe. They made a striking pair that was the talk of the capital.

Their notoriety exploded in the summer of 1879, when Conkling secretly visited Kate while her husband was out of town. When Sprague unexpectedly returned to the house two nights later, armed with a shotgun, Conkling, gossips whispered, escaped out of a bedroom window, clutching his trousers. The affair ended abruptly, as did Conkling's pretensions. Lord Roscoe, to the delight of his Washington critics, had been caught, in flagrante, in the act of looking ridiculous.

———

There was no doubt that President Hayes was straightlaced. He never smoked, swore, or drank liquor, and his wife, who banned alcohol from the White House, was known in the capital as "Lemonade Lucy." But Hayes was surprisingly broadminded when it came to his first cousin John Humphrey Noyes. As governor of Ohio, Hayes told visiting Oneidans that he had "no prejudices" about their peculiar religious beliefs, "and was well pleased" at having a visit from them. He even toured the Community's branch in Wallingford, Connecticut. Later, when he was president, Oneidans came to see him in the White House and presented him with a huge bear trap—although they were always careful not to embarrass him about their connection.

With his close family ties to the president, Noyes publicly downplayed his religious vision of the Oneida Community as an outpost of God's heaven on earth. He recast the colony, instead, as a model of successful collective living and renamed its newspaper *The American Socialist*. His son Theodore, meanwhile—a devoted spiritualist—became his full-fledged deputy. In May 1877, Noyes declared that Theodore would be his successor and formally stepped down as Community leader.

But there was resistance. Even his devoted niece Tirzah Miller worried about the future and his son's capacity for leadership. "The course Theodore has pursued for the last few years makes it utterly impossible for us to receive him as leader, unless he undergoes a vast change," she wrote.

> It is unlikely that we shall ever allow anyone the absolute control which has been exerted by Mr. Noyes—certainly not unless his mantle falls on a successor who shall equal him in spiritual power. An aristocracy of the Noyes blood has grown up in the Community. . . . But look at the second generation of Noyeses! Where is there one among them who has inherited anything like the original faith?

Still, despite her unhappiness and growing fear that Noyes was just "a crazy enthusiast . . . experimenting on human beings," she felt that she had to stand by him and support his right to run the community "not by vote of the members but by the will of God."

Theodore, as its new leader, repeated his success as business manager—adding a new wing to the Mansion House and building a factory to make tin-plated spoons at Wallingford. But he adopted a management approach that exasperated and offended many Oneidans. Each day, he required them to file written reports of all their activities—work-related, sexual, and recreational. Even youngsters, one later recalled, "were given little pads, printed and lined, so that we could record each hour of the day."

The Community soon had enough. In January 1878—only seven months after Theodore's appointment as "Father"—John Humphrey

Noyes was obliged to take back control of the colony. By then, however, there were intractable internal conflicts. Seventy-five percent of Oneidans, Noyes admitted, had lost confidence in him. He grew accustomed to watching Community members turn their faces away from him when they crossed paths, avoiding even a casual hello.

There were also growing threats from the outside. Since 1873, Oneida had been besieged by attacks from a publicity-hungry academic named John Mears, a professor of intellectual and moral philosophy at nearby Hamilton College. In his lectures and articles, Mears took aim at "a set of men banded together for the purpose of . . . shameful immoralities," leading the young "into impure and shocking practices." The Oneida Community, he declared, was a monstrous "Utopia of obscenity" visited by "the throngs of curious or the indifferent, by picnic parties . . . and . . . Sunday-School excursions."

After Mears sounded the alarm, Methodist ministers in upstate New York excoriated the Community for its harlotry and "free and licensed indulgence," reveling in "debauchery and shame." In Utica, the Synod of Presbyterians of New York appointed a committee to investigate the "dark and slimy depths" of depravity practiced by the Oneidans. Local newspapers, however, were unimpressed by all the outrage. The *Fulton Times* complimented the Community for being "clean and thrifty," respectable and peaceful, and the *Utica Herald* had nothing but praise for its leader:

> For the Oneida Community there is but one John Humphrey Noyes. It has reached the zenith of its prosperity under the impulse of his guiding mind and hand; its decay and disintegration will have begun when these are finally removed. . . . It has . . . accumulated broad acres and a large bank account, it has built fine buildings and

commanded ready markets for its goods and manufactures, not because of its religion, nor its Communism, but in spite of them.

Local law enforcement was equally unmoved. The Oneida County district attorney admitted that

> For the life of me, I don't see how they can ever get a legal hold on those people. . . . They are planted as firm as a rock . . . if indictments could be procured on the ground of general immorality, who wouldn't be liable? I don't believe they can ever be indicted for their belief, in this State. . . . Not a word has been said to me about prosecuting them or about an arrest. I feel safe to predict that none will occur. They are good citizens, mind their business, have the respect of their neighbors and the confidence of their customers all over the country, own a large property and valuable industries, furnish employment to hundreds of people at good wages, and are altogether too serviceable to warrant either county in doing anything to risk their displeasure without very good cause.

Frustrated but not silenced, Mears and his fellow antagonists gathered together on Valentine's Day 1879 to demand action against Oneida's "Epicurean sty." Although Mears banned reporters from the meeting, he likely leaked some dubious information—published by the *Syracuse Morning Standard* in late June—that Noyes was about to be arrested.

In 1847, when he was charged with fornication in Vermont, Noyes had swiftly and secretly abandoned his devoted followers. Now, thirty-two years later, with his health failing and his power over the Community crumbling, he faced another stark moment of truth. His closest advisers urged him to leave immediately. "Tonight!" they begged him. "Tomorrow it may be too late." One of his counselors—Myron Kinsley, a member of Oneida for thirty years—was especially worried about publicity that could tarnish the future prospects of Community members. While Noyes contemplated his options, they hitched up a buggy to carry him outside the jurisdiction of New York State. Finally, after midnight on June 23, 1879, Noyes slipped out of his room in the South Tower of the Mansion House, past the darkened bedrooms of his sleeping and rebellious flock, climbed into the waiting carriage, and secretly fled west to Canada.

10

SERPENTS IN THE GARDEN

By 1879, James Garfield—in his ninth term as a US congressman—had built a home in Washington, D.C., and he had rebuilt his marriage. After confessing his infidelity to his wife, Crete, he had lost his taste for extramarital adventures. Garfield became a family man—in love, at last, with his own wife and enchanted by his surviving children, Harry, Jim, Mollie, Irvin, and Abram.

Their three-story brick house, at the corner of Thirteenth and I Streets, was a happy nest. Garfield had built it a decade earlier, and his youngsters grew up tearing through its rooms and racing around his desk as he dictated letters. Harry and Jim attended classes just up the block at the Franklin School, while Garfield headed to Congress around noon, carrying his own spartan lunch of raw beef on stale bread to soothe his delicate digestion. The family gathered together for dinner, when Garfield would try—with little success—to tame his lively brood's "animal spirits" with serious conversations about their lessons.

During the sultry, stinking, malarial Washington summer, the family escaped to the Ohio countryside. In 1876, Garfield had purchased a broken-down farm with one hundred twenty acres in the town of Mentor. The property was in a "general state of chaos," with "shaky old barns . . . heaps of rubbish" and a malodorous pigsty, a visitor sniffed. But Garfield welcomed the challenge and distraction of pitching hay, raising cattle, rehabilitating the down-at-the-heels farmhouse, and building himself a library in a small cottage behind it. The refreshing simplicity of life in Mentor was a calming counterweight to the intense political turmoil that had gripped Washington.

As minority leader in the Democratic-controlled House, Garfield had won institutional power and influence—even though he was considered as "helpless as a child" when it came to his grasp of parliamentary rules and he was never, like Blaine or Conkling, a compelling leader. Still, he was widely admired, though the hurly-burly of the House had taken its toll. On his forty-eighth birthday, in November 1879, he noted that his whiskers were "considerably sprinkled with gray." He had little touches of rheumatism in his shoulders, too, reminding him that the years were leaving their mark. Happily, two months later, he was elected a US Senator—a role that he hoped would be less demanding—for a term set to begin over a year later, in March 1881.

Until then, Garfield would have his hands more than full with the upcoming presidential election. Although President Hayes would not run again, he had weakened the Republican party. His stern, rigidly correct manner did little to endear him to voters, and he had pursued, according to Garfield, "a suicidal policy toward Congress and is almost alone without a friend." He had split the party by ending Reconstruction and removing Chester Arthur as New York collector. The Republicans were splintered into feuding factions, and the race for the White House was wide open.

Senator James Blaine of Maine was competing for the nomination. So was Secretary of the Treasury John Sherman, who, like Garfield, hailed from Ohio. Sherman had supported Garfield's Senate candidacy. In return, Garfield promised to be his floor manager at the Republican National Convention. But this time, Roscoe Conkling was out of the running. His goal, instead, was to install his political patron, Ulysses Grant, in the White House for a third, nonconsecutive term.

In May 1877, after his second term ended, Grant had set off on a world tour for two and a half years, received by heads of state and cheering crowds throughout Europe, the Middle East, and Asia. The trip had improved his image in the United States—so much so that he began contemplating a third term. In Paris, Grant indicated to Mississippi senator Blanche K. Bruce—a former slave who was elected to the Senate in 1874—that if his services were demanded by the American people, it would be his duty to accept the Republican nomination.

Conkling's ambitions for a third Grant term had less to do with loyalty than political power. If Grant won the White House in 1880, the New York senator would regain his iron grip on federal patronage. Once more, he would be the most powerful political boss in the country. As a result, the *New York Times* commented, "the whole contest is a vulgar and selfish scramble for the spoils of office, rather than a struggle for any well-defined requirements of public interest." But it looked like it might be a safe bet.

When Grant arrived in San Francisco at the end of his tour, in September 1879, it seemed like Americans would carry him into the White House on their shoulders. Foghorns and cannons blasted a welcome as his ship entered the Golden Gate, and he was greeted by ecstatic crowds. From California, he traveled by train across the country, past mobs of well-wishers at every stop. In Chicago, he was honored with a grand banquet and a parade celebrating the "Man of Destiny, our General Grant." In Philadelphia, he presided over a mile-long procession marking a brand-new holiday in his honor. The prospect of a third term was increasingly tantalizing. Grant craved the prestige of the presidency, and the money that came with it. He had no fortune to fall back on, and his wife, Julia, was longing to be First Lady again.

By late May, the *New York Times* predicted that Grant's nomination was a sure thing, and, according to a close friend, the former president was "extremely anxious" to receive it. He counted delegates and calculated how every move would affect his chances. But as the date of the June convention approached, the ex-president's surge began to wane. Voters grew hesitant to award him a third term, something that no other president had achieved. And they became wary of the bosses who promoted him and the obvious self-interest of their support. His backers called themselves the Stalwarts, while Blaine's supporters were known as Half-Breeds. Blaine remained extremely popular, but there was something slightly distasteful about his ambition and suspected avarice. As Garfield observed, "I like Blaine, always have, and yet there is an element in him which I distrust." Sherman, meanwhile, was known as "the Ohio Icicle"—unfriendly and aloof, with a reputation for using patronage for political power.

The Republican showdown was held from June 2 to June 8 in Chicago's new International Exposition Building. Dubbed the "Glass Palace," the huge iron, brick, and glass structure was draped with flags, banners, and giant color portraits of renowned Republicans. Nearly fifteen thousand delegates, reporters, and spectators crowded into the building on the convention's opening day, and fifty thousand Americans swarmed into Chicago for the event. Rooms were so scarce that Garfield had to share his narrow hotel bed with a total stranger. The city, still rebuilding after the Great Fire, was "boiling over with politics," he wrote. Fresh crowds arrived on every evening train, and the mood at the convention was intense, hostile, and "very fatiguing."

Garfield was pledged to place Sherman's name in nomination, but many delegates, he told Lucretia, would prefer him to be Ohio's candidate. "Many are fully of the belief," he wrote, "that all the candidates will be dropped and that I will be taken up." Garfield, however, batted away their entreaties and denied seeking the nomination. "I long ago made a resolution," he declared, "that I would never permit myself to let the Presidential fever get any lodgement in my brain. I think it is the one office in this nation that for his own peace no man ought to set his heart on."

In the noisy chaos of the convention hall, only two men commanded the crowd's attention, although neither of them were potential nominees. One was Roscoe Conkling. With his mountainous stature and booming voice, he was trailed by whispers of power plays and titillating gossip. The other standout was James Garfield. Tall, burly, and athletic, with his leonine head and shining, intelligent gray eyes, Garfield warmly worked his way through the crowd, slapping the backs and shaking the hands of his many friends and acquaintances. Both men, though opposites in many ways, were applauded and cheered whenever they entered the hall.

When Conkling delivered his carefully memorized speech nominating Grant—in magnificent voice, standing on top of a table—he brought down the house. It was a barn burner. He was followed by Garfield, who had neglected to prepare his remarks. His brief, ad-libbed speech nominating Sherman made Conkling "sea-sick," the New Yorker grimaced. But it moved the delegates—so much so that someone shouted, "We want Garfield!" when he finished. And when, after thirty-three exhausting ballots, the candidates remained deadlocked—with Grant leading, but far short of the 379 votes he needed to win—momentum suddenly shifted to drafting Garfield as a dark-horse candidate. Three ballots later, the weary delegates voted for Garfield in a landslide, awarding him 399 votes to

Grant's 306. Stunned, he protested that he was never a candidate, but the hall erupted in deafening cheers and exultant chants of "Garfield!"

He was an accidental nominee, the Republican candidate for president, and the focus now shifted to the choice of his running mate. Nine men were nominated for the vice presidency, including Senator Blanche K. Bruce—the first Black American to be short-listed for that office. But it was clear that only a New York Stalwart could help bring the party together and deliver the crucial Empire State for Garfield. Without consulting Conkling, Republicans settled on his loyal deputy, Chester Arthur. Ever since President Hayes had removed him as New York collector, Arthur—known as the "Gentleman Boss" of New York's political machine—had served as chairman of its Republican Central Committee. He was considered an elegant stooge—tall, well-mannered, sharply dressed in vanilla trousers and tall white beaver hats, and always at the command of Conkling. He had never expected to be offered the vice presidency; it was, he declared, "a greater honor than I ever dreamed of attaining." But Conkling demanded that he decline it. Garfield was now the senator's enemy in his drive to put Grant back in the White House, and his deputy would be nothing less than a traitor if he accepted. But Arthur held firm, despite Conkling's fury.

At eleven o'clock that night, in Chicago's Grand Pacific Hotel, the two Republican nominees—James Garfield and Chester Arthur—stepped onto a small stage and shook hands under the harsh glare of calcium lights. For the next two hours, they shook so many other hands that Arthur dislocated a finger. The *New York Times* was bullish about Garfield's nomination, noting that he represented, with "his own eminent qualities and his distinguished career," all of the party's most valued principles. But many were less kind about Arthur. John Sherman quipped that the "only reason for his nomination was that he was discharged from an office that he was unfit to fill." And

E. L. Godkin, editor of *The Nation*, commented that at least the vice presidency would keep Arthur out of mischief—unless "Garfield, if elected, may die during his term of office"—but that, to be sure, he added, was an unlikely prospect.

⁓

In Boston, Charles Guiteau had closely followed the news from the convention. He had set his sights on politics again. Swept up in the early enthusiasm for a third Grant term, he had rewritten his campaign speech for Horace Greeley as a stump speech for the former president. Politics, he reckoned, would be a better-paying opportunity than his indigent four-year career as a traveling preacher. Calling himself "the Little Giant from the West," Guiteau had become a threadbare evangelist, delivering theological lectures that the *Chicago Tribune* called a laughingstock. In front of stupefied audiences, he would give sermons that were, according to an observer, "disconnected and random, just as an insane person would talk." He even wrote a book called *The Truth, A Companion to the Bible*, that merely plagiarized a book by John Humphrey Noyes. Wearing shabby clothes and, as usual, moving from one town to another whenever his boarding bills came due, Guiteau claimed that he worked for Jesus Christ & Co., driven by heavenly inspiration. But by the spring of 1880, at the age of thirty-eight, he felt inspired to enter politics again. So he decided to go to New York to offer his services to the Republican National Committee.

Three days after the convention, on Friday, June 11, he boarded an overnight steamer from Boston to New York. The paddle wheeler, called the *Stonington*, left the dock at about nine thirty at night with a full load of passengers, including many women and children. By eleven o'clock, as the ship entered Long Island Sound, it was enveloped in a cold sea fog that made it impossible to see ten yards ahead. When Guiteau took a walk on deck, he recalled, the night was as "black and dark as tar. You couldn't see an inch before your face." The *Stonington* whistled frequently as it approached the Cornfield Light off the Connecticut coast. Then suddenly, its bow smashed through the side of another vessel—the *Narragansett*, which was steaming from New York City to Providence, Rhode Island, with over four hundred passengers and crew.

The jolt threw passengers out of their berths, as seawater rushed into the splintered hull of the *Narragansett*. The sharp iron bow of the *Stonington* had cut through its gas lines, and within minutes the ship was ablaze. Its lights had gone out, and men, women, and children blindly groped their way to the deck in complete darkness. With few life preservers and rotted lifeboats that were full of holes, its passengers screamed for help. Many, clutching their children, ran to the rails and jumped into the black water. More than fifty burned to death or perished in the cold sea as the *Narragansett* sank in less than half an hour. From the *Stonington*'s deck, Guiteau said he heard "the wailing of the poor people, but we were utterly powerless to do anything. Our boat was badly damaged, and . . . we had our life-preservers on. We thought we were going down, too." After two or three hours, though, they were transferred to another boat and reached New York at about ten in the morning.

As he recovered from the calamity in a rented room, Guiteau was certain that God had saved him for a special mission. He began rewriting his Greeley and Grant speech for James Garfield and "felt sure," he said, "that I was on my way to the White House."

———

For Garfield, a veteran stump speaker, the campaign was quiet. He was advised to spend most of his time in Mentor, where, as President

Hayes put it, his job was "to sit crosslegged and look wise until after the election." Although Garfield was kept off the hustings, he was frantically busy with visitors and reporters. It was a "front porch" campaign, and trainloads of Americans arrived to pay their respects daily, including five hundred members of the Indianapolis Lincoln Club, all in matching dusters and straw hats, and the Jubilee Singers of historically Black Fisk University. Businessmen, children, suffrage campaigners, politicos, and prohibitionists trampled his lawn and climbed his fences. So many came that the railroad built a special spur right to his farm.

Despite the crush of visitors, he still managed to enjoy a frenetically pleasant summer—looking after his farm; harvesting oats, corn, and beets; carousing with his boys; and enjoying some quiet family time. Still, he confided to a friend, he felt "a streak of sadness . . . that no one else can understand." For one thing, there were still lingering tensions from the convention. Conkling remained bitter about Grant's defeat and so reluctant to campaign for Garfield that he would rather, he declared, spend the time in jail.

But Conkling's backing was crucial to attract New York money and voters. When Garfield took a brief trip back to Washington in June, he found a note from the senator, who had stopped by to see him when he was out. Garfield, hoping to warm up their frosty relations, replied right away, but Conkling never responded to him. It was a calculated snub that threatened to stall the campaign and perhaps even poison it from within. In July, word was out that Conkling had gone off on a cozy fishing trip with Garfield's running mate, Chester Arthur. The New York senator was deliberately flexing his power over Garfield's sputtering presidential campaign.

Advisers were now pressuring him to meet with Conkling in New York. But Garfield worried that such a meeting, behind closed doors, would make him look like a supplicant and worry his Half-Breed supporters. "If they shall now think I am in any way surrendering unduly to the N.Y. regulars," he wrote in his diary, "it will alienate them still more." So Garfield's advisers devised a ploy to arrange a meeting between the candidate and the New York senator. They decided to organize a large party meeting on August 5 at New York's Fifth Avenue Hotel. Conkling and Garfield would both be invited, along with leading Republicans from every state. It would be the perfect public vehicle for arranging a private chat between Conkling and the candidate for president.

Garfield was uneasy with the plan. It was "an unreasonable demand," he believed, "that so much effort should be made to conciliate one man." But, he was told, there would be "serious trouble with Conkling and his friends if I do not go." So, on August 3, Garfield left Mentor for New York aboard a private railroad car, the "Northern Star," making more than two dozen campaign stops en route to New York. The crowds and brass bands were fortifying, but nothing like the reception he experienced in the metropolis when he arrived the next evening. Cannons and fireworks blasted, and hordes of New Yorkers jammed the sidewalks around Grand Central Depot as the candidate stepped off the train. After a police escort to the hotel, on Fifth Avenue between Twenty-Third and Twenty-Fourth Streets, he watched from his second-floor balcony as women waved their handkerchiefs at him and men, shouting his name until they were hoarse, tossed their hats up in the air.

At noon the next day, the Republican conference opened. Although Garfield met with a parade of visitors—include Senator James Blaine, whom he now considered "the prince of good fellows"—Conkling, strangely, was nowhere to be found. He had checked into his suite the night before, but he made no appearance at the convention, and his room was empty. He had dodged Garfield and slipped away again. Still, five of Conkling's friends managed to corner Garfield behind closed doors, in a private room. Chester Arthur, his own ticket mate, was one of the Stalwarts who wanted Garfield to promise control of New York patronage to Conkling's machine in exchange for its support of his campaign. Over whiskey and cigars, Garfield believed that Conkling's friends showed "zeal and enthusiasm" about stumping for him, but he was sure that he had promised nothing that would bind him.

The following night, ten thousand people gathered on Fifth Avenue, outside the hotel, to cheer a torchlight parade of mounted and marching Republican veterans in full regalia. When Garfield appeared on the hotel's balcony, lit by bright calcium lights, the 7th Regimental Band struck up the rousing strains of "Hail to the Chief" before he addressed the throng. Only a few steps away from Garfield, amid the crush of dignitaries on the hotel balcony, was an empty chair, reserved for Roscoe Conkling, and a slight, shabbily dressed supporter who delivered the concluding speech—a small, ginger-bearded man from Illinois named Charles Guiteau.

He had finally found an audience, and a grand one. Although Guiteau had tried to give his campaign speech for Garfield in Saratoga and Poughkeepsie, it "didn't draw," he admitted. Returning to Manhattan, he tried to introduce himself to Chester Arthur, the vice presidential nominee, at the candidate's home on Lexington Avenue, but the doorman never admitted him inside. The Fifth Avenue Hotel gathering, however, offered him the perfect opportunity to hobnob with top Republicans. Wearing a threadbare coat, he haunted the hotel's lobbies, cheekily walking up and introducing himself to party leaders, including Arthur, and personally handing them copies of his speech. Everyone, Guiteau reported, was very polite to him—"delightful and pleasant in every way." And despite his seediness and odd demeanor, the party's leaders gave him a chance to debut his recycled stump speech before an audience of thousands at the massive Fifth Avenue rally.

He was on his way, he believed, to his own future election as president of the United States. "I shall be nominated and elected . . . by the act of God," he predicted. It was his fate, he was certain, to "unify the entire American people."

The next day, Conkling's entourage—still missing their leader—cornered Garfield again, this time with a less friendly manner. Behind a locked door, Chester Arthur and the boss's other minions—led by former New York congressman Tom Platt, "a cold-blooded, mousy, fidgeting little man"—pressed Garfield to give Conkling control over New York's patronage as the price for his political support. According to Platt's recollections, Garfield agreed. But the candidate, in his own diary, wrote that there were "no trades, no shackles" and "no serious mistakes" that he had made. It was a long meeting, he reported, but both sides believed—inaccurately, as it turned out—that they had come to an understanding. Conkling's faction was sure that Garfield would make no move in New York without their approval—while Garfield was sure that he had ceded none of his authority and freedom.

Conkling believed his underlings—later sneering to a reporter that Garfield was willing "to concede anything and everything to the Stalwarts if they would only rush to the rescue and save the day!" And he held up his end of the bargain, to a degree. While Garfield returned to his farm in Mentor, Conkling hit the hustings in New York, Indiana, and Ohio. But he never said anything flattering about Garfield in his stump speeches, except that he might make a "competent" chief executive. Garfield, insulted, judged Conkling "a singular compound of a very brilliant man and an exceedingly petulant, spoiled child."

The election was close. On November 2, more Americans than ever—nearly 80 percent of the voting public—turned out at the polls. The popular vote was a nail-biter. Only about seven thousand votes separated Garfield from his Democratic opponent, General Winfield Scott Hancock, a Civil War hero who had led the Union Army at Gettysburg but later supported white supremacists in the South. Garfield, however, had a commanding lead in the electoral college, with 214 votes to Hancock's 155. Conkling's support had been critical to his win in New York State. If Garfield had lost there, Hancock would have won the election.

Now, Conkling's coterie waited for their reward. But Garfield asserted that he owed them nothing. He even nominated Conkling's arch enemy, James Blaine, to serve as his secretary of state, the most powerful cabinet member. Garfield and Blaine had known each other now for more than twenty-five years, since they first served together in Congress, and they had become close friends. Both were exceptionally well-read, but Garfield lacked Blaine's focused, calculating ambition. As Massachusetts senator Henry Dawes put it, "Garfield is a grand, noble fellow, but fickle, unstable . . . brilliant like Blaine, but timid and hesitating." Garfield was affable and deeply articulate, but even Blaine considered him "a big good-natured man that doesn't appear to be oppressed by genius." He also, John Sherman remarked, "easily changed his mind, and honestly veered from one impulse to another." More and more, Garfield had come to rely on Blaine's counsel to anchor and guide him through political storms. At the end of December, Blaine accepted his appointment as secretary of state.

There were few others Garfield could trust or turn to. "The personal aspect of the presidency," he realized, "are far from pleasant. I shall be compelled to live in great social isolation." Almost everyone who came to him, he knew, would want something from him, poisoning the pleasures of friendship. He had to confront, he acknowledged, "the problem of trying to survive the presidency." He was sleeping badly, his head ached, and he was suffering from digestive problems again, forcing him to stick to a highly restricted diet. He had only two tasks to complete before his inauguration on March 4: forming a cabinet and writing his inaugural speech. But both those goals seemed frustratingly out of reach.

The heart of the cabinet conundrum was that his party was split into three factions—the independents, the Stalwarts, and the Half-Breeds. Garfield wanted to include all three groups in his cabinet. Blaine, however, wanted him to ignore the independents and shut out the Stalwarts, who, he said, represented "all the desperate bad men of the party, bent on boot and booty." They must, Blaine urged, "have their throats cut with a feather." Although Garfield did not follow Blaine's advice, it seemed like an inscrutable puzzle to recruit cabinet members from all three factions and every major region of the country.

Conkling, meanwhile, insisted on selecting the secretary of the treasury, the appointee who controlled the New York Custom House—the lucrative seat of his power—as well as all the nation's other custom houses and subtreasuries, revenue bureaus, and financial offices. President Hayes had crippled Conkling's power by removing Chester Arthur as New York's collector. Now, Conkling—who saw Blaine's appointment as a deliberate humiliation—demanded to restore his patronage power by installing a New York Stalwart as head of the Treasury. Although Garfield refused this demand, he briefly considered appointing Conkling himself to a cabinet post. Blaine, however, warned him bluntly that the New York senator "would act like strychnine" on the administration—causing convulsions, "followed by death."

As the date of the inauguration approached, Garfield was still far from completing his list of cabinet nominations. He was also struggling with his inaugural speech. In late December, he began reading the addresses of former presidents. John Adams, he thought, was too verbose—"His next to the last sentence contains more than seven hundred words," and most of them, he added, were "dreary reading." But Garfield was "strangely disinclined" to work on his own speech. "It is difficult to understand," he wrote, "the singular repugnance I feel in regard to doing this work. . . . It drags heavily and does not please me." Three days before the inauguration, he looked over his draft and was so dissatisfied with it that he decided to start over again. He had accidentally attained the presidency, without the fire and vision for it that drove other candidates. Tormented by his lack of clarity and indecision, he and his family arrived in Washington on Tuesday, the first of March.

The vice president–elect, meanwhile, was happily engaged in his own preparations—buying half a dozen new suits and a dress coat to upgrade and expand his wardrobe—while he prepared for his move from New York to Washington. He would have no official residence in the capital, so he gratefully accepted his master Roscoe Conkling's offer of accommodation. Arthur would move into Conkling's personal apartment at Wormley's Hotel—providing him comfort and companionship in their shared space and giving Conkling access, day and night, to his protégé, the vice president of the United States, while he worked to control Garfield's appointments.

Conkling's suite was known in Washington as "the morgue," for reasons discovered by disloyal deputies. On the night of Tuesday, March 1, Conkling learned that one of his lieutenants—New York congressman Levi P. Morton—had secretly accepted Garfield's appointment as secretary of the navy without Conkling's knowledge and assent. Morton lived in a townhouse just across the street from Wormley's. Hours before dawn, Conkling, in a fury, dispatched another Stalwart congressman to pull the treasonous Morton out of bed and deliver him to Wormley's immediately, which he did. In the senator's suite, Conkling and Arthur savaged the hapless Morton until sunrise. At last, the broken and bedraggled congressman trudged three blocks over to the Riggs House, where Garfield and his family were staying, to ask the president-elect to withdraw his nomination. "Morton broke down on my hands," Garfield wrote in his diary, with some disgust, "under the pressure of his N.Y. friends, who called him out of bed at four this morning."

To fill the now-vacant cabinet slot, Garfield settled on Thomas James, New York's postmaster, who immediately accepted the appointment without consulting Conkling. James had to promise to keep his nomination secret and even quietly left the capital to escape Conkling's pressure tactics. But on Wednesday night, March 2, the New York senator learned about the appointment. With Arthur at his elbow, he marched through a freezing blizzard over to Riggs House and burst unannounced into Garfield's bedroom, where the president-elect was working on his inaugural speech. Conkling exploded in fury, accusing Garfield of cheating and insulting him by appointing New Yorkers behind his back. Garfield remained silent, seated on the side of his bed, while Conkling screamed for an hour and finally left. He finished his speech, at last, at two thirty that morning.

—⁓—

Snow was still falling, hours later, as parade marchers gathered in the icy wind, shivering in their dress uniforms. Eight years earlier, during President Grant's second swearing-in, the temperature had plunged to a record low of four degrees below zero. Marching bandsmen were too frigid to play, and at the unheated celebration that night, even the wine froze. But the sky began to clear as Garfield, bleary-eyed from little sleep, prepared for his inauguration.

At ten thirty, President Hayes rode over to meet him at Riggs House, and they drove back to the White House together. A group of senators then escorted them to the Capitol, past bunting, bleachers, and benches that were filling with spectators. After they entered the Senate chamber, packed with legislators, diplomats, and Supreme Court justices, Vice President Chester Arthur took the oath of office. The entire entourage then paraded out onto the East Portico. As thousands strained for a glimpse of their new president-elect, Garfield—in a black suit, satin tie, and silk top hat—dryly delivered spiritless remarks. Roscoe Conkling, seated directly behind him, applauded flamboyantly throughout the speech. When Garfield finished and cheers died away, he placed his hand on a Bible held by the chief justice and took the presidential oath of office. Then, after lunch at the White House, he and Crete took their places on the reviewing stand, as Grand Marshal William Tecumseh Sherman, riding a great white horse, led a stately inaugural procession—including a hearse that was ominously trapped in the parade.

That night, invited revelers gathered inside the new Smithsonian Museum, under the bright blaze of novel electric lights and a huge plaster statue of the Goddess of Liberty. They consumed a hundred gallons of oysters, fifty hams, fifteen hundred pounds of turkey, and fifteen thousand desserts. Garfield, who had never learned to dance, shook hundreds of hands as guests whirled to the strains of his favorite Gilbert and Sullivan tunes. Finally, "very weary" at eleven o'clock, he retired to the White House, his new home.

Despite the heady celebrations, he was exhausted by the preparations and sadly wary of the months to come. He had the grim conviction, he wrote, "that I am bidding goodbye to the freedom of private life, and to a long series of happy years," which, he feared, had ended forever in 1880.

11
THE REMOVAL

The rising sun on Garfield's first morning as president illuminated the shabby appearance of the White House. The drapes were ragged and the carpets so worn that furniture had to be placed over the holes. The stench of mold permeated the rooms, and rats scuttled around the basement, with its ancient plumbing. No improvements had been made since the Grants were in residence. The Democrats in Congress, as punishment for the Hayes presidency, had withheld any funding for its upkeep. Now, at last, repairs could be made, thanks to an appropriation. But Garfield, like past presidents, would personally have to pay for White House coachmen, stables, cooks, and waiters. Since he had no private wealth beyond his fifty-thousand-dollar-a-year presidential salary, he had to ask former president Hayes to loan him a carriage and a lame horse. Garfield inherited the former president's personal steward—a man named William T. Crump, who had been Hayes's orderly in the Union Army. The White House also came with a government-funded staff of fifty, including doorkeepers, maids, laundresses, gardeners, and a barber.

For the young Garfield children, the White House was a diverting playground. Eight-year-old Abram and ten-year-old Irvin raced around the East Room on their high-wheeled bicycles. Irvin liked to steer his bike down marble staircases and hallways, banging into the woodwork and carving deep tracks in the carpets. Their older siblings were more decorous. Mollie, a fourteen-year-old student at Madame Burr's school, liked to practice on the mansion's grand piano, while Harry, seventeen, and Jim, fifteen, studied with a tutor to prepare for college.

Over the past few years, in Congress, Garfield had sometimes played hooky from the Capitol to watch the Nationals play baseball, enjoy boat racing on the Potomac, and attend Gilbert and Sullivan operettas. Now, in the White House, he and his family were still able to enjoy some diversions. The First Lady, along with the wives of cabinet officers and senators, attended the opening of Washington's brand-new National Natatorium—a pioneering aquatic school operated by "Professor of Swimming" Robert Odlum. Considered the largest swimming gymnasium in the country, it featured indoor freshwater pools heated by huge steam boilers. Odlum's pupils included the Garfield boys, the sons of Secretary of State Blaine, and former president Hayes's daughter, Fannie. Odlum taught his students—dressed in gray flannel swimming suits—how to float and swim by strapping a belt around their chests, attached to a pole, and pulling them along through the water.

P. T. Barnum, too, was captivating the capital that season. He was launching the most thrilling production of his career, called Barnum and Bailey's "Greatest Show on Earth." In August 1880, he had joined forces with James Bailey, another American showman, who had toured Australia, Java, Brazil, and Peru with his gigantic circus. The thirty-three-year-old Bailey was a genius at logistics, and Barnum, at age seventy, saw the wisdom of forming a partnership.

Since 1870, he had refocused his show business career from museums to circuses. In 1871, he opened what he called the biggest outdoor circus in history. Under three tented acres in Brooklyn, New York, he showcased animals, clowns, daredevils, and human curiosities such as the towering seven-foot-five Colonel Goshen; Esau, a bearded boy; and the twenty-five-inch-tall comedian, Admiral Dot. He then took his show on the road, filling more than eighty railcars with his marvels. In 1874, he built a permanent home for the circus—Barnum's Great Roman Hippodrome—in New York City. The venture was a celebrated success, but when Bailey came on the scene, Barnum opted to hedge his bets. The two impresarios merged their circuses into a mammoth, three-ring production—originally called the Barnum and London Circus—that astounded New Yorkers when it debuted in March 1881.

Half a million people crammed the streets and gaped from windows as the spectacular Barnum and Bailey circus paraded through the city to the new Madison Square Garden, recently built on the site of the hippodrome. The dazzling torchlight procession included glittering golden chariots; twenty elephants; colorful floats pulled by zebras and camels; cages of wild leopards and tigers; four brass bands; more than three hundred horses; and nearly four hundred costumed performers, including acrobats, daredevils, trapeze artists, and General and Mrs. Tom Thumb in a tiny carriage. Before the circus traveled to Washington, D.C., Barnum wrote to the president on March 12, with the tongue-in-cheek heading: *"No office wanted!"*:

> My dear Mr. President,
>
> About all the favor I ask from you is, do please have the kindness to *live*, & then I know our country will be blessed. . . . This last great crowning effort of my managerial life so far surpasses all similar exhibitions in the world that I am extremely anxious to have it visited by

you and Mrs. Garfield *in person* at the commencement of
my traveling season. Hence I take this liberty of preparing
your mind for the *great occasion!*"

The Garfield children attended the extravaganza, which, according
to the *Washington Post*, was making the capital "circus crazy."

Another event was the annual Easter egg roll on the South Lawn.
And although the president and First Lady hosted no state dinners
that season, there seemed to be an endless number of receptions. In
his first week in office, Garfield and his wife, Lucretia, greeted thousands of supporters, the diplomatic corps, and officers of the army
and navy. Then, on Saturday, March 12, they opened the doors of the
White House "for all the great roaring world to enter"—continuing
a tradition, started by Lucy Hayes, of welcoming the public for two
hours on Saturday afternoons. They steeled themselves for the duties
of the receiving line. "Before the first hour was over," Lucretia wrote
in her diary, "I was aching in every joint, and thought how can I ever
last through the next long sixty minutes. But the crowd soon made
me forget myself, and though nearly paralyzed, the last hour passed
more quickly than the first." Harriet Blaine, the wife of the secretary
of state, stood next to her, shaking hundreds of eager hands. "I stood
up with Mrs. Garfield," she recalled, "while all the American people
who wanted to, came to pay their respects to her and the President."
It was "not any of it so bad as I expected, and much of it," she added,
"was really amusing."

As the long line of callers snaked slowly in front of them, a slight,
scruffy man took Lucretia's hand and asked her, "How do you do,
Mrs. Garfield?" He told her that he hailed from Chicago, although
he had not lived there for two or three years. He had been in New
York, he informed her, and took a very active part in the presidential
campaign.

"I was one of the men that made General Garfield President," he boasted as he gave her his card. When she read his name—Charles Guiteau—she told him that she remembered it and added, with a very polite smile, that she was "glad to see him."

—⁓—

He had traveled from New York to Washington on March 5, the day after the inauguration, to claim what he believed to be the just reward for his campaign service—a patronage appointment as the minister to France or Austria. His speech "Garfield vs. Hancock," he claimed, was "the first shot" in the strategy that had elected Garfield. Although the streets in the capital were still banked with snow when he arrived, Guiteau, an observer noted, was oddly dressed for the weather. He had no socks on, and instead of boots or shoes, he wore rubber sandals on his bare feet. Still, he made himself a regular figure in the White House, as he had at New York's Fifth Avenue Hotel. Before the election, Chester Arthur recalled, he had seen Guiteau in his suite there "at least ten and possibly as often as twenty times."

Guiteau had pestered Arthur for campaign speaking assignments and succeeded in getting one on the night of August 21, at a mass meeting of Black voters on Twenty-Fourth Street. But after reading the beginning of his speech, he suddenly stopped. "It was a very hot, sultry night," he later explained, "and I didn't fancy speaking, with the . . . gas-lights and all that. . . . There were plenty of other speakers there, so I retired." He knew that the campaign gave its prime speaking slots to "men of reputation," he admitted. Still, after the election, he was convinced he was entitled to a consular appointment "as a personal tribute" for all the work that he had done in the campaign—even though, according to one witness, Guiteau "seemed to have no special purpose nor employment. I don't know that I ever saw him doing anything except reading papers."

But, determined to be a foreign minister, he even lobbied ex-president Grant, who often stayed at the Fifth Avenue Hotel. Guiteau frequently sent his card up to Grant's room. "I always returned the same reply that I would not see him," the former president recalled. "Several times he waylaid me on the street or in the corridor of the hotel when I was passing through, but I would not talk to him. Finally, he wrote me a letter saying that he wanted me to help him obtain the appointment of minister to Austria." Even though Grant refused to let Guiteau into his suite, "he subsequently forced himself in one day, but I refused to talk with him and dismissed him speedily."

Guiteau, though, was undeterred and wrote directly to President-Elect Garfield. Although he had written to him before the election— enclosing a copy of his speech and declaring that he "could represent the United States Government at the Court of Vienna with dignity and grace"—he soon determined that the Paris ministry, now held by Hayes appointee Edward Noyes, was likely to become more available than the Vienna post.

Arriving in Washington after the inauguration, the strange, shabby little man became a regular fixture at the White House. According to Garfield's personal secretary, Joseph Stanley-Brown,

> Mr. Guiteau's visits began about the 8th or 9th of March. His first appearance was in the office of the private secretary at the Executive Mansion, one morning. The room was very crowded and his card was sent in with those of the other guests and he took his seat. His visits were repeated in the following weeks quite regularly at intervals of about three or four or five days, sometimes only two

or three days apart. . . . If the President did not see him he would go away.

Strangely, Guiteau did, one day, have an audience with Garfield. The office seeker was ushered into the president's private office, and Garfield, he claimed, "recognized me at once." Guiteau handed him a copy of his speech—on which he had scrawled the words "Paris consulate." He then "left him reading the speech and retired," Guiteau recalled. He continued to return to the White House, day after day, leaving notes for the president to press his case. People pitied the "wild looking" little man, in his tattered clothing and rubber sandals. He seemed perfectly harmless, though a bit off in his head.

—⁓—

Political assassination was in the air. On Sunday, March 13—the day after the first public reception at the White House—a rebel threw a bomb at the feet of Czar Alexander II of Russia as he stepped out of his carriage, tearing off the emperor's legs and killing him. President Garfield learned the news by telegraph that day after he returned from church. It was a tragic incident, but the President refused to boost security at the White House, which was regularly open to the public. "Assassination," he declared, "can no more be guarded against than death by lightning; and it is best not to worry about either."

The crowds at the White House were crushing. On Tuesday, March 8, Garfield wrote in his diary, "It is said that no day in twelve years has witnessed such a jam of callers. . . . Again and again, we were compelled to shut the doors—with the files of people extending to the avenue." Worst of all, he remarked, were the "disciplined office hunters who drew papers on me as highway men draw pistols." Personnel issues distressed him. "I love to deal with doctrines and events," he explained. "The contests of men and about men I greatly dislike." He struggled, he confessed, "to keep from despising the office seeker" and suspected he was "wholly unfit for this sort of work." He had to resist, he added, "a very strong tendency to be dejected and unhappy at the prospect which is offered by the work before me."

He continued to sleep badly, and he and Lucretia battled nausea and headaches from the stench of sewage rising out of the malarial mudflats behind the White House. He tried to raise his spirits by taking long horseback rides along the river, carousing with his children, riding in his carriage with Lucretia or Blaine, and playing billiards in the White House basement. But his gloomy pessimism always returned.

Relentless office seekers were annoying, but high-level appointments were even more troubling. The Senate had approved all his cabinet nominees after the inauguration. Now Garfield, in a magnanimous mood, felt it was time to specially reward the New York Stalwarts for the vital role they had played in his election. So on Tuesday, March 22, he sent the Senate five administration nominations—all of them close allies of Conkling. Although Blaine typically advised Garfield on every decision, the secretary had been in bed with rheumatism. So on his own initiative, Garfield had put together the list to gratify his Stalwart supporters. When Blaine learned about it, he was apoplectic. At ten thirty that night, he dragged himself out of bed and over to the White House, where he vented his anger at the appointment of Conkling's cronies. After the secretary left around midnight, Garfield conceded that he had "broken Blaine's heart with the nominations. . . . He regards me as having surrendered to Conkling. I have not but . . . perhaps I should have consulted Blaine before sending in some of those New York appointments." He resolved to appease the secretary of state by submitting a new list that would prove he had not capitulated to Conkling.

The next day, he sent the Senate another round of nominations. The name that riveted everyone's attention was New York State senator William Robertson, Garfield's nominee for collector of the New York Custom House. Robertson was a declared enemy of Conkling and a devoted ally of Blaine. It was, according to the *New York Herald*, "a very lively bombshell." The *St. Louis Globe-Democrat* accused Garfield of being "a willing instrument for the execution of James G. Blaine's private vengeance," and former president Grant said Garfield lacked "the backbone of an angleworm." Three cabinet members threatened to resign. And Conkling, of course, was outraged at the appointment of his political enemy as head of the custom house, the seat of his patronage power. He was also incensed that Garfield had not consulted him first—which, he believed, the president had pledged to do. But the criticism simply stiffened Garfield's resolve; this time, he refused to waver. "The President is authorized to nominate—and did so," he asserted in his diary on March 27. Conkling may have considered it "a personal affront that he was not previously told," but Garfield stood "joyfully" on that issue. "Let who will," he declared, "fight me."

He and Conkling were now at war. Garfield believed his nomination of Robertson was a stand for principle and presidential power. The editor of the *New York Tribune* urged him to stay firm: this was the turning point of his whole administration, "the crisis of his Fate." If he surrendered, Conkling would be "President for the rest of the term," and Garfield would be "a laughing-stock. . . . The least wavering would be fatal." Blaine, too, said that backing down would be "a deep damnation personally and politically." Robertson was also ready to do battle. Under no circumstances, he stated, did he want Garfield to withdraw his nomination, which, he predicted, would make the president "Conkling's abject slave." Garfield agreed, declaring that he would never withdraw the appointment and that it was a test of friendship or hostility to his presidency. "I do not propose to be dictated to," he warned. "Senators who dare to oppose the Executive will henceforth require letters of introduction to the White House."

Conkling wielded every weapon that he could to block Robertson's confirmation, excoriating Garfield for hours before a Senate committee. But as the battle extended through April and early May, there was a growing sense that Conkling was trying to bully the president and the Senate. Public sentiment began leaning strongly toward Garfield; in New York State, only eighteen newspapers supported Conkling, compared to ninety-four that backed the president.

Frustrated and furious at his shrinking power, Conkling, in early May, decided to publicly embarrass and shame the president. He invited the editor of the *New York Herald* to his apartment at Wormley's, where he and Vice President Arthur denounced Garfield to the journalist in a scathing rant. On May 11, the newspaper published their remarks in an article entitled "The Wriggler." The *Herald*, parroting Conkling and Arthur, declared that

> it is doubtful if ever there was an occupant of the White House who has been so completely fooled and blinded as the twentieth President of the United States. There is something supremely ridiculous between the promise and performance of his administration. . . . Every movement he has made since the 4th of March has been a blunder. . . . In the end he may succeed in confirming Mr. Robertson and crushing Mr. Conkling . . . but the ruin of his own party and the prostitution of his great office will be the price.

Conkling believed that the public lashing would bring the Senate to his side, but its effect was the opposite. Senators were now fed up with his bitter posturing, and they knew that voters were supporting

Garfield. By May 15, the *New York Times* reported, it was certain that Robertson would be confirmed.

Conkling was running out of strategies to regain his patronage power. Backed into a corner, he and his lackey Tom Platt—now the junior senator from New York—made the shocking decision, on May 16, to resign from the US Senate. It was the act, according to Massachusetts senator Henry Dawes, of a "great big baby boohooing because he can't have all the cake and . . . runs home to his mother." From any point of view, judged the Utica *Herald*, "it is the act of a man who has lost his head, or at least has devised a dramatic episode in order to hide . . . his complete and utter rout." It was, *The Times* of Indiana noted, the "confession of Conkling's complete failure and Garfield's complete success." Conkling was "so infernally selfish and so thoroughly contemptible" that his resignation should be "the end of his political career."

Garfield and Blaine supporters were jubilant over Conkling's downfall, and Robertson was confirmed, two days later, by a huge margin. Garfield, however, had been too distracted by a personal crisis to pay close attention to the Senate drama. On Wednesday, May 4, Lucretia had suddenly come down with chills and a high fever. By Saturday, she was so much worse that her doctor, Susan Edson, was summoned to stay with her at the White House. The first female doctor in Washington, Edson, from Ohio, had taken care of the Garfields' youngest child, Neddie, when he died in 1876 of whooping cough at only twenty-two months of age. Deeply trusted by the family, she quickly diagnosed Crete's illness as malaria.

Garfield moved into a guest bedroom, and his anxiety for his wife, he admitted, consumed all his thoughts. According to the president's steward, William Crump, Garfield spent hours at her bedside, staying up with her as late as four in the morning and pacing the floor with worry at other times. He refused to see anyone on business. All of his thoughts centered on Crete, he wrote; everything else was insignificant. He had "no heart" to think about his battle with Conkling—although on the evening of May 12, he did read the senator's tirade in the *New York Herald*.

Lucretia's pain and headaches worsened steadily; by May 13, her temperature had jumped to 104, and she was losing handfuls of hair. Garfield brought in another trusted physician—his first cousin Silas Boynton. Dr. Boynton agreed with Edson's diagnosis and gave Lucretia "heroic" doses of medicine to reduce her fever. That night, as Garfield was sobbing on his knees over Crete's condition, she began turning the corner. By the morning of May 15, her temperature had fallen to 100.5, and at breakfast, Garfield recounted, he and his children laughed for the first time in weeks. "The little ones," he noted, "have been very brave."

There was good news from the Senate, too. On Monday, May 16, Garfield learned that Conkling had resigned his seat. It was ironic, he later wrote, that the New York Senator, who always suspected people of trying to humiliate him, had inflicted "measureless humiliation on himself." By Wednesday, when Robertson was confirmed and Crete continued to improve, the president celebrated with a twelve-mile ride on Denmark, his new horse. His grueling personal and political crises were behind him, and he was now, at last, able to sleep soundly.

———

That night, on Wednesday, May 18, Charles Guiteau lay in bed in his rented room, feeling depressed and upset about the war in the Republican party. He had read "The Wriggler" in the *New York Herald* and agreed with every indictment of Garfield. He had closely followed the battle over Robertson and had even written to the president about it on April 29:

> General Garfield: I wish to say this about Mr. Robertson's nomination: Would it not be well to withdraw it on the ground that Mr. Conkling has worked himself to a white heat of opposition? . . . I am on friendly terms with Senator Conkling and the rest of our Senators, but I write this on my own account and in the spirit of a peacemaker.

Then, when Conkling and Platt resigned from the Senate, Guiteau was shocked by what he saw as Garfield's total betrayal of his Stalwart supporters. He would never have become president, Guiteau was certain, without the extraordinary efforts of Conkling and Arthur. The president's greatest insult, Guiteau believed, was to make "Mr. Blaine—the worst enemy that . . . Conkling had—his Secretary of State and bosom friend."

Guiteau also felt personally betrayed by Blaine. In March, the White House told him that they had sent his consulship application to the State Department. Guiteau then became a regular there, asking to see Secretary of State Blaine. Those requests were always ignored, but he managed to corner Blaine one day inside an elevator. "I gave him my speech," Guiteau recalled, "and he pricked up his ears and was very cordial. He knew all about me as soon as he heard my name."

Over the next four to six weeks, Guiteau persisted in sending Blaine notes and attending his public receptions. Secretary Blaine remembered seeing the strange little man there "repeatedly" and politely put off his requests for the Paris mission. But finally, on Saturday, May 14, Blaine lost his patience and warned Guiteau to "never speak to me again on the subject of the Paris consulship." Although Blaine maintained that he "did not do it with any special harshness," Guiteau felt deeply wounded by Blaine's dismissal. As a last resort, he wrote to President Garfield, implying that Blaine was disloyally planning to run against him in the next election. He even advised Garfield that "Blaine is 'a vindictive politician' and 'an evil genius,' and you will 'have no peace till you get rid of him.' . . . you ought to demand his *immediate* resignation; otherwise you and the Republican party will come to grief."

Guiteau received no reply to his letters and began formulating a solution. The president, he believed, "was doing great wrong to the Stalwarts and was wrecking the Republican party." But if he took action to remove the president, Guiteau realized, he would solve everything. His good friend Chester Arthur would become president and surround himself with Stalwarts like Conkling, and "the Blaine element"—the cause of all the party's troubles—would disappear.

———

Lucretia, at last, was starting to recover. Although she still had a slight fever, every day brought some improvement, and the household was filled with "a deep strong current of happy peace," Garfield wrote gratefully. By Thursday, June 2, she was well enough to sit up and have a bite of steak. According to Crump, Garfield would pick her up and "carry her about the house from one room to another, down into the conservatory and dining room. . . . Every moment that he could spare from his official duties he would tear himself away from the hungry office seekers who were after him continually, like a pack of wolves," and attend to his wife. At lunchtime on Sunday, June 12, Garfield and his son Harry made a chair of their arms and carried Crete down to the dining room, where she sat at her place for the first time in more than a month.

Garfield had gone to services that morning at Washington's small wooden Disciples of Christ church. It was a "very stupid sermon," he complained. Even more disquieting, he noted, was an outburst by "a dull young man with a loud voice" who interrupted the preacher by shouting, "What think ye of Christ?" from the back of the room. Congregants swiveled their heads to look at the slight, bearded man lurking behind them at the door. The president may even have recognized him as the strange, shabby office seeker who had come into his office and handed him a speech a few months earlier—asking, absurdly, to be appointed minister to France.

As Guiteau skulked by the church door—studying the president, who was sitting in a pew with Boynton and his wife—he nervously touched the new pistol in his pocket. He had bought it from a gun shop for ten dollars, with a box of cartridges. It was a distinctive English Bulldog five-shooter, with a fancy ivory handle—a weapon that was worthy, he imagined, to be preserved for history. Since Guiteau knew nothing about weapons and had never held a gun, the store owner suggested that he practice firing it outside the city, on the muddy banks of an old canal. So, at sunset, Guiteau made his way there to an abandoned spot, loaded ten bullets into the Bulldog, and aimed it at a sapling on the bank to get used to the feel and handling of the revolver.

He came back for more practice a few nights later. He then began tracking the president whenever he left the White House, even to church—deciding, that Sunday, that the little Disciples of Christ sanctuary would be the perfect place to dispatch Garfield. He planned to shoot him through the back of the head on the following Sunday, June 19.

But Garfield did not go to church that day. Instead, he had taken Lucretia and his family to the seashore at Long Branch, New Jersey. The bracing salt air, he hoped, would speed Crete's recovery. He, too, was eager to get away for a few days—far from the "terrible strain" of relentless office seekers. His time, he complained, was "frittered away by the personal seeking of people, when it ought to be given to the great problems which concern the whole country. Four years of this kind of intellectual dissipation," he worried, "may cripple me for the remainder of my life."

So on Saturday morning, June 18, he and his wife—along with Mollie, Irvin, Abram, and the Boyntons—had arrived at Washington's Baltimore and Potomac railroad station to start their excursion to the ocean. As they walked through the depot to the platform, they passed a small, haggard man who sat watching them from a quiet corner. He had learned about their trip from newspapers and was waiting for them, patiently, with his revolver. But, Guiteau later explained, "Mrs. Garfield looked so thin and clung so tenderly to the President's arm" that he lost his nerve. He decided to wait, instead, for another opportunity and try again.

The Garfields took rooms at the Hotel Elberon, with a view of the ocean, and the worry and work of Washington seemed far away. Crete seemed to be gaining strength every hour, the president noted, and the sea always brought him a feeling of repose and peace. The only bitter note of the trip was their treatment by former president Grant, who was staying at his son's cottage across the street. Grant had dinner at the hotel one night and saw the Garfields, but he ignored them, still bitter about Conkling and Robertson. One of the only courtesies he showed the First Family was briefly raising his hat to them as they passed him one evening in a carriage.

The next Monday, on June 27, Garfield traveled back to Washington, leaving his family in Long Branch. Crete would join him on

Saturday, July 2, in Philadelphia to begin a full month's vacation away from Washington, with planned travels to New York, Virginia, Maine, and Ohio. Garfield would have five days in the White House before the trip to catch up with mail and meetings, consular appointments, and consultations with his cabinet. He was now, finally, rested and free of the partisan battles that had strangled the first months of his presidency. He especially enjoyed talking with Blaine about future plans for the administration. They were extremely close—Garfield called Blaine "his old friend Jim"—and on the evening of Friday, July 1, his last day in Washington before the trip, the president stepped out the front door of the White House, without a bodyguard, and strolled a few blocks over to Blaine's townhouse, directly across the street from Wormley's.

Harriet Blaine glanced out her window and saw Garfield bounding up the front steps. "A President ought never to be kept waiting," she said to herself, so she ran to the door to open it herself, almost before he had rung the bell. "It was a very handsome and happy looking man who sat down with me" in the drawing room, she recalled. Garfield was dressed in a gray summer suit, with a cheerful pink flower in his coat—"his face beaming with anticipation of the enjoyment of freedom away from the White House." Their relationship was so affectionate that she called him "Gaffy." He sat with her for an hour and gave her an autographed, bound copy of his inaugural speech. Then, when her husband arrived, Garfield said a gracious goodbye and left the house with him—declining to stay for supper because he had promised to go to his daughter's little French play. He and Blaine then walked back to the White House together, arm in arm.

They never noticed the small, stealthy figure behind them. Guiteau had shadowed Garfield from the White House over to Blaine's. He then waited on a stoop outside of Wormley's Hotel while the president went inside, fingering the pistol in his pocket as he watched the house. After Blaine and Garfield left together, he trailed them as they ambled back to the White House "in the most delightful and cozy fellowship possible," he recalled, "just as hilarious as two young schoolgirls. . . . They had their heads together . . . and Garfield listening very intently . . . laughing and joking." The friendly scene only confirmed what Guiteau had read in the papers, that the president had sold himself body and soul to Blaine, and that the wily secretary of state was using Garfield to destroy the Stalwarts.

He intended to remove the president the next morning at the railroad depot, before he embarked on his vacation. Guiteau made careful preparations for the shooting—walking to the edge of the city, near the poorhouse and Congressional Cemetery, to see the District of Columbia Jail and the quarters he would soon occupy. He was not allowed inside the jail, but by peering through the front door, he could tell that it was an "excellent" facility, as prisons go. He also wrote "An Address to the American People" that justified the shooting of the president. "I conceived the idea myself and kept it to myself," he wrote.

> I read the newspapers carefully for and against the administration, and gradually the conviction settled on me that the President's removal was a political necessity, because he proved a traitor to the men that made him, and thereby imperiled the life of the Republic. . . . The President, under the manipulation of his Secretary of State, has been guilty of the basest ingratitude to the Stalwarts. . . . He has wrecked the grand old Republican party, and for this he dies. . . . I had no ill will to the President. This is not

murder. It is a political necessity. It will make my friend Arthur President, and save the Republic.

He also penned a personal letter to William Tecumseh Sherman, commanding general of the US Army, for release right after the assassination: "I have just shot the President . . . several times," he explained, "as I wished him to go as easily as possible. His death was a political necessity. . . . I am a Stalwart of the Stalwarts. . . . I am going to the jail. Please order out your troops," he urged him, "and take possession of the jail at once."

———

Garfield was in high spirits when he awoke early the next morning. It was a bright, clear day, and he was going to catch the nine-thirty train from Washington. He was "unusually cheerful and jolly," Crump remembered, "cracking jokes and laughing heartily. I had never before seen him so merry and full of fun." After breakfast, he and the steward went upstairs to open the safe. Garfield took out five hundred dollars, then turned to Crump and thanked him for his service.

"I am going out of this old prison for a month," he said, and "we are going to have a good time; now, you lock up the house, and take your family and go off and enjoy yourselves like the rest of us." Crump thanked Garfield for his kindness. Then, as they passed the president's bedroom, Crump recounted, they saw his sons Harry and Jim turning handsprings over his bed. Garfield said, "Those boys think they are smart, don't they?"

He then walked up to the bed and turned a complete handspring over it as nimbly as either of the boys had done. We all looked at him with astonishment, while both the boys clapped their hands, and gleefully shouted,

"Hurrah for Papa!" . . . running up and kissing him with
much joy.

After the bedroom antics, they went downstairs to the first floor of
the White House. At the foot of the staircase, by the pantry, was a large
set of scales. Garfield stepped onto them, asking Crump to weigh him
so he would know whether he had lost or gained weight on vacation.
Crump announced that Garfield weighed two hundred ten pounds,
"which caused him to clap his hands with satisfaction," he recalled.
"He then shook my hands very warmly, bid me goodbye, and passed
out to the front door."

Blaine was already there to drive Garfield to the station. Before he
had left his house, he had asked his wife to hold breakfast until
he returned. Harriet told him she would wait until nine thirty, as Blaine
climbed into a State Department carriage to drive it himself over to
the White House. At a few minutes past nine, the president joined
him in the two-seater, and together they left for the Baltimore and
Potomac station, chatting, as usual, the entire way. When they got to
the depot, they were still engrossed in conversation. Garfield had his
hand on Blaine's shoulder, and then, as he turned to leave, the secretary
decided to escort him to the train. So the two men stepped down from
the carriage—the president pausing for a moment to say hello to a few
waiting supporters and ask a police officer how much time they had
before the train's departure—"About 10 minutes, Sir," he said. Then,
side by side, he and Blaine walked into the brick depot, passing through
the ladies' waiting room on their way out to the platform.

Suddenly, they heard a sharp bang, like an exploding firecracker.
Garfield threw his hands up in the air, jolted his head back, and said,
"My God! What is this?" They heard another loud blast, and Garfield's
legs buckled beneath him, throwing him forward as he dropped,
bleeding, onto the floor.

12
END TIMES

Harriet Blaine had finally sat down to breakfast at nine thirty that morning when she heard the shrill ring of the telephone. A servant answered it, then raced into the dining room, saying, "The President has been assassinated," and when Harriet rushed to look out the front door, she "saw that it must be true," she recalled—everybody was "on the street, and wild." She sent her daughter next door to tell Ellen Sherman, the wife of the army's commanding general, who immediately summoned a carriage to take them to the White House. The streets in front of the Executive Mansion were jammed with crowds and traffic, and the doors were closed, but "they let us through and in," Harriet recounted. The shooter had been arrested and her husband was safe, she learned with relief, but he was still with the wounded president at the station.

Inside the depot, collapsed on the floor, Garfield was drifting in and out consciousness. He was pale and vomiting. His summer suit was stained with blood, his smashed top hat lay beside him, and his legs were quivering. The first bullet had grazed his elbow, but the second shot penetrated his back, shattering two ribs. Within minutes, a doctor, the city's health officer, was on the scene, giving him brandy and spirits of ammonia. Meanwhile, Garfield's secretary of war,

Robert Todd Lincoln—the son of President Abraham Lincoln—had been at the station and seen the shooting. It was tragically familiar. In 1865, he had been with his father when he died from an assassin's bullet. Now, as another president clung to life, Lincoln immediately sent a carriage to fetch a well-known Washington physician, D. Willard Bliss. He came quickly, and eight other doctors also rushed to the scene. The president said he felt pain and tingling in his right calf and foot, so they wrapped blankets around his legs and inserted their unwashed fingers and instruments into the wound, probing for the bullet without success.

A few strong men had placed the president on a coarse mattress and carried him upstairs to a room on the second floor. But Garfield asked to be taken back to the White House. So they gently loaded him into a horse-drawn police ambulance cushioned with mattresses. As it carried him, at a slow walk, from the station, solemn onlookers gathered on the sidewalks in frightened silence.

William Crump, meanwhile, was preparing a room for the president on the second floor and transforming the White House into a makeshift hospital. When the ambulance arrived, Harriet Blaine stood in the hallway and watched as a dozen men carried the president over their heads, stretched out on a mattress. Garfield lay, without his coat and shoes, under a gray blanket, his right arm resting above his head. When he saw Harriet, he kissed his hand to her. "I thought I should die," she remembered. He was carried upstairs and placed on his bed as Harriet stood watching. "He turned his eyes to me, beckoned, and when I went to him," she recalled, he "pulled me down, kissed me again and again, and said, 'Whatever happens, I want you to promise to look out for Crete. . . . Don't leave me until Crete comes.'" She took off her bonnet and stayed there the rest of the day, she recounted. "I never left him a moment."

Meanwhile, Garfield's secretary, Joseph Stanley-Brown, had the gates of the grounds closed and arranged for a detail of police officers. Only officials and journalists, he instructed, would be admitted, but the White House was already a scene of chaos. More than twenty doctors, cabinet officers and their wives, army and navy officers, and family friends filed in and out of the president's room. "They all believed him to be . . . dying, as he did himself," Crump recalled. "Secretary of War Lincoln entered the room with a deathlike countenance," tears rolling down his cheeks until his wife took him away. "But the most affecting meeting," he added, occurred when Secretary of State Blaine finally arrived. After Garfield had left the station, Blaine had briefly gone home to alert foreign capitals about the shooting. Now, by the president's bedside, he was sobbing and shaking. Garfield threw both of his arms around Blaine's neck and said, "My God! Jim, why did that wretch shoot me?"

The president could hear all the doctors whispering to one another around his bed, predicting that he would die within hours. They continued to insert their fingers into the small, red-edged hole in his back, causing it to gush blood onto the bedsheets. He was vomiting every thirty minutes and given injections of morphine to dull his pain. Few of the doctors believed he would live. The president asked Crump to move them to another room, but he was grateful to see Dr. Susan Edson, who had rushed over to the White House to help. When Garfield saw her, he said with anguish, "What will this do for Crete? Will it put her to bed again? I had rather die."

In Long Branch, Lucretia was nearly ready to leave the hotel to meet her husband in Philadelphia when a messenger arrived with news that he had been shot and seriously injured. Almost frantic, with Mollie in tow, she boarded a special train to take her back to Washington. As the engine raced full-speed for the capital, it nearly derailed and screeched to a stop, throwing Crete out of her seat and barely averting a deadly accident. Still fragile from her long illness, she then waited for hours in the remote countryside for another train that would carry her to Washington. It was six thirty in the evening by time she and Mollie reached the White House.

Leaning on the arm of her son Harry, she stepped through the front door, looking, Harriet recounted, "frail, fatigued, desperate, but firm and quiet and full of purpose." When she got to her husband's bedside, they embraced each other silently for several minutes. Then, Garfield began talking to her calmly about his approaching death, but Crete stopped him, saying that he should only think about getting well. It was now her turn, she said, to nurse him.

His spirits lifted, but he was in pain, especially in his calves and feet—like they were on a red-hot stove, he said. Harriet piled pillows beneath them, while Edson put pressure on his knees, which helped a bit. For hours on end, Crump squeezed the president's feet between his hands until he made them numb, bending himself almost double over the low bedstead.

After Crete finally went to bed, four cabinet members stayed with Garfield throughout the night. He woke every half hour to vomit, but he seemed better, surprisingly, in the morning. A team of physicians returned to the White House to plan his treatment, but Dr. Bliss quickly dismissed them. He was assuming complete control over the patient, on his own initiative. He had known Garfield in Ohio, and he claimed that the president and First Lady had personally asked him to take charge. The Garfields later denied that, according to Silas Boynton. But in the chaos after the president's shooting, no one thought to question Bliss's authority. He had assumed control at the depot, too, after the shooting. Now, on Sunday, he asked only a few doctors to continue, on a limited basis. Edson and Boynton were also permitted to stay with the president, but only as nurses, not physicians.

Despite the pain and prodding, Garfield never complained, Edson recalled. They would dress his wound at eight o'clock every morning. Then he was "carefully lifted from the bed by six men," she recounted, while nurses changed all the bedclothes, including the mattress. He was sponged and fanned frequently in the summer heat, and doctors were constantly going in and out of his room. Garfield was "a remarkable patient," she reported—"never complaining, and never allowing a groan to escape him, no matter how great or severe his sufferings." He lay on his back nearly all the time and was never able to raise his head from his pillow without support.

The doctors issued multiple updates each day about his condition. The public was extraordinarily anxious and followed the reports closely. Part of their worry, no doubt, was that Chester Arthur would become president if Garfield died. There were serious questions about the vice president's character. The optics were very bad. It was widely known that he shared an apartment with Roscoe Conkling, and his slavish loyalty to the former senator made him seem especially unfit for the presidency. Guiteau claimed that he shot Garfield so Arthur would become president. There were even suspicions that Conkling had arranged the assassination. Former president Rutherford Hayes reflected the feelings of many Americans when he wrote that "the death of the President at this time would be a national calamity," with results that were impossible to predict. Public anger at the Stalwarts was so venomous in New York, a journalist noted, that men were going around "with clenched teeth and white lips. . . . Any Stalwart . . . seen rejoicing . . . would be immediately lynched."

On the morning that Garfield was shot, in fact, Arthur and Conkling had been together. They had just stepped off a steamer from Albany, and when they learned the news, they went directly to the Fifth Avenue Hotel. That evening, Arthur spent hours huddled with Conkling and his deputies. Then, at the urging of the secretary of state, he traveled to Washington on the midnight train. Conkling accompanied Arthur—carrying the vice president's bags in a rare gesture of respect. Aware, at last, that it was unseemly for him to live with Conkling, Arthur moved into the Washington townhouse of a Nevada senator. In truth, Arthur was shaken by the prospect that he might become president. It was an office that he had never wanted. A journalist who interviewed him soon after he arrived in Washington reported that his bloodshot eyes were teary, and he was so overwhelmed with emotion that he could barely speak.

<hr />

After an anxious, subdued Fourth of July, there seemed to be new hope for Garfield's survival. Although he took only liquids—milk, ice water, and chicken broth—in the first days, his appetite was beginning to return. On July 6, Harriet Blaine reported that it looked "as though Gaffy would live. He is now, six o'clock, still comfortable, and has asked for beefsteak. They will not, of course, let him have it, but if they would," she remarked, "it ought not to come from the White House kitchens. Such tough leather as they had there for breakfast the other morning, is a disgrace to the cattle on a thousand hills." Garfield's bowels were also functioning with no signs of blood—suggesting that his major internal organs were undamaged. So the doctors began giving him a little solid food. To Garfield's disgust, it was oatmeal, which he detested.

James Wormley was enlisted to prepare his special chicken broth recipe for the president, made from his own Tenleytown chickens. Wormley was also asked to supply the White House with his "patented" beef broth—made, according to the *New York Herald-Tribune*, by broiling a tenderloin until it was smoking, then putting it into a heated iron device. "A crank was then turned which brought hundreds of pounds of pressure on the steaming steak, causing every particle of its juice to stream forth." With a little seasoning, the extract was ready—"the pure juice of the beef."

"At times," Crump recalled, "the President's appetite would be very keen," and he would ask for certain foods, "but I could not always yield to his wishes." By mid-July, however, he had fewer dietary restrictions. One morning, Crump recalled, Garfield was "hungry as a bear" and asked for two lamb chops and a baked potato. "I was so delighted at the marked improvement in his appetite and general condition," he added, "that I fairly flew down the stairs to execute his order. . . . After eating all I had prepared for him with great relish, he asked permission to smoke a cigar. . . . But the doctor very promptly refused him this luxury."

Everything, Harriet Blaine noted, seemed to be going well now—"no danger now for the President, no anxiety about paralysis or bullet in the liver, and every prospect of a speedy recovery in all his parts." Chester Arthur, she added, could even return to New York, since the president was now past the crisis. He was visibly improving, but he was also suffering from isolation, with screens around his bed and guards at the door. "He might as well be . . . a prisoner," a visitor said. Garfield was also plagued by Washington's oppressive heat. Doctors tried to cool down his sickroom by bringing in large blocks of ice, but they only worsened its stifling humidity. Finally, navy engineers ingeniously invented a crude air conditioner. They loaded a large container with tons of ice and blew air over it, which passed through a box filled with absorbent cotton filters that was connected to a vent in the sickroom. The cool, dry air brought the temperature down twenty degrees.

By late July, however, Garfield's condition began to decline again. He was showing signs of infection—fever, vomiting, sweats, and convulsive chills. On July 24, the doctors decided to operate on a sac full of pus that had erupted beneath the wound. Without anesthetic, they made a two-inch incision, an inch and a half deep, inserted a drainage tube, and set one of his broken ribs. Despite the pain of the procedure, Garfield stoically made no sound or movement. Afterward, though, he was no longer able to keep down any solid food. The news was worrying. "I cannot tell you what a state we are in," Harriet Blaine reported. "I am as disappointed as though a re-set bone had to be rebroken." People around the president, she said, were as despairing as "lost children."

On July 25, she wrote,

> We are doing nothing but wait, and despair and hope. Five minutes ago, we had talked ourselves into an abyss of misery. . . . Dr. Agnew had put his finger into the wound more than an inch further than yesterday, [and] pieces of bone had come away.

Meanwhile, the doctors were still trying to locate the bullet in Garfield's back. There was no reason to find it—it was causing no harm to the president, and they would not have been able to remove it safely. But on July 26, Bliss enlisted the help of Alexander Graham Bell, the inventor of the telephone, who had developed an early metal detector. He came to the White House and used his contraption to try to locate the bullet in the president's body, without success.

By August 15, Garfield could no longer keep down any kind of nourishment. So doctors began trying to feed him through "nutrient enemas," which introduced animal blood or liquified food into his body anally. They believed that these could be an effective way to nourish and sustain the president. For the first few days, Bliss experimented by introducing egg yolks, but the infusion resulted in "offensive flatus." He then used fresh cow's blood, but that liquid, too, had foul effects. Finally, he came up with a recipe for specially prepared beef extract, which was injected every four hours, night and day. The president retained the infusions, but his weight began dropping precipitously. He was, in fact, starving to death and weakened by a raging infection caused by the dirty hands and instruments of the doctors.

A week later, Harriet Blaine admitted, even Dr. Edson had abandoned hope. On August 25, the outlook was so bleak that doctors told Crete that her husband had little chance of recovery. Even Bliss felt "very anxious now," he acknowledged. The outlook was "less promising than ever before." Harriet conceded that hope was over. Every night when she went to bed now, she tried to brace herself for the dreaded telephone call that would bring them news of the president's death. Chester Arthur was standing by in New York, and Lucretia summoned all her children to Washington.

Meanwhile, conditions in the capital were noxious in the late-summer heat. When one of Garfield's consulting surgeons got a pungent whiff of the mudflats behind the White House, he said, "We must get the President out of this. . . . It's enough to kill a well man in a week." On September 1, Blaine suggested moving the president to Long Branch. Garfield loved the sight and sound of the ocean and hated the suffocating boredom and loneliness of the White House. Crete agreed with Blaine's idea, but it would be no small matter to transport "poor dear Gaffy," Harriet knew. "He is very weak, and there is little to build on." Nevertheless, Bliss agreed, and over the course of the next few days, highly complex plans and logistics were put in place to move the fragile president from the White House to the New Jersey seashore.

ABOVE: The free-love Oneida Community, in upstate New York, prospered for more than three decades. It was the most successful utopian experiment in American history. *Courtesy of the New York Public Library.* **BELOW LEFT:** John Humphrey Noyes founded the Oneida Community in 1848. He was, writer Aldous Huxley later observed, "a born prophet, a missionary in the bone." *From Wikimedia Commons.* **BELOW RIGHT:** Charles Julius Guiteau joined the Oneida Community in 1860, when he was nineteen years of age. Guiteau was known for his odd personality and behavior and permanently left the Community in 1866. He assassinated President Garfield in 1881. *Courtesy of the Library of Congress.*

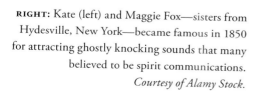

James Garfield and his wife, Lucretia, had a difficult early marriage while he served as a school principal and state senator in Ohio, as an officer in the Union Army, and as a young US congressman. *From Wikimedia Commons.*

TOP LEFT AND RIGHT: In 1863, while Garfield was serving as chief of staff for Major General William Rosecrans in Tennessee, he became one of the "most constant companions" of a cross-dressing actress and Union spy named Pauline Cushman. Garfield later persuaded President Lincoln to give Cushman the honorary title of "major" in the Union Army. *Both images from Wikimedia Commons.*

BOTTOM LEFT: P. T. Barnum met Horace Greeley in 1841 and became one of the editor's closest friends. The masterful showman, famous for his popular museums and circuses, invested in Greeley's utopian venture in Colorado. *Courtesy of the Library of Congress.*

LEFT: In 1849, Roscoe Conkling began his political career, at age twenty, as district attorney of Oneida County in New York. At twenty-nine, he was elected to Congress from Oneida County, and in 1867, he was elected a US senator. Conkling became the most powerful Republican power broker in the country and the fierce political enemy of Horace Greeley, President Rutherford B. Hayes, and President James Garfield. *Courtesy of Alamy Stock.*
BELOW: General Ulysses S. Grant, shown here in 1865, was elected US President in 1868. He was a devoted ally of Roscoe Conkling and, in 1880, vied unsuccessfully against James Garfield for the Republican presidential nomination. *Courtesy of the Library of Congress.*

RIGHT: John Humphrey Noyes, shown here in 1867, exerted power over his followers in the Oneida Community by controlling their sexual relations. *From Wikimedia Commons.* **BELOW LEFT:** President Rutherford B. Hayes, elected in 1876, was a first cousin of John Humphrey Noyes and received visits from members of the Oneida Community in the White House. *Courtesy of the Library of Congress.* **BELOW RIGHT:** James Wormley, a respected, successful Black entrepreneur, owned Wormley's Hotel—Washington, D.C.'s most elegant and expensive place for lodging, dining, and political dealing. Roscoe Conkling and Chester Arthur both resided at Wormley's Hotel, located two blocks from the White House. *From Blackpast.org.*

LEFT: James Garfield, shown here in 1880, was inaugurated as president of the United States on March 4, 1881. Charles Guiteau shot him on July 2, and he died on September 19. *Courtesy of the Library of Congress.*

RIGHT: Senator Blanche Kelso Bruce of Mississippi, a former slave elected in 1874, was the second Black American to serve in the US Senate. In 1880, he became the first Black American to be shortlisted for nomination as vice president of the United States. In 1881, President Garfield appointed him register of the Treasury, and Bruce became the first Black American to have his signature printed on all US currency. *Courtesy of the Library of Congress.*

RIGHT: Chester Arthur, a crony of Roscoe Conkling, served as controller of the lucrative New York Custom House. In 1880, he was chosen as the Republican nominee for vice president, sharing the ticket with presidential candidate James Garfield. After Garfield won the election, he was assassinated after six months in office. Arthur succeeded him as the twenty-first president of the United States. *Courtesy of the Library of Congress.*

LEFT: Senator James G. Blaine of Maine, a political enemy of Roscoe Conkling, served as President Garfield's secretary of state. *Courtesy of the Library of Congress.*

On September 5, all the detailed preparations were ready. At six o'clock in the morning, four specially trained men carried Garfield—whose wasted body had shrunk to only one hundred thirty pounds—out of the wide front door of the White House on his low walnut bed, covered by a white lambswool blanket with red borders. A white cloth was wrapped around his pale forehead. As Garfield passed the assembled White House staff, he raised his right hand to them with a weak smile. He was then gently loaded into a large, two-horse Adams Express wagon, normally used for transporting bullion. The horses pulled it slowly down Pennsylvania Avenue to Fifteenth Street. For a brief moment, the president opened his eyes and gazed at the crowds lining the sidewalks, doffing their hats and weeping as he passed. He whispered, "How good it is to see the people," before drifting back into unconsiousness.

The express wagon stopped at a railroad car that was specially outfitted to circulate cool, filtered air as it carried the president. The refitted car stood on a new spur that ran from the main track to the street. Garfield was gently lifted from the wagon and placed on a special Indian rubber waterbed inside the railcar. Bliss and Crete were there to receive him, and she fanned him constantly in the heat. His walnut bedstead was stowed, and at nearly six thirty, the train started on its journey to Long Branch.

All night long, three hundred railroad workers had labored to lay a thirty-two-hundred-foot track that ran from the Elberon depot at Long Branch directly to the front door of the president's cottage on the ocean. They had driven the last spike at three in the morning, and then started laying the track bed, lit by huge locomotive headlights and hundreds of small lamps. At one twenty-three in the afternoon, when the president's train reached Elberon, workmen carefully detached his special car and pushed it by hand along the new track, until its door came right up to the cottage porch. They then placed planks from the car door to the veranda, under an awning set up to shade the president from the hot sun. Soldiers carried his walnut bed into the cottage and then, at one thirty, others carried the president out of the railcar on a stretcher. Five minutes later, Garfield was lying comfortably in his own bed, in a room that looked out over the ocean.

All of his cabinet members were in Long Branch, and every evening they gathered with Crete and the doctors. The Blaines felt discouraged about Garfield's condition. "All our journey through," Harriet wrote, "we were cheered by bulletins from the President's car, telling us of the comfortable progress he was making. . . . But after getting here. . . . He is just the same. I do not believe he will recover." Still, the move, at first, seemed to have a reviving effect on Garfield. Bliss was so encouraged on September 8 that he almost declared him in a state of recovery. The next day, in fact, the president's appetite was so improved that they stopped his anal infusions. Six days later, he even got out of bed and sat in a chair by the window, gazing out at the rolling surf for more than an hour. He seemed to be improving daily—until September 17, when he was suddenly shaken by convulsive chills. The president had another fit the next day, and on September 19, he was suddenly too weak to lift a glass.

That morning, the attorney general sent Chester Arthur a telegram warning him about the president's abrupt decline. Finally, at ten thirty that night, Garfield awoke with piercing chest pains before losing consciousness. Bliss gave him stimulants and sent for Lucretia. For twenty minutes, she kept one hand on her husband's forehead and the other on his heart, until, at last, his breathing stopped, and his limbs stiffened. She then collapsed in a chair by his bed, shaking silently to the sound of waves heaving and crashing on the beach.

Hours later, an autopsy revealed that Garfield had died from a burst aneurysm near his heart. The bullet, it turned out, was safely encased in scar tissue near his spine.

On September 21, two days after the president died, a casket containing his withered body—dressed in the black suit and black satin tie he had worn for his inauguration just six months earlier—was carried out of the cottage and placed aboard a funeral train, waiting on the specially laid track by the front door. Sitting alone, at the rear of the passenger car, sat the new president of the United States, Chester Arthur. The day before, at twelve thirty-five in the morning, he had received a telegram alerting him to the president's death. At two fifteen that morning, two judges of the New York State Supreme Court administered the oath of office to Arthur in the front parlor of his home. Now, dressed in a Prince Albert coat, a black silk tie, and a silk hat banded with black crepe, he rode with Garfield's coffin from Elberon to Washington's Baltimore and Pacific station, where the assassin, Guiteau, had shot the president.

At the depot, soldiers carried Garfield's coffin from the funeral car to a hearse drawn by six gray horses, accompanied by two hundred army and navy officers. To the sound of solemn music and muffled drums, the president's remains were then taken to the Capitol and placed under its immense dome, on the same catafalque that had held the coffin of President Lincoln sixteen years earlier. Arthur was sworn in again, formally, the next day, and thousands of people, in lines that stretched far from the Capitol, came to gaze at the ravaged face of the late president, lying in an open casket in the Rotunda. Two days later, on September 23, Garfield's coffin—surrounded by crowds that were greater than those at his inauguration—was marched out of the great bronze doors of the Capitol and carried, in a solemn procession of dignitaries, citizens, soldiers, and black-plumed horses, to the Baltimore and Potomac station, to start its final journey home, back to Ohio.

At the jail, Guiteau dropped to his knees when he learned of Garfield's death. It was God's will, he believed, and proof of the soundness of his inspiration. His friend Arthur would now be in the White House, exactly according to plan.

On September 20, the day after Garfield's death, he wrote President Arthur that the assassination of Garfield was "a God send to you and I presume you appreciate it. It raises you from $8,000 to $50,000 a year. It raised you from a political cypher to President of the United States with all its powers and honors." He then suggested that Arthur name Roscoe Conkling as his secretary of state.

He had set out to heal the Republican party, and he had done so. It was his duty to God and country. The newspapers, after all, had implied that Garfield had caused the split in the Republicans. They were "bitterly denouncing the President for wrecking the Republican party by the unwise use of patronage," he explained. "Gradually as the result of reading the newspapers the idea settled on me that if the President was removed it would unite the two factions of the Republican party." The papers, he declared, had practically compelled his actions. "In attempting to remove the President," he remarked, "I only did what the newspapers said was . . . to be done. . . . I certainly should never have shot him on my own account."

He had risen early on the day of the shooting, at four o'clock in the morning. After donning a black coat, dark trousers, and a soft black hat, then eating breakfast and charging the meal to his hotel room—knowing he would never pay for it—he felt excellent in body and spirit. He went to the river and practiced firing his gun, then walked over to the train station. Guiteau had his boots blacked and asked a hack driver to wait for him until he came out of the depot. At about nine twenty, he entered the station and took a seat in the corner of the ladies' waiting room, near the door. President Garfield appeared shortly, and Guiteau fired two shots at him to execute "the divine will for the good of the American people."

He then wheeled around and calmly walked to the door. He was swiftly intercepted by Officer Patrick Kearney of the District police, who had heard the shots from outside and rushed into the depot. After witnesses quickly identified Guiteau as the shooter, the slight man looked Kearney squarely in the eye and said, "I did it, and will go to jail for it. I am a Stalwart, and Arthur will be President."

Kearney hurried him over to police headquarters, a few blocks away on Fourth Street. The officers there searched Guiteau—finding his pistol, still loaded with three live cartridges; the screeds he had written; clippings from forty or fifty newspapers around the country; and a copy of "The Wriggler" from the *New York Herald*. They then loaded him into a police wagon and took him to the District of Columbia Jail. When it was all over and he was finally in his cell, Guiteau said he was happier than he had been in weeks

He was delighted to be in the well-protected prison, guarded by troops who kept curious visitors, and vigilantes, at a distance. For once, he could count on regular meals—enjoying a breakfast, on his first morning, of wheat bread, salted herring, potatoes, and coffee. Guiteau's appetite was so lusty that he gained more than ten pounds that summer. He was also enjoying the notoriety. When a photographer arrived to take his pictures, Guiteau instructed him to make them very flattering. "I don't want to appear strained and awkward," he insisted. "If my picture is taken at all it must be a good one." But he missed having access to the daily newspapers, and his safety was not guaranteed. On September 11, as he was looking out his cell window, one of his own guards took a shot at him—an act that won the officer the admiration of many, along with a court-martial and a prison sentence of eight years.

In a strange turn of events, Guiteau's brother-in-law, attorney George Scoville, had arrived in Washington right after the shooting. He visited Guiteau in his jail cell and was appointed sole counsel for the assassin, even though he had no experience in criminal law. Guiteau insisted on serving as assistant counsel and was the main architect of his own defense. Part of his courtroom argument was the perceptive claim that Garfield had died not from the gunshot wounds but from his doctors' medical malpractice. The physicians killed him, Guiteau insisted. "I simply shot at him."

Scoville also lost no time in linking Guiteau's derangement to his membership in the Oneida Community. After interviewing Guiteau at the jail, Dr. John Gray, head of New York's Utica Asylum, declared that "Whatever the religious fanaticism which brought him into the Community, it was there developed in the midst of sensualism, contentions and self-conceit and laid the foundation for the after character of religious ranting, hypocrisy and his dishonorable conduct." On November 4, the *New York Herald* trumpeted the scandalous connection between Guiteau and Oneida. Three days later, John Humphrey Noyes penned a response.

<hr />

He had been living in Canada ever since his middle-of-the-night flight from Oneida in June 1879. After escaping thirty miles in a buggy, he had taken a train to a port on the St. Lawrence River, then crossed into Canada by ferry. At first, Noyes took shelter in Ontario with the Bretts, a family of religious sympathizers. They lived on their primitive farm, surrounded by a monotonous landscape, and ate mainly potatoes. Their drinking water, Noyes complained, was "no better than slush." But he remained with the Bretts for more than six months, while the Community collapsed in his absence.

Noyes had been a magnetic leader, holding the Oneidans together for thirty years. But now, as Aldous Huxley later put it, his current switched off, and all "the iron filings" flew apart. Infighting increased, and young people in the Community, according to an elder, had fallen into an "awful state of disrespect and rowdyism"— sleeping with whomever they wanted, without the control of Community leaders. The "sexual grab bag" alarmed Noyes so much that in late August, he wrote from Canada proposing that Oneidans would now be allowed to marry in the traditional manner. Instead of the supervised promiscuity that had characterized the colony, Oneidans would now be able to choose between marriage and celibacy. His proposal, announced on August 26, "was like the explosion of a bomb-shell," according to Tirzah Miller. But Community members voted to approve it. The new regime of celibacy or monogamy would go into effect on August 28, 1879, at ten o'clock in the morning—leaving two full days for members to enjoy their last flings. Frequent sexual farewells took place over those frenzied forty-eight hours. Tirzah herself reported that she had sex with three different partners in a single day.

It was a torrid end to a unique social system that had thrived for three full decades. Soon after, in a letter to President Rutherford Hayes, a relative recounted the dramatic changes to the Community:

> They have abandoned "complex" family life. And good . . . marriages have occurred. There is a serious defection from John H. Noyes authority and he is presently absent probably in Canada though his whereabouts are unknown to most members of the Community. He can probably never come back again. The community has lost its religious character almost wholly and seems likely to drift into a co-operative industrial association.

The social changes led, in fact, to a financial and structural transformation. A year after the new marriage rules, in August 1880, more than two hundred Oneidans signed an "Agreement to Divide and Reorganize" the Community—turning it into a corporation called the Oneida Community, Limited. Members held shares in the joint-stock company, whose profits came from Oneida's fruit-canning business and its spoon factory, which had moved to the Niagara Gorge in Canada. The Mansion House itself was divided up by square feet and allocated for rental to members. Furnishings were priced for purchase, although every member was entitled to thirty dollars' worth of items, as well as a small annual sum of money for expenses. The Oneidans' communal dining room was turned into an à la carte restaurant, where even pats of butter were priced by the piece.

Meanwhile, in January 1880, members agreed to give Noyes a house in Niagara, Canada, called Stone Cottage—with a view of the falls, a horse and carriage, and fifty dollars a month. The Oneidans sent him furniture from the Mansion House, and his wife, Harriet, traveled there to join him. At his desk in the cottage, in November 1881, Noyes considered the strange circumstances that had made his Community the former home of a presidential assassin. Guiteau was about to go on trial for his "exhibition of holy horror and righteous zeal," he wrote. There was "no danger of my going [to Washington] if I can help it," he explained in his letter of testimony. "I am seventy years old, and have long been disabled by laryngitis and deafness, so as to be quite unfit for service as a witness. But I can write a little yet, and it is no more than fair to the memory of the defunct Community." Early in life, he explained, the president-killer had exhibited tendencies that "naturally led him to fasten himself on the Oneida Community, first as a lascivious hypocrite, and afterward as a pettifogging plunderer."

Soon after, in mid-November, another Oneidan was subpoenaed to testify about the assassin. James Vaill had been Guiteau's roommate in the Community. The murderer "was not evenly balanced," Vaill remembered. "We considered him a 'little off.'" But the night before Vaill planned to leave for Washington to testify, he was arrested on a charge of arson—supposedly for burning down the Community's large stables. His trial, it turned out, ended with a hung jury, and there are indications that Vaill was framed by some Oneidans, including Myron Kinsley, to prevent him from sharing salacious details about the Community in the federal courtroom.

Vaill and his sister had been raised in the Community since their early childhood. And although he never actually testified at Guiteau's trial, he did give a jailhouse interview to the *Syracuse Sunday Herald* in January 1882. He publicly told the reporter stories that Oneidans would have liked to suppress—especially in light of their persecution by Professor Mears. Vaill specifically told the reporter of his sister's experience with John Humphrey Noyes when she was a young child.

> My sister told me that when but nine years old she, with five other children, were forced into a room by this monster and assaulted by him, and she knew of several instances where girls, whose ages ranged anywhere from ten to fourteen years, were taken from their beds at night and carried to Noyes that he might work their ruin . . . covered with the cloak of religion. . . . The Community had a summer-house at Oneida lake, about twelve miles away. In the summer Noyes would spend a season of fishing there. . . . To this place he would take half a dozen girls, whose ages ranged anywhere from twelve to sixteen years, and would compel them to sleep in his room. My

sister has been among the number and she has told me of the dreadful scenes she has witnessed there.

Noyes, Vaill continued, "had a peculiar influence over all of us. He was a large, fleshy man, weighing two hundred and twenty-five pounds; the animal predominated in him to a terrible extent; he was brutal beyond measure in a great many ways; and had almost a complete control over those who were under him. He was an able man; there's no doubting that, and he made the women and most of the men believe that the moon was made of green cheese. Like Guiteau," Vaill said, "he claimed to do everything by inspiration."

———

The assassin's trial began on November 14, 1881, two months after the president's death. Guiteau was eager to make a "racy, stirring" opening statement—blasting Arthur, Conkling, and Grant for not coming forward and taking their share of responsibility. The dingy criminal courtroom in Washington, D.C., was jammed with lawyers, spectators, and reporters. The jury, including a member of the Wormley clan—plasterer Ralph Wormley—was seated three days later. Guiteau, wearing a new black suit, had a rather "pleasant and ingratiating" courtroom countenance, according to one observer, while another saw him as "a puny, white-faced, insignificant little fellow, with a peculiar look in his eyes, and a rather anxious expression on his face." He managed to make a spectacle of himself—interrupting the proceedings with manic, erratic remarks and gestures "like a half-tamed chimpanzee" in a traveling circus, according to *Harper's Weekly*.

There were other dramatic moments during the trial. On Saturday, November 19, Dr. Bliss took the stand and submitted, in evidence, a gory five-inch length of the late president's spine, with bits of his ribs still attached to it. As they handled the piece of bone, many jurors burst into tears. Then, as the trial concluded for the day and Guiteau was returning to prison in a police van, a drunken farmer on horseback rode up to the vehicle and fired a pistol at the assassin through the bars, missing Guiteau but blowing a hole right through his coat.

Six weeks later, on January 5, 1882, at four thirty-five in the afternoon, the jury came to a verdict in just an hour. "Guilty as indicted," they announced. On February 4, Guiteau returned to court, where the judge pronounced his sentence. He would be taken

> to the common jail of the District from whence you came, and there to be kept in confinement, and on Friday, the 30th of June, 1882, you will be taken to the place prepared for the execution, within the walls of said jail, and there, between the hours of 12 A.M. and 2 P.M., you will be hanged by the neck until you are dead.

⁓

Over the next four months, Guiteau stayed cheerful—confident that he would win an appeal for a new trial and that President Chester Arthur would grant him a pardon. His cell was comfortable, he wrote his sister; he was dining happily on meals of fried potatoes and steak, and he was sleeping well. On May 22, however, Guiteau lost his appeal, and on June 24, he learned that President Arthur would not intervene. Guiteau was enraged by what he called Arthur's treachery, cowardice, and ingratitude. But he took consolation in the belief that someday, "instead of saying 'Guiteau the assassin,' they will say 'Guiteau the patriot.'" The worst that men could do, he reflected, was kill you, but "whatever the mode of my exit from this world, I have no doubt but that my name and work will roll thundering down the ages."

He recovered his good humor. As the warden of the jail mailed specially printed invitations to a small fraction of the twenty thousand hopefuls who had asked for tickets to the execution, Guiteau began preparing a dramatic spectacle for his departure. He planned to wear a white robe to the gallows, which he would then drop in front of the assembled witnesses and swing to his death in his underwear. He was persuaded to drop that plan, but he did compose a poem to read from the scaffold, and he sent his shoes out to be shined.

On the day of his execution, Guiteau quickly devoured a large meal at eleven thirty in the morning. Then, when he heard the squad of soldiers entering the yard, he fell over in a dead faint. Worried that they would not be able to get him to the gallows, prison officials revived him and gave him a large dose of brandy. At noon, Guiteau managed to mount the scaffold and drunkenly read fourteen verses from the tenth chapter of Matthew. Then, in a high-pitched, squeaky voice, he recited a strange, childlike poem he had written that said, in part, "I am going to the Lordy, I am so glad. . . . I saved my party and my land. . . . But they have murdered me for it, And that is the reason I am going to the Lordy."

Partway through, Guiteau suddenly stopped speaking and stood up straight. The executioner placed a black hood and noose over his head. Then, dropping the papers in his hand, Guiteau shouted, "Glory, ready, go!" and the platform suddenly gave way beneath him. He dangled from the rope for half an hour, his feet just grazing the ground.

Finally, Guiteau's body was taken down and placed in an open coffin. Crowds of people came forward to view his corpse, as flies swarmed around his face and spectators eagerly snapped up "guaranteed" bits of the coffin lining from an enterprising officer. Before the year was out, prison guards predicted, the gallows themselves would be hacked into pieces for ghoulishly profitable souvenirs.

13

OVER THE FALLS

Guiteau's corpse was quickly taken out of its cheap coffin so that doctors from the Army Medical Museum could conduct an autopsy. George Scoville had hoped to take possession of the body, freeze it, and exhibit it around the country, but the army took charge of it. The doctors removed the assassin's spleen, which was greatly enlarged from chronic malaria, along with several pieces of his brain. They planned to preserve those relics for the museum's historical and educational collection, which also included three vertebrae from the cadaver of John Wilkes Booth. The rest of the assassin's body was thrown into a huge boiler, where, according to the Columbia, South Carolina, *State*, it was allowed to "boil and bubble" until "all the flesh had fallen" from his skeleton. The bones were then picked out, bleached, and also prepared for exhibit at the museum.

The assassin's head, however, received special treatment. The skin on the skull, including Guiteau's face, was preserved in alcohol and then stuffed "so skillfully," according to the *Cleveland Leader*, that it looked just like the living assassin, "with the scraggly beard, scar on the scalp," and even marks on his neck from the hangman's rope. The army's official anatomist then preserved the stuffed head in a clear eight-inch-by-twelve-inch glass jar. For many months, according to the *New York Herald*, the doctors had it "on exhibition for the gratification of curious friends."

In 1887, however, Guiteau's stuffed head came into the possession of an impresario, "Professor" E. M. Worth, who was known in New York as the founder of Worth's Museum and Congress of Living and Inanimate Curiosities. Worth took Guiteau's head on tour—along with a Monster Devil Fish and Transparent Baby—before showcasing it, in 1908, as a permanent exhibit in his Indiana museum. In September 1916, however, the museum—with Guiteau's face and thousands of other curiosities—burned down to the ground. The assassin's skeleton, meanwhile, remained in the Army Medical Museum. A portion of his brain still resides in Philadelphia's Mütter Museum, along with the brain of Albert Einstein and the livers of Cheng and Eng, famous conjoined twins who toured with P. T. Barnum.

———

Amateurs, too, tried to profit from gruesome mementoes of the assassination. When Chester Arthur moved into the White House on December 7, 1881, William Crump continued on as his personal steward, although he complained to former president Rutherford Hayes that there was "nothing like it ever before in the Executive Mansion—liquor, snobbery, and worse," as well as "outbursts of ill temper, caused by drink, no doubt." Work hours, too, were grueling because of Arthur's penchant for late-night soirées.

Crump permanently left his post as White House steward in 1886, during Grover Cleveland's administration. He began running a hotel outside the capital that, according to a reporter, was "filled with ghastly memories of Garfield's untimely taking off"—including part of the shirt he wore when he was shot, the chair he sat in in his room at Elberon, and his whisk broom, ink stands, and other morbid souvenirs. The displays failed to entice many paying guests.

Washington's "Professor of Swimming," Robert Odlum, also got into the murder memento business. After his expensive natatorium failed financially in 1882 and shut down, Odlum worked as a lifeguard on the Virginia shore. He then managed a touring museum that exhibited relics of Garfield's assassination, including Guiteau's clothing and a piece of the executioner's rope. The museum, like Crump's bloody tourist hotel, failed to attract the paying public. So Odlum eventually decided to make a stunning, potentially profitable spectacle of himself.

In January 1883, New Yorkers had celebrated the opening of the Brooklyn Bridge, then the longest suspension span in the world, from Brooklyn to Manhattan across the East River. A year later, P. T. Barnum had demonstrated its stability and strength by parading twenty-one elephants across it, led by Jumbo, his most famous pachyderm. Odlum resolved to be the first person to jump from the Brooklyn Bridge into the water one hundred thirty-five feet below. He was confident that he would survive. In Washington, D.C., he had dived from steamships into the Potomac River, and on July 4, 1881—two days after Garfield's shooting—he had jumped from a bridge ninety feet above the Occoquan River in Northern Virginia. He was a jumping evangelist—encouraging people to jump from burning buildings into safety nets at a time when many people believed that if they jumped from a great height, they would perish in midair.

Odlum was inspired by Sam Patch, an earlier jumping daredevil. In 1827, when Patch was a worker at a cotton mill in New Jersey, he jumped eighty feet from a ledge over the Passaic Falls into the water. He survived, and as his fame spread, he tried even more spectacular stunts. In October 1829, as thousands watched, Patch—dressed all in white, his hands held close to his body and his legs together—jumped feet first from a height of one hundred twenty-five feet into the churning Niagara River at Niagara Falls. According to the *Buffalo Republican*, it was "the greatest feat of the kind ever effected by man." Patch was an overnight sensation.

Looking for his next triumph, a month later, Patch jumped nearly ninety-four feet from a ledge above the churning High Falls of the Genesee River in Rochester, New York. Unhappy with the amount of cash he had collected from spectators, he decided to up the ante. Patch had a platform erected twenty-five feet higher than the ledge he had jumped from the first time. On November 13, in front of an audience of thousands, he climbed up the platform, delivered a short speech comparing himself to Napoleon, then jumped over the Genesee Falls. But this time his leap was not as controlled as usual. His arms suddenly flew out from his sides and his legs parted before he slammed into the foaming water. The crowd strained their eyes to glimpse Patch rising to the surface, but he never appeared. His frozen body was found four months later, seven miles downstream.

Still, Patch was a working-class American hero, inspiring future thrill seekers like Robert Odlum. If Patch's jumps over Niagara and the Genesee Falls were showstoppers, Odlum's inaugural jump from the Brooklyn Bridge would go down in history. It would put his name in headlines across the country, making him more famous than Sam Patch or any other leaping daredevils.

Odlum chose May 19, 1885, as the date of his death-defying plunge. It was against the law to jump from the Brooklyn Bridge, and police knew all about his plan. So Odlum and his friends devised a ruse to trick the New York coppers. One of his accomplices pretended to be the jumper, and when the cops swarmed him, Odlum—dressed in gray tights and a red shirt—stepped out onto the railing of the bridge. As he spotted a tugboat jammed with spectators positioned near the span, Odlum filled his chest with air, pulled his feet together, placed his left arm firmly against his body, raised his right arm straight up in the air, then stepped off the railing and plunged straight down, in perfect position, for a hundred feet. Suddenly, however, he appeared to lose his balance, perhaps from a rogue gust of wind. As his body began falling at a slant, he bent slightly forward. Odlum smashed into the water with a gigantic splash and met the same final, watery fate as Sam Patch.

There is something seductive about an approach to danger—"an irresistible attraction that fairly drags one into peril," observed George Cragin, one of the first members of the Oneida Community. So often, he mused, people venture "too near the brink of a waterfall, a precipice, or some other dangerous situation. . . . They simply can't keep away."

John Humphrey Noyes was now living at the edge of Niagara Falls, gazing out at its tumbling, crashing water. Even in the safety and comfort of his second-floor bedroom at Stone Cottage, he could feel the torrent rattling the lead windowpanes, and its powerful roar lulled him to sleep at night. He liked to pace back and forth on the veranda, gazing into the white cloud of mist that sometimes rose so high that it enveloped the large, rambling house.

It was a gabled home with seven bedrooms, a large parlor, and a big dining room with French windows facing the Niagara River. It had two kitchens, two pantries, a stable, a barn, and a Turkish bath that Noyes had built inside a woodshed. Seven members of the Oneida family lived with him in Stone Cottage, including his wife, Harriet. Called "Mother Noyes" by all, she was three years older than her husband. Now physically frail, she had trouble walking and climbing stairs. But three times a day, she insisted on sitting in a special high chair at the kitchen sink, humming to herself while she washed up all the family dishes, and she spent hours reading aloud and making artificial flowers out of silvery fish scales.

Every day at supper, Noyes would sit at the head of the long table, smiling and aloof. There were always guests from Oneida in the house, and the table was routinely set for at least a dozen. Afterward, Noyes would return to his room, while the others read, chatted, and played games. On Sunday afternoons, there was always a crowd. Oneida's tableware factory was located on the American side of the gorge, at the brink of the falls, and the joint stock company also made steel chains on the Canadian side. Managers of those enterprises had built homes close to Stone Cottage, and they brought their families to visit Noyes every Sunday. Although he was able to speak only in whispers, Noyes would sit in his armchair in the parlor, surrounded by his still-loyal followers, and give them one of his "home talks," with cookies and lemonade.

There were so many Community children in Niagara that the Oneidans organized their own school. Students studied Greek, mathematics, dancing, and shorthand, and Noyes himself taught Hebrew lessons, rising at four in the morning for a while to learn the language. The children also had chores—feeding animals, chopping wood, hoeing potatoes, cleaning sheds, and carrying coal. But they also had ample free time to play sports and flirt with the locals, roam the woods, and explore the riverbanks and rock ledges above the gorge.

It seemed like a sylvan paradise. But despite the apparent serenity Noyes seemed to have reached, he was often tormented and depressed. He "suffered dreadfully from fear," he wrote in 1883. "I know very well what that aching death at the pit of the stomach is which listens for bad news and haunts one day and night, making sleep impossible." But he took comfort in the belief that he was now inspired, not by

St. Paul, but by loving female spirit guides—perhaps manifestations of the Virgin Mary, Mary Magdalene, or even Queen Victoria and her fetching daughter, Princess Louise.

John Humphrey Noyes was still following his own truth. It had carried him from Vermont to Oneida to Niagara Falls, in a lifelong pursuit of perfection and self-invention. And then, in April 1886, at the age of seventy-four, Noyes at last gave up his long struggle for control in life and died in his bed, alone, at the edge of the falls.

NOTES

1: The Secret History

p. 4   underclothes were "inexpressibles": Reynolds, *Waking Giant*, 201.

p. 4   from church groups and journalists: Fogarty, *Desire and Duty*, 16.

p. 4   "They seemed pleased that I was shocked": "The New Radical Platform: Free Love, Free Lovers and Perfection," *New York Tribune*, May 1, 1867, 4.

p. 4   Their aim was to convert the world: Parker, *A Yankee Saint*, 190.

p. 4   "a born prophet": Huxley, *Adonis and the Alphabet*, 276.

pp. 4–5   Lovemaking in Oneida: Noyes, *Male Continence*, 16.

p. 5   the most successful utopian experiment: Martin, "Saints, Sinners and Reformers."

2: A Revolution of the Senses

p. 6   "I could face a battery of cannon": Parker, *A Yankee Saint*, 13. According to Parker, Noyes's father and his four Noyes uncles all suffered from such profound shyness toward women that they each married a cousin or other relative (see Parker, *A Yankee Saint*, 6).

p. 6   the feeble, emaciated Rutherford B. Hayes: Parker, *A Yankee Saint*, 10.

p. 6   John Humphrey was a precocious student: Thomas, *The Man Who Would Be Perfect*, 3.

p. 6   his shyness was so paralyzing: Parker, *A Yankee Saint*, 15.

p. 6   he felt transformed: Parker, *A Yankee Saint*, 17–18.

p. 7   Andover Theological Seminary: Parker, *A Yankee Saint*, 17–18.

p. 7   A liberal theologian there: Thomas, *The Man Who Would Be Perfect*, 3; Fogarty, *Special Love/Special Sex*, 5. Nathaniel William Taylor encouraged his divinity students "to go for the truth themselves to its sources," to think for themselves "in light of their own intelligence," and to "follow truth if it carries you over Niagara."

p. 7   He was stripped of his license: Thomas, *The Man Who Would Be Perfect*, 48–49.

p. 7   the "Brimfield Bundling": George Wallingford Noyes, *Religious Experience*, 195-199; Parker, *A Yankee Saint*, 36–37; Cross, *The Burned-Over District*, 243.

p. 8   His declaration was published: Parker, *A Yankee Saint*, 36–37; Thomas, *The Man Who Would Be Perfect*, 83–84.

p. 8   The newlyweds spent their honeymoon: Parker, *A Yankee Saint*, 64.

p. 8   Newspapers were a thriving: Williams, *Horace Greeley*, 33.

p. 9   "John H. Noyes," they pledged: Robertson, *Oneida Community*, 10.

p. 9   Although the arrangements were an open secret: Parker, *A Yankee Saint*, 131.

p. 9   charged with adultery and fornication: Parker, *A Yankee Saint*, 133.

p. 9   he fled the village: Parker, *A Yankee Saint*, 133.

p. 9   Noyes purchased the land: Parker, *A Yankee Saint*, 160.

p. 9   On an icy March day in 1848: Parker, *A Yankee Saint*, 160.

p. 10   as many as a million Americans: Cross, *The Burned-Over District*, 287.

p. 10   The frenzy of anticipation: Knight, *Millennial Fever*, 144.

p. 10   "The Great Disappointment": Reynolds, *Waking Giant*, 156; Knight, *Millennial Fever*, 217.

p. 11   In America's new democracy: Kern, *An Ordered Love*, 25.

p. 11   The individual was the world: Reynolds, *Waking Giant*, 157.

p. 11   Americans launched more than seventy utopian experiments: Noyes, *History of American Socialisms*, 10–12.

p. 11   "to promote the happiness of the world": Lockwood, *New Harmony*, 84.

p. 11   the Kingdom of Matthias: Reynolds, *Waking Giant*, 149–50.

p. 12   By the end of the year: Cross, *The Burned-Over District*, 334.

p. 12   They divided the space: Parker, *A Yankee Saint*, 171–74.

p. 12   a boatman, approaching a waterfall: Noyes, *Male Continence*, 8.

p. 12   Noyes was eager: Parker, *A Yankee Saint*, 187; Stoehr, *Free Love in Utopia*, 67, 72.

p. 13   So when a fire: Parker, *A Yankee Saint*, 191; Habegger, *The Father*, 284–85.

p. 13   "teacher and father": Parker, *A Yankee Saint*, 93.

p. 13   A towering presence: Conkling, *The Life and Letters of Roscoe Conkling*, 10–21.

NOTES

p. 14   "we, the undersigned": George Wallingford Noyes, *Free Love*, 140.

p. 14   "so loathsome in its details": George Wallingford Noyes, *Free Love*, 147.

p. 14   "free love": Klaw, *Without Sin*, 175.

p. 15   "The Sexes should sleep apart": Fogarty, *Special Love/Special Sex*, 9.

p. 15   Each morning at precisely ten: Parker, *A Yankee Saint*, 208–09.

p. 16   the devil knew where to find people: *Handbook of the Oneida Community*, 20; Klaw, *Without Sin*, 15.

p. 16   hunter and trapper named Sewell Newhouse: Klaw, *Without Sin*, 82.

p. 16   a new brick Mansion House: Jennings, *Paradise Now*, 328.

p. 16   It was also drawing hordes of visitors: *The Circular*, July 11, 1861; Klaw, *Without Sin*, 165; Jennings, *Paradise Now*, 358.

p. 16   "infidels, spiritualists, irresponsible free lovers": Klaw, *Without Sin*, 194.

p. 16   William Mills: Parker, *A Yankee Saint*, 222–23.

p. 17   "by an irresistible power": *Report of the Proceedings*, 318.

p. 17   "known to all the world": Letter from Guiteau to Charles Olds, Ann Arbor, February 5, 1860, Inventory of Letters from C. J. Guiteau Sent to District Attorney Corkhill, Oneida Community Collection, Syracuse University Special Collections, Box 45, Guiteau, Charles J.

p. 17   "Why do you put business responsibilities on me": Letter from Guiteau to J. H. Noyes, Inventory of Letters from C. J. Guiteau Sent to District Attorney Corkhill, Oneida Community Collection, Syracuse University Special Collections, Box 45, Guiteau, Charles J.

p. 17   "felt like a slave": *Report of the Proceedings*, 554.

p. 17   "Git Out": Rosenberg, *Trial of the Assassin*, 19.

p. 17   he felt "crucified": Guiteau's answers to a questionnaire from Charles Olds, Oneida Community, NY, 1861, Inventory of Letters from C. J. Guiteau Sent to District Attorney Corkhill, Oneida Community Collection, Syracuse University Special Collections, Box 45, Guiteau, Charles J.

p. 18   "moody, self-conceited, unmanageable": Noyes, *Guiteau vs. Oneida Community*, 9, reproduction of the original from the New York City Bar.

p. 18   "aspired to the position of Mr. Noyes": *Report of the Proceedings*, 448.

p. 18   "famous in this world": Hayes, Hayes, Dunmire, and Bailey, *A Complete History*, 89–90.

p. 18   "paralyzing to my brain": Letter from Guiteau to Oneida Community, Hoboken, July 12, 1865, Inventory of Letters from C. J. Guiteau Sent to District Attorney Corkhill, Oneida

Community Collection, Syracuse University Special Collections, Box 45, Guiteau, Charles J.

p. 18 "expedient to withdraw": Guiteau to his father, Luther Guiteau, April 10, 1864, in *Report of the Proceedings*, 536–37.

p. 18 books and a new wardrobe: *Report of the Proceedings*, 538.

p. 18 dried beef, carrots, crackers, and lemonade: *Report of the Proceedings*, 538, 685.

p. 18 *The Theocrat*: *Report of the Proceedings*, 553.

p. 18 "the organ of the deity": *Report of the Proceedings*, 663.

p. 18 "to do a big thing": *Report of the Proceedings*, 661.

p. 18 "Jesus Christ & Co.": *Report of the Proceedings*, 681.

p. 18 "under the power of God's inspiration": *Report of the Proceedings*, 685.

p. 19 "why may not I?": *Report of the Proceedings*, 685.

p. 19 "usually deemed insane": Letter from Guiteau to Oneida Community, Inventory of Letters from C. J. Guiteau Sent to District Attorney Corkhill, Oneida Community Collection, Syracuse University Special Collections, Box 45, Guiteau, Charles J.

3: H. Greeley & Co.

p. 23 Greeley was nearly bankrupt: Parton, *Life of Greeley* (1855), 192.

p. 23 Despite heroic treatments: Collins, *William Henry Harrison*, 123; William Freehling, "William Harrison: Death of the President," Miller Center, University of Virginia, https://millercenter.org/president/harrison/death-of-the-president.

p. 24 flags flapped at half mast: "Funeral Obsequies of the Late President Harrison," *New York Tribune*, April 10, 1841, 3–4.

p. 24 two thousand paid subscribers: Linn, *Greeley, Founder*, 61; Tuchinsky, *Horace Greeley's* New York Tribune, 9.

p. 24 From early childhood: Greeley, *Busy Life*, 34–42, 54–62.

p. 24 Greeley read almost every book: Parton, *Life of Greeley* (1855), 82–97.

p. 25 *The Northern Spectator* failed financially: Williams, *Horace Greeley*, 21; Greeley, *Busy Life*, 84.

p. 25 Greeley stepped off the boat: Parton, *Life of Greeley* (1855), 119.

p. 25 squalid and filthy: Leadon, *Broadway*, 31.

p. 25 The stench of tanneries: Burrows and Wallace, *Gotham*, 588.

p. 25 he found a cheap bed: Greeley, *Busy Life*, 84–86.

p. 25 His co-workers called him "The Ghost": Parton, *Life of Greeley* (1855), 125–26.

p. 25 "The season was sultry": Greeley, *Busy Life*, 88.

pp. 25–26 Every day, privies: Burrows and Wallace, *Gotham*, 591.

p. 26   "industry languished": Greeley, *Busy Life*, 88–89.

p. 26   a young medical student named Horatio Sheppard: Parton, *Life of Greeley* (1855), 139–41.

p. 26   hawked on the streets: Ingersoll, *Greeley, Founder*, 108.

p. 26   New Year's Day 1833: Parton, *Life of Greeley* (1855), 143–44.

p. 27   Story went boating: Parton, *Life of Greeley* (1855), 148.

p. 27   H. Greeley & Co.: Williams, *Horace Greeley*, 27.

p. 27   *The New York Sun*: Schudson, *Discovering the News*, 18; Snay, *Politics of Reform*, 52.

p. 27   Unlike the *Sun*: Parton, *Life of Greeley* (1855), 153.

p. 27   *The New Yorker*: Parton, *Life of Greeley* (1855), 161.

p. 27   Greeley printed the first issue: Parton, *Life of Greeley* (1855), 152–53.

p. 27   "the best newspaper of its kind": Parton, *Life of Greeley* (1855), 152.

p. 27   above the initials "H.G.": Parton, *Life of Greeley* (1855), 155.

p. 27   "sitting at a small table": Williams, *Horace Greeley*, 33.

p. 27   never became profitable: Parton, *Life of Greeley* (1855), 170.

p. 27   passionate about politics: Greeley, *Busy Life*, 106; Williams, *Horace Greeley*, 29.

p. 29   "The country was in a wretched condition": Williams, *Horace Greeley*, 30.

p. 29   "I saw three widows": Greeley, *Busy Life*, 145.

p. 29   Poverty is "a hard master": Greeley, *Busy Life*, 192.

p. 29   It was a "year of ruin": Parton, *Life of Greeley* (1855), 169.

p. 29   stooping and nearsighted: Williams, *Horace Greeley*, 46.

p. 29   battling bedbugs: Parton, *Life of Greeley* (1855), 179.

p. 29   a circulation of fifteen thousand: Greeley, *Busy Life*, 126.

p. 30   indiscreet and vain: Shafer, *Carnival Campaign*, 6.

p. 30   It was a harsh attack: Greeley, *Busy Life*, 132; Ingersoll, *Greeley, Founder*, 93–94.

p. 31   if Van Buren won a second term: Ingersoll, *Greeley, Founder*, 98.

p. 31   the people's candidate: Greeley, *Busy Life*, 132.

p. 31   the *Log Cabin*: Shafer, *Carnival Campaign*, 100–02; Ingersoll, *Greeley, Founder*, 95.

p. 31   more Americans than ever: Williams, *Horace Greeley*, 54.

p. 31   thousands of new, lower-income voters: Shafer, *Carnival Campaign*, 16.

p. 31   The nation's first grassroots political campaign: Williams, *Horace Greeley*, 52.

p. 31   campaigns were restrained affairs: Shafer, *Carnival Campaign*, 77.

p. 31   a mammoth structure in Manhattan: Burrows and Wallace, *Gotham*, 623.

p. 31   "keep the ball rolling": Shafer, *Carnival Campaign*, 23.

p. 32   gargantuan quantities of free food: Shafer, *Carnival Campaign*, 75–80.

p. 32   E. G. Booz: Freehling, "William Harrison: Campaigns and Elections."

p. 32   Harrison glee club: Ingersoll, *Greeley, Founder*, 91–100.

p. 32   Greeley, in awkward excitement: Williams, *Horace Greeley*, 53.

p. 32   pioneered political swag: Williams, *Horace Greeley*, 53; *The American Heritage History of the Presidency*, 142.

p. 32   "I doubt," he noted: Greeley, *Busy Life*, 135.

p. 33   Newspaper readership: Reynolds, *Waking Giant*, 241–42.

p. 33   almost every driver: Burrows and Wallace, *Gotham*, 527.

p. 33   three hundred thousand residents: Burrows and Wallace, *Gotham*, 576.

p. 33   the *New York Herald* dwarfed: Williams, *Horace Greeley*, 57.

p. 33   every class and station: Burrows and Wallace, *Gotham*, 526.

p. 33   the *New York Tribune*, promoting: Ingersoll, *Greeley, Founder*, 111.

p. 33   "His Accidency": Williams, *Horace Greeley*, 56.

p. 33   "Fame is a vapor": Greeley, *Busy Life*, 143.

p. 33   It was usually midnight: Parton, *Life of Greeley* (1855), 432.

p. 34   Sylvester Graham: Williams, *Horace Greeley*, 38.

p. 34   "prophet of bran bread and pumpkins": Ralph Waldo Emerson dubbed Graham "the prophet of bran bread and pumpkins"; Nissenbaum, *Sex, Diet, and Debility*, 3.

p. 34   Such dietary discipline: Sphrintzen, *The Vegetarian Crusade*, 27–29.

p. 34   the most deadly form of gratification: Whorton, "The Solitary Vice," 66–68.

p. 34   "crazy for knowledge": Parton, *Life of Greeley* (1855), 165. The friend was Margaret Fuller.

p. 34   "ate furiously, and fast, and much": Parton, *Life of Greeley* (1855), 94.

p. 34   a big platter of doughnuts: Ingersoll, *Greeley, Founder*, 366.

p. 34   When she moved to North Carolina: Parton, *Life of Greeley* (1855), 166.

p. 34   Mary taught and kept a Graham table: Greeley, *Busy Life*, 104.

p. 34   Thomas Sawyer: Williams, *Horace Greeley*, 26; Parton, *Life of Greeley* (1855), 426.

p. 35   Barnum had been convicted: Barnum, *The Life of P. T. Barnum*, 138–39.

p. 35   "gangling, wispy-haired, pasty-cheeked man": Williams, *Horace Greeley*, 60.

p. 35   "My recent enterprises": Barnum, *The Life of P. T. Barnum*, 216.

p. 35   The huge edifice: Wallace, *Fabulous Showman*, 47.

p. 35   taxidermy shop: Lehman, *Becoming Tom Thumb*, 22.

p. 35   New Year's Day 1842: Wallace, *Fabulous Showman*, 53.

p. 36   "I felt considerably sheepish about it": Barnum, *The Life of P. T. Barnum*, 226.

p. 36   "General Tom Thumb": Barnum, *The Life of P. T. Barnum*, 243.

p. 36   "It was a great act": Lehman, *Becoming Tom Thumb*, 22–24.

p. 36   On a third-floor balcony: Wallace, *The Fabulous Showman*, 63–64.

p. 36   When they reached the roof: Barnum, *The Life of P. T. Barnum*, 228.

p. 36   "dusty halls of humbug": James, *Henry James*, 89.

p. 37   "startlingly original thinker": After hearing Emerson speak in Massachusetts, James Garfield wrote these words in a letter on August 22, 1854, in Fuller, *Reminiscences*, 27.

p. 37   "the thinker and the worker": Swift, *Brook Farm*, 16.

p. 37   "numberless projects of social reform": Ralph Waldo Emerson to Thomas Carlyle, October 1840, in Norton, *Correspondence*, 308.

p. 37   "chief of all the experiments": Noyes, *History of American Socialisms*, 103, 117–18.

p. 37   "rich and brilliant genius": Emerson, *Lectures*, 342.

p. 37   "knot of dreamers": Hawthorne, *The Blithedale Romance*, 20.

p. 38   "the Greek and Latin": Charles A. Dana in Wilson, *Life of Charles A. Dana*, 527.

p. 38   miniature French Revolution: Emerson, *Lectures*, 364.

p. 38   "cruel surgical delivery": Von Mehren, *Minerva and the Muse*, 200.

p. 38   "quite solitary": Williams, *Horace Greeley*, 68–69.

p. 38   "so light that it was almost white": Swift, *Brook Farm*, 276.

p. 38   "only to angelic natures": Delano, *Brook Farm*, 98.

4: Muggletonians and Mystics

p. 39   like a bird of prey: Channing, *Memoirs of Margaret Fuller Ossoli*, 9, 17.

p. 39   "like the sun shining on plants": Gornick, "A Double Inheritance."

p. 39   "You stretch your limbs": Thurman, "Desires of Margaret Fuller."

p. 40   there were seventy members: Packer, *The Transcendentalists*, 155.

p. 40   Its deficit exceeded a thousand dollars: Packer, *The Transcendentalists*, 134.

p. 40   a Frenchman named Charles Fourier: Jennings, *Paradise Now*, 156–66.

p. 41   Five years before he died: Jennings, *Paradise Now*, 176.

p. 41   Fourier's ideas soon "swept the nation": Noyes, *History of American Socialisms*, 25.

p. 41   their library carried: Jennings, *Paradise Now*, 202.

p. 41   "nothing less than Heaven on Earth": Dana, *A Lecture on Association*, 26.

p. 41   "Transcendental nonsense and humbuggery": Jennings, *Paradise Now*, 212.

p. 42   On a cold evening that March: Jennings, *Paradise Now*, 231–34.

p. 42   the North American Phalanx: Williams, *Horace Greeley*, 72.

p. 42   The Sylvania Association: Williams, *Horace Greeley*, 71.

p. 42   "the conceited, the crotchety, the selfish": Greeley, *Busy Life*, 154.

p. 42   thirty-four phalanxes: Noyes, *History of American Socialisms*, 15–17.

p. 43   "Utopia is impossible to build up": Marshall, *Margaret Fuller*, 187.

p. 43   "Castle Doleful": Weisberg, *Talking to the Dead*, 115.

p. 43   "entirely charming": Parton, *Life of Greeley* (1855), 255.

p. 43   Fuller liked comfort and luxury: Parton, *Life of Greeley* (1855), 256–57.

p. 44   hair that was "the color of sunshine": Parton, *Life of Greeley* (1855), 261; Marshall, *Margaret Fuller*, 242.

p. 44   "great-souled friend": Parton, *Life of Greeley* (1855), 261; Marshall, *Margaret Fuller*, 243.

p. 44   "to a surprising extent": Murray, *Margaret Fuller*, 236; Higginson, *Margaret Fuller Ossoli*, 209.

p. 44   America's first female foreign correspondent: Marshall, *Margaret Fuller*, 269.

p. 44   the deadly disease: Pyle, "The Diffusion of Cholera."

p. 45   cholera panic swept the capital: Maizlish, "The Cholera Panic in Washington."

p. 45   the epidemic killed more than five thousand: John Noble Wilford, "How Epidemics Helped Shape the Modern Metropolis," *New York Times*, April 15, 2008.

p. 45   "we were never utterly desolate till now": Williams, *Horace Greeley*, 117.

p. 45   "rivers of tears": Parton, *Life of Greeley* (1855), 263.

p. 45   Fuller felt "absurdly fearful": Higginson, *Margaret Fuller Ossoli*, 275.

p. 46   he believed in the "superusual": Greeley, *Busy Life*, 234.

p. 47   Frightened, the family asked their next-door neighbor: *A Report of the Mysterious Noises*, 42.

p. 47   "The questions were put in every shape": *A Report of the Mysterious Noises*, 39.

p. 48   He, too, attended a séance with Kate and Maggie Fox: "An Hour with the Spirits," *New York Tribune*, June 5, 1850, 1.

p. 49   "Rochester Knockings": Weisberg, *Talking to the Dead*, 109.

p. 49   Kate stayed on with the Greeleys: Braude, *Radical Spirits*, 16; Linn, *Greeley, Founder*, 106.

p. 49   movements of their anatomy: Barnum, *Humbugs*, 62.

p. 49   the spirit rappings had "something in them": Linn, *Greeley, Founder*, 122.

p. 49   Jumpers and Sandemanians: Fornell, *The Unhappy Medium*, 159.

p. 49   "knee joint rattling": Greeley, *Busy Life*, 238.

p. 49   "real and momentous communications": Linn, *Greeley, Founder*, 122.

p. 50   The editor's white coat: Parton, *Life of Greeley* (1855), 347.

p. 50   Noyes secretly learned: Noyes, *Free Love*, 191–92.

p. 51   It was a bit more agreeable below: Parker, *A Yankee Saint*, 194.

p. 51   Greeley was familiar: Jennings, *Paradise Now*, 337.

p. 51   "absolute torture": Reavis, *A Representative Life*, 395–97.

p. 51   Americans should stay on their own continent: Parker, *A Yankee Saint*, 194.

5: Garfield's Crucible

p. 52   Garfield nuzzled his two horses: James Garfield to J. Harrison (Harry) Rhodes, Camp Chase, October 26, 1861, in Williams, *Wild Life*, 41.

p. 52   Ohio had a quota of thirteen regiments: Peskin, *Garfield*, 87.

p. 52   Inside his tent, which was swarming with flies: Garfield to friends, Camp Chase, August 3, 1861, in Williams, *Wild Life*, 34; Peskin, *Garfield*, 94; Balch, *Life of James Abram Garfield*, 125.

p. 53   The young men, dreaming of glory: Peskin, *Garfield*, 93; Garfield to Lucretia Garfield, Columbus, OH, December 9, 1861, in Williams, *Wild Life*, 48.

p. 53   On December 14, 1861: Balch, *Life of James Abram Garfield*, 126.

p. 54   "The work will be positively enormous": Garfield to J. Harrison (Harry) Rhodes, Louisville, KY, December 17, 1861, in Williams, *Wild Life*, 49.

p. 54   "ragged, greasy, and dirty": Peskin, *Garfield*, 107.

p. 54   "Our forces were very much exhausted": Garfield to Lucretia Garfield, Paintsville, KY, January 13, 1862, in Williams, *Wild Life*, 54.

p. 54   "the bold lion" of the Union Army: Peskin, *Garfield*, 120.

p. 54   "stacks of wheat and hay, gigantic trees": Garfield to Lucretia Garfield, Piketon (now Pikeville), KY, February 23, 1862, in Williams, *Wild Life*, 71.

p. 54   "I tremble": Peskin, *Garfield*, 127.

p. 55   "more depressed": Garfield to Lucretia Garfield, Camp Buell, Paintsville, KY, February 15, 1862, in Williams, *Wild Life*, 68.

p. 55   "This fighting with disease": Garfield to Lucretia Garfield, Piketon, KY, March 10, 1862, in Williams, *Wild Life*, 74.

p. 55   "The thought . . . of taking command": Peskin, *Garfield*, 133.

p. 55   "I never suffered such acute and crushing pain": Garfield to Lucretia Garfield, Field of Shiloh, TN, April 21, 1862, in Williams, *Wild Life*, 83.

p. 55   he lost forty-three pounds: Peskin, *Garfield*, 146.

p. 56   "wild, passionate heart": Peskin, *Garfield*, 42.

p. 56   "unpardonable neglect": Peskin, *Garfield*, 54.

p. 56   he felt as though he "died daily": Peskin, *Garfield*, 75.

p. 56   "should go before a convention": Garfield to Harmon Austin, Tuscumbia, AL, June 25, 1862, in Williams, *Wild Life*, 116.

p. 56   "spontaneous act of the people": Peskin, *Garfield*, 147.

p. 57   "There is a settled gloom": Peskin, *Garfield*, 160.

p. 57   life with "thunder in it": Peskin, *Garfield*, 21.

p. 57   shuffled and sulked: Garfield to J. Harrison (Harry) Rhodes, Washington, D.C., November 16, 1862, in Williams, *Wild Life*, 179.

p. 57   the smell of rotten potatoes: Garfield to Lucretia Garfield, Washington, D.C., November 21, 1862, in Williams, *Wild Life*, 183.

p. 58   "I know fully and sadly": Garfield to Lucretia Garfield, Washington, D.C., January 6, 1863, in Williams, *Wild Life*, 208.

p. 58   "We met at the War Department": Garfield to Lucretia Garfield, Washington, D.C., January 2, 1863, in Williams, *Wild Life*, 206.

p. 58   "had a screw . . . loose in him somewhere": Peskin, *Garfield*, 169.

p. 58   "mingling of spirits": Peskin, *Garfield*, 171.

p. 58   "Rosecrans shares all his counsels": Peskin, *Garfield*, 175.

p. 59   "sharp, clear sense": Peskin, *Garfield*, 170.

p. 59   "a tall, deep-chested, sinewy built man": James Gilmore, *Down in Tennessee*, 198.

p. 60   "more commanding and attractive appearance": Villard, *Memoirs of Henry Villard*, 66–68.

p. 60   "striking, striking and striking again": Peskin, *Garfield*, 180.

p. 60   "I have been married four years": Garfield to Eliza Ballou Garfield, Murfreesboro, TN, June 12, 1863, in Williams, *Wild Life*, 277.

p. 60   Her real name was Harriet Wood: Christen, *Pauline Cushman*, iii, 17, 49.

p. 60   dramatic and comic ability: Christen, *Pauline Cushman*, 49.

p. 61   posing as a Southern gentleman: Sarmiento, *Life of Pauline Cushman*, 70.

p. 61   Traveling alone, armed with a six-shooter: Christen, *Pauline Cushman*, 110.

p. 61   she was captured in Shelbyville, Tennessee: Christen, *Pauline Cushman*, 131.

p. 61   they found her gravely ill: Christen, *Pauline Cushman*, 137.

p. 61   "most constant companions": Christen, *Pauline Cushman*, 138–42.

p. 61   "I love every bone in his body": Peskin, *Garfield*, 196.

p. 62   "We have been watching for twelve hours": Garfield to Harmon Austin, Hiram, OH, December 1, 1863, in Williams, *Wild Life*, 299.

p. 62   "after the death of Trot": Peskin, *Garfield*, 219.

p. 63   "wickedly and maliciously false": Garfield to Lucretia Garfield, Washington, D.C., May 8, 1864, in Shaw, *Crete and James*, 206.

p. 63   "lawless passion": Peskin, *Garfield*, 279.

p. 63   "when you think over my trip home": Garfield to Lucretia Garfield, New York, June 12, 1864, in Shaw, *Crete and James*, 210.

p. 63   "the greatest heroine of the age": Christen, *Pauline Cushman*, 5–6.

p. 64   "charming and intelligent": Christen, *Pauline Cushman*, 6–7.

6: Dreams and Disasters

p. 65   suddenly engulfed in flames: "Disastrous Fire," *New York Times*, July 14, 1865, 1, 8.

p. 65   Huge anacondas and pythons: "Disastrous Conflagration," *New York Sun*, July 14, 1865, 1.

p. 65   So did two beluga whales: Bosworth, "Barnum's Whales"; Wallace, *The Fabulous Showman*, 209–10.

p. 66   his huge minareted palace: Wallace, *The Fabulous Showman*, 149–50, 160, 184–85.

p. 67   "a national loss": Wallace, *The Fabulous Showman*, 219.

p. 67   "When the head of thirty millions": "Highly Important! The President Shot!" *New York Tribune*, April 15, 1865, 4.

p. 67   "of transcendent genius": "Mr. Lincoln's Fame," *New York Tribune*, April 19, 1865, 4; Greeley, *Busy Life*, 404.

p. 67   in spite of "all his awkward homeliness": Peskin, *Garfield*, 83.

p. 67   "so broken with our great national loss": James Garfield to Lucretia Garfield, New York, April 17, 1865 in Shaw, *Crete and James*, 218.

p. 67   "I do not believe it is in the American character": "Address of Gen. Garfield," *New York Tribune*, April 17, 1865, 3.

p. 68   "They all laughed at the idea": *Report of the Proceedings*, 553.

p. 68   They put Guiteau to work: *Handbook of the Oneida Community,* "Financial Experiences and Conditions," 13; *Report of the Proceedings,* 554.

p. 68   He also carried water and wrung mops: "Moral Monstrosities," *The Sunday Herald* (Syracuse, NY), January 29, 1882, 5.

p. 68   Noyes, he noted, was about the only man: *Report of the Proceedings,* 689.

p. 68   "We took you in out of charity": Charles Guiteau to E. H. Hamilton, New York, December 6, 1866, Oneida Community Collection, Syracuse University Special Collections, Box 45, Guiteau, Charles J.

p. 69   "one of the trap-packers shipped himself": "An Exit," *Daily Journal of Oneida Community* 2, no. 106, Friday, November 2, 1866, Oneida Community Collection, Syracuse University Special Collections, Box 45, Guiteau, Charles J.

p. 69   on Printing House Square: "The Tribune Has Had Five Buildings, Including One of City's Earliest Skyscrapers," *New York Herald Tribune,* April 13, 1941, 124.

p. 69   Newsboys crowded its steps: Parton, *Life of Horace Greeley* (1872), 358–60.

p. 69   rapidly scrawling editorials: Parton, *Life of Horace Greeley* (1872), 368–72.

p. 69   Greeley was out of the office: *Report of the Proceedings,* 557.

p. 70   Like "Mr. Lincoln and Mr. Greeley": Hayes, Hayes, Dunmire, and Bailey, *A Complete History,* 90.

p. 70   "to learn what they want to know": Williams, *Horace Greeley,* 265.

p. 70   a destitute German writer named Karl Marx: Hale, "When Karl Marx Worked for Horace Greeley."

p. 71   Clemens agreed to mail the *Tribune*: "Mark Twain and the Tribune Partners in Humor of 1860's," *New York Herald Tribune,* April 13, 1941. For Twain's comic portrait of Greeley, see Mark Twain, "Horace Greeley, A Humorous Description of Him," [from Wilkes's *Spirit of the Times*], *Mariposa Gazette* 13, no. 25, December 18, 1868.

p. 71   "my first notoriety": Williams, *Horace Greeley,* 265.

p. 71   the Trumbull Phalanx: Williams, *Horace Greeley,* 284; Noyes, *History of American Socialisms,* 349–51.

p. 72   After the failure of this experiment: "Biographical Note of Nathan Cook Meeker," Guide to the Meeker Manuscript Collection, Hazel E. Johnson Research Center, Greeley History Museum, Greeley, Colorado.

p. 72   "healthful and free of distractions": "History of the College," *Hiram College*, https://www.hiram.edu/about/history-of-the-college/.

p. 72   "a small store, kept by a man named Meeker": Fuller, *Reminiscences*, 26.

p. 73   a friend had told him: Boyd, *Greeley and the Union Colony*, 15.

p. 73   the newspaper published an announcement: Boyd, *Greeley and the Union Colony*, 30.

p. 73   "a location which I have seen": Boyd, *Greeley and the Union Colony*, 32–34.

p. 73   Meeker advised interested readers: Boyd, *Greeley and the Union Colony*, 30.

p. 73   On the frosty night of December 23: Boyd, *Greeley and the Union Colony*, 33–38.

p. 74   five dollars to join the project: Boyd, *Greeley and the Union Colony*, 38.

p. 74   after Meeker invested his own funds: Williams, *Horace Greeley*, 286.

p. 74   Union Colony Number One: Boyd, *Greeley and the Union Colony*, 84.

p. 74   The committee traveled west: Boyd, *Greeley and the Union Colony*, 39.

p. 74   The scenery, organizers gushed: Boyd, *Greeley and the Union Colony*, 51.

p. 75   Arthur's Round Table: Boyd, *Greeley and the Union Colony*, 84.

p. 75   "three-fourths of a mile wide": Boyd, *Greeley and the Union Colony*, 42.

p. 75   a hundred thousand acres: Williams, *Horace Greeley*, 286.

p. 75   The town that would arise there would be called "Greeley": Williams, *Horace Greeley*, 286–88.

p. 75   There were no shelters: Boyd, *Greeley and the Union Colony*, 382–84; Williams, *Horace Greeley*, 287.

p. 75   in the fall of 1870: Williams, *Horace Greeley*, 287.

p. 76   the "Great Ditch" was a total failure: Boyd, *Greeley and the Union Colony*, 52–54.

p. 76   "with the greatest care": Boyd, *Greeley and the Union Colony*, 81.

p. 76   "All the women tried to have lawns": Uchill, *Howdy, Sucker!*, 16–17.

p. 77   Although Horace Greeley was treasurer: Boyd, *Greeley and the Union Colony*, 79.

p. 77   Just weeks after the fire of 1865: Wilson, *Barnum*, 220, 217–19; Van Deusen, *Horace Greeley*, 157.

p. 77   his new American Museum burned down: Wallace, *The Fabulous Showman*, 221–22.

p. 77   He sold the lots: Wilson, *Barnum*, 223; Wallace, *The Fabulous Showman*, 221.

p. 78   the two-story Barnum's Hotel: Williams, *Horace Greeley*, 288.

p. 78   Brussels carpet and bedsprings: "Mr. Barnum's Hotel," *Greeley Tribune*, May 17, 1871, 2.

p. 78   Although he had once been known to guzzle: Wallace, *The Fabulous Showman*, 156–58; Uchill, *Howdy, Sucker!*, 22.

p. 78   He employed one of his cousins: Uchill, *Howdy, Sucker!*, 23; Williams, *Horace Greeley*, 288.

p. 78   But in 1870, she abandoned her husband: Uchill, *Howdy, Sucker!*, 19–22.

p. 78   the Colony Drugstore: *Greeley Tribune*, September 20, 1871, 3.

p. 78   The deed banned liquor on the site: "A Tax Payer on the Liquor Traffic," *Greeley Tribune*, January 24, 1872, 2.

p. 79   "Just across the border of Greeley": Uchill, *Howdy, Sucker!*, 16, 25.

p. 79   the "skillful apothecary": "A Tax Payer on the Liquor Traffic," *Greeley Tribune*, January 24, 1872, 2.

p. 79   the good citizens of Greeley organized a sting: "The Liquor Business," *Greeley Tribune*, February 14, 1872, 2.

p. 79   "doses of damnation": "A Tax Payer on the Liquor Traffic," *Greeley Tribune*, January 24, 1872, 2; August 7, 1872, 2.

p. 79   "place our hands upon a long rope": "Alcohol Again," *Greeley Tribune*, July 31, 1872.

p. 79   his son-in-law was a "shyster": Uchill, *Howdy, Sucker!*, 27, 40–42.

p. 79   Barnum also built Greeley's first auditorium: Lenore Harriman, "Historic Hindsights: How P. T. Barnum Helped Shape Early Greeley," *Greeley Tribune*, August 4, 2018; Peggy A. Ford, "Dullsville, U.S.A.: Finding Something to Do in Greeley Has Been a Historical Quest," *Weld County Past Times*, September 19, 1998; Uchill, *Howdy, Sucker!*, 94.

p. 79   His son-in-law Dr. Buchtel: Angela Alton, "Historical Hindsights: P T. Barnum and the 'Flaming Swords of Sobriety,'" *Greeley Tribune*, August 14, 2009.

7: Horace Greeley for President

p. 81   As a Whig representative from New York: Tuchinsky, *Horace Greeley's New York Tribune*, 145.

p. 81   "the most detested man": Maihafer, *The General and the Journalists*, 50.

p. 82   He was also a crack shot: Chidsey, *The Gentleman from New York*, 6.

p. 82   He was temperamental and aloof: Chidsey, *The Gentleman from New York*, 11; Jordan, *Roscoe Conkling*, 21.

p. 82   "air of a Prince": "The Lordly Roscoe," New York *Commercial Gazette*, June 18, 1883.

p. 83   "the giant of Oneida": Chidsey, *The Gentleman from New York*, 1, 135.

p. 83   Conkling stage-managed the convention: Chidsey, *The Gentleman from New York*, 135.

p. 83   when Greeley ran again for governor in 1870: Chidsey, *The Gentleman from New York*, 147.

p. 83   "the pose of [his] majestic figure": Chidsey, *The Gentleman from New York*, 148.

p. 83   Greeley had backed the Civil War: Maihafer, *The General and the Journalists*, 105.

p. 83   he had doubts that the Union Army could beat the rebels: Van Deusen, *Horace Greeley*, 310.

p. 84   On April 9, 1865: Van Deusen, *Horace Greeley*, 318.

p. 84   But when he saw that Johnson: Van Deusen, *Horace Greeley*, 342–44.

p. 84   an "angry man, dizzy with the elevation": Conkling, *Life and Letters*, 270.

p. 84   "that slavery shall never range this continent": Jordan, *Roscoe Conkling*, 23.

p. 84   he might run for mayor of his hometown: Maihafer, *The General and the Journalists*, 107.

p. 85   with "honor and esteem": Maihafer, *The General and the Journalists*, 219.

p. 85   "as plain as an old shoe": Smith, *Grant*, 233.

p. 85   "the most modest": Maihafer, *The General and the Journalists*, 145.

p. 85   "Liquor seemed a virulent poison": Chernow, *Grant*, 80.

p. 86   "He was shabbily dressed": Chernow, *Grant*, 108–09.

p. 86   he "would go behind the counter": Chernow, *Grant*, 115.

p. 86   Grant's "dress was seedy": Chernow, *Grant*, 130.

p. 86   "if he knew enough to find cows": Chernow, *Grant*, 130, 137.

p. 86   Grant "knew his business": Chernow, *Grant*, 134.

p. 86   "So intelligent were his inquiries": Chernow, *Grant*, 313.

p. 86   "natural, severe simplicity": Chernow, *Grant*, 360.

p. 87   "an expression as if he had determined": Chernow, *Grant*, 360.

p. 87   Thanks to Conkling's support: Jordan, *Roscoe Conkling*, 112.

p. 87   his homespun habits: Chernow, *Grant*, 652.

p. 87   attempted to translate his grunts: Chidsey, *The Gentleman from New York*, 141.

p. 88   regarded him "as the greatest mind": Chernow, *Grant*, 734.

p. 88   "Conkling and my father loved each other": Chernow, *Grant*, 734.

p. 88   Grant had a "romantic affection": Chernow, *Grant*, 734.

p. 88   With jurisdiction: Chernow, *Grant*, 735.

p. 88   Its granite building on Wall Street: Reeves, *Gentleman Boss*, 67.

p. 89   "a hack politician": Chernow, *Grant*, 736.

p. 89   Murphy swindled importers: Reeves, *Gentleman Boss*, 56.

p. 89   he "came upon hundreds": Jordan, *Roscoe Conkling*, 152–53.

p. 89   "as rotten as his hats": Greenberger, *The Unexpected President*, 78.

p. 90   "Tom Murphy under another name": Greenberger, *The Unexpected President*, 79.

p. 90   He almost always arrived late: Greenberger, *The Unexpected President*, 80–82.

p. 90   "as corrupt a band of varlets": Greenberger, *The Unexpected President*, 85; "Mr. Murphy's Confederate," *New York Tribune*, October 1, 1872, 4;

p. 91   "too small a man for the presidency": Seitz, *Horace Greeley*, 364.

p. 91   no one "outside of a lunatic asylum": Maihafer, *The General and the Journalists*, 238.

p. 91   "Grant," he wrote, "is not fit to be nominated": Peskin, *Garfield*, 350.

p. 91   "Boozy Brown": Maihafer, *The General and the Journalists*, 244.

p. 92   "he has the largest head": Maihafer, *The General and the Journalists*, 244.

p. 92   "one of those stupendous mistakes": Chernow, *Grant*, 744.

p. 92   They were marvels of impromptu oratory: Williams, *Horace Greeley*, 302.

p. 92   "He had a poor and somewhat squeaking voice": Benton, "Reminiscences."

p. 93   "From that grand and costly building": "The Dead-Beats' Funeral," *The Horace Greeley Campaign Songster*, 30.

p. 93   "inspired idiot": Williams, *Horace Greeley*, 302.

p. 93   "just now a feeling": Hayes, *Diary and Letters*, July 16, 1872, vol. III, 206.

p. 93   "nightly, innocent *girls*": *Report of the Proceedings*, 543; Klaw, *Without Sin*, 163.

p. 94   "exemplary young man": Hayes, Hayes, Dunmire, and Bailey, *A Complete History*, 71, 113.

p. 94   "He was rather peculiar": Hayes, Hayes, Dunmire, and Bailey, *A Complete History*, 71.

p. 94   "everybody that he came in contact with": Hayes, Hayes, Dunmire, and Bailey, *A Complete History*, 74–75.

p. 94   "nothing but the best": Hayes, Hayes, Dunmire, and Bailey, *A Complete History*, 85.

p. 94   He "wore the best of everything": Hayes, Hayes, Dunmire, and Bailey, *A Complete History*, 113.

p. 94   their baggage was detained: Hayes, Hayes, Dunmire, and Bailey, *A Complete History*, 83–85.

p. 95   "get out of the law business": Hayes, Hayes, Dunmire, and Bailey, *A Complete History*, 93–95.

p. 95   "He used to walk back and forth": Hayes, Hayes, Dunmire, and Bailey, *A Complete History*, 89–90.

p. 95   "He read it over and over": Hayes, Hayes, Dunmire, and Bailey, *A Complete History*, 94.

p. 95   he was the first speaker: "A Greeley and Brown Ratification Meeting," *New York Times*, August 14, 1872.

p. 96   "If I were to be attacked by anybody": Hayes, Hayes, Dunmire, and Bailey, *A Complete History*, 135–36.

p. 96   "peevish, eccentric, grotesque and harmless": "Issues of the Day," *New York Times*, July 24, 1872.

p. 96   a "domestic hell": Goldsmith, *Other Powers*, 280.

p. 97   "almost insane melancholia": Tom Miller, "The Much-Altered Horace Greeley House—No. 35 East 19th St.," *Daytonian in Manhattan*, June 15, 2013, http://daytoninmanhattan.blogspot .com/2013/06/the-much-altered-horace-greeley-house.html.

p. 97   "souring the temper": Goldsmith, *Other Powers*, 281.

p. 97   she gave birth to a little girl: Goldsmith, *Other Powers*, 60–61.

p. 97   He told Margaret Fuller: Van Deusen, *Horace Greeley*, 157.

p. 98   There was no furniture: Goldsmith, *Other Powers*, 58–60.

p. 98   Mary took their two surviving children: Van Deusen, *Horace Greeley*, 321; Goldsmith, *Other Powers*, 62.

p. 98   He found his wife in her stateroom: Van Deusen, *Horace Greeley*, 409.

p. 98   "I wish she were to be laid": Hale, *Horace Greeley*, 346.

p. 99   Bankrupt and "out of his head": Seitz, *Horace Greeley*, 399; Brown and Williams, *The Diary of James A. Garfield*, 2:120. On November 29, 1872, Garfield wrote of Greeley, "His death raises curious questions for the Electoral College which meets next Wednesday. It is the first time I believe that a presidential candidate has died between the election of the electors and the meeting of the Electoral College."

p. 99   With his reputation "seriously shattered": Williams, *Horace Greeley*, 308.

p. 99   His body, dressed in black: Williams, *Horace Greeley*, xii–xiv.

p. 99   draped in black: Williams, *Horace Greeley*, xiii–xv.

p. 99   President Grant rode: Linn, *Greeley, Founder*, 258.

p. 99   "If I cannot get notoriety for good": *Report of the Proceedings*, 2028.

8: The Master of Love

p. 103   "the only father I have known": Fogarty, *Desire and Duty*, 63.

p. 103   she bore a child: Fogarty, *Desire and Duty*, 30.

p. 103   "He said he believed it to be his duty": Fogarty, *Desire and Duty*, 72.

p. 103   Noyes successfully sired a baby: Klaw, *Without Sin*, 207.

p. 104   "breeding in and in": Thomas, *The Man Who Would Be Perfect*, 174.

p. 104   "I am conquering": Fogarty, *Desire and Duty*, 21.

p. 104   "We shall never have heaven": Fogarty, *Desire and Duty*, 22–23.

p. 104   "regulated promiscuity": Thomas, *The Man Who Would Be Perfect*, 174.

p. 104   a "female man": Parker, *A Yankee Saint*, 169.

p. 105   "Perhaps we don't look as well": Klaw, *Without Sin*, 137.

p. 105   Liberated from traditional marriage: Kern, *An Ordered Love*, 244.

p. 105   Like a cello: von Zeigesar, "Reinventing Sex."

p. 105   "There is as much difference": Fogarty, *Desire and Duty*, 58.

p. 105   "As a man is said to know a woman": Noyes, *Free Love*, 311.

p. 105   Those communions would last all night: Kern, *An Ordered Love*, 244.

p. 106   "Talk less, love more!": Fogarty, *Desire and Duty*, 31, 57, 170.

p. 106   By early 1874: Charles Nordhoff and Paul Royster (Depositor), "The Perfectionists of Oneida and Wallingford" (1875), *Electronic Texts in American Studies* 5, http://digitalcommons.unl.edu/etas/5.

p. 106   "They even had a Turkish bath": Kephart, "Experimental," 261–71.

p. 107   "I was a child in the old Community": Kephart, "Experimental," 261–71.

p. 107   "All with whom I had occasion to speak": Nordhoff and Royster, "The Perfectionists of Oneida and Wallingford."

p. 107   "We believe the time will come": Parker, *A Yankee Saint*, 253–54.

p. 108   "It is very probable": Parker, *A Yankee Saint*, 255.

p. 108   "Weighing the Babies": Fogarty, *Desire and Duty*, 15.

p. 108   "all the children seemed happy enough": Kephart, "Experimental," 261–71.

p. 109   when he stood at the edge of a frozen pond: Parker, *A Yankee Saint*, 261.

p. 109   "exquisite little romance": Fogarty, *Desire and Duty*, 32.

p. 110   "I have never made free with girls": Fogarty, *Desire and Duty*, 43.

p. 110   "The seduction of a young girl": Fogarty, *Special Love/Special Sex*, 215–16.

p. 110   regulating the sexual relations: Robertson, *The Breakup*, 16.

p. 111   "inclined to apoplexy": Robertson, *The Breakup*, 37.

p. 111   "Our Home on the Hillside": *The Jackson Health Resort*.

p. 112   "to conquer his doubts": Klaw, *Without Sin*, 215.

p. 112   "those who are swallowing": George W. Noyes Papers, 196–201, Oneida Community Collection, Syracuse University Special Collections.

p. 112   "simply absurd to attempt": Shusko, "Spiritualism and the Oneida Community."

p. 113   "we sat around a table": Roach, "The Loss of Religious Allegiance among the Youth of the Oneida Community."

p. 113   ghostly sessions of mutual criticism: Shusko, "Spiritualism and the Oneida Community."

p. 113   there was "conclusive evidence": Robertson, *The Breakup*, 32–33; Klaw, *Without Sin*, 217.

p. 113   His research, he specifically noted, took him to Vermont: Robertson, *The Breakup*, 37.

p. 114   "sensitive, distant and curt with strangers": Olcott, *People from the Other World*, 23.

p. 115   "every imaginable variety of costume": Olcott, *People from the Other World*, 163.

p. 115   "various solos, duos, trios, and concerted pieces": Olcott, *People from the Other World*, 217.

p. 117   the ghost of Benjamin Franklin: Weisberg, *Talking to the Dead*, 219.

p. 117   "I have heard [the sounds] in a living tree": Weisberg, *Talking to the Dead*, 225.

p. 118   At their wedding breakfast: Doyle, *The History of Spiritualism*, 48.

p. 118   "intensely high-tempered": Hayes, Hayes, Dunmire, and Bailey, *A Complete History*, 123-29.

p. 118   "very much reduced in circumstances": Hayes, Hayes, Dunmire, and Bailey, *A Complete History*, 29.

p. 119   "a fit subject for a lunatic asylum": *Report of the Proceedings*, 2065–66.

p. 119   "committed a fearful crime": Noyes, "Guiteau vs. Oneida Community."

9: Prizes of Power

p. 120   the elder John Noyes: Barnard, *Rutherford B. Hayes*, 50, 60, 64.

p. 120   they decided to sell their shares: Barnard, *Rutherford B. Hayes*, 66–69.

p. 120   They settled in the town of Delaware: Barnard, *Rutherford B. Hayes*, 19–20.

p. 120   "It would be a mercy if the child would die": Barnard, *Rutherford B. Hayes*, 36.

p. 120   "timid as a girl": Barnard, *Rutherford B. Hayes*, 74.

p. 121   "a pleasure tour": Barnard, *Rutherford B. Hayes*, 216.

p. 121   "From the sunny, agreeable, the kind": Barnard, *Rutherford B. Hayes*, 219.

p. 122   "discouraged rather than encouraged": Barnard, *Rutherford B. Hayes*, 278.

p. 122   "It seems to me that good purposes": Morris, *Fraud of the Century*, 68.

p. 122   "cheap swagger": Brigham, "Blaine, Conkling and Garfield," 6–7.

p. 123   "Had he been a woman": Morris, *Fraud of the Century*, 51.

p. 123   Conkling brought fifteen hundred workers: Reeves, *Gentleman Boss*, 92–93.

p. 123   "the Ticket That Pays": Morris, *Fraud of the Century*, 71–72.

p. 123   his cousin and campaign manager, Edward Noyes: Morris, *Fraud of the Century*, 81.

p. 123   Although some critics called him "a plaster saint": Barnard, *Rutherford B. Hayes*, 287, 299; Morris, *Fraud of the Century*, 83.

p. 124   "flat and tame": Morris, *Fraud of the Century*, 136.

p. 124   sporting a cheery red carnation: Morris, *Fraud of the Century*, 162.

p. 124   But three crucial states were still in play: "The Electoral Vote Count of the 1876 Presidential Election," *History, Art, and Archives: United States House of Representatives*, https://history.house.gov/Historical -Highlights/1851-1900/The-electoral-vote-count-of-the-1876 -presidential-election.

p. 125   "He was taken from his house": Chernow, *Grant*, 843.

p. 126   offered to certify the election: Barnard, *Rutherford B. Hayes*, 331.

p. 126   "to calm the public agitation": Brown, *The Diary of James A. Garfield*, 3:379–80.

p. 127   "Another civil war": Morris, *Fraud of the Century*, 172.

p. 127   There were rumors of a coup d'état: Barnard, *Rutherford B. Hayes*, 341.

p. 127   "fully armed and ready for business": Morris, *Fraud of the Century*, 214.

p. 127   steal weapons from federal arsenals: Barnard, *Rutherford B. Hayes*, 342.

p. 127   "fixed ammunition, enough to supply": Barnard, *Rutherford B. Hayes*, 344.

p. 127   President Grant would use the military: Barnard, *Rutherford B. Hayes*, 341.

p. 127   "It will not do to fight": Morris, *Fraud of the Century*, 214.

p. 128   "a tribunal whose authority": Morris, *Fraud of the Century*, 202.

p. 128   "a day of the most nervous strain": Morris, *Fraud of the Century*, 226.

p. 128   Garfield heard whispers: Morris, *Fraud of the Century*, 231.

p. 129   Born in Washington in 1819: Gelderman, *A Free Man of Color*, 10.

p. 129   Wormley Alley: Gelderman, *A Free Man of Color*, 10.

p. 129   His son James had the benefit: Gelderman, *A Free Man of Color*, 2–13; Donet D. Graves, "Wormley Hotel," The White House Historical Association, January 26, 2016, https://www.white househistory.org/wormley-hotel-1.

p. 129   Then, in the 1850s: Gelderman, *A Free Man of Color*, 13–20, 46.

p. 130   When James opened his grand hotel: Gelderman, *A Free Man of Color*, 20–21, 46–48.

p. 131   an incendiary eighteen-hour session: Barnard, *Rutherford B. Hayes*, 394–95; Morris, *Fraud of the Century*, 235–37.

p. 131   Weeks earlier in Columbus: Morris, *Fraud of the Century*, 238–39.

p. 131   "There were many indications of relief and joy": Brown, *The Diary of James A. Garfield*, 3:454.

p. 131   "His Fraudulency": Morris, *Fraud of the Century*, 2.

p. 132   "the endless whine of office-seekers": Benton, *Greeley on Lincoln*, 42.

p. 132   his home was besieged: Brown, *The Diary of James A. Garfield*, 3:454.

p. 132   it promoted and protected the unworthy: Reeves, *Gentleman Boss*, 98.

p. 132   "There is no duty": Chernow, *Grant*, 731.

p. 132   the first Civil Service Commission: Chernow, *Grant*, 731–32.

p. 133   "the most complete and offensive example": Reeves, *Gentleman Boss*, 113.

p. 133   "in the management of": Reeves, *Gentleman Boss*, 123–25; Barnard, *Rutherford B. Hayes*, 348.

p. 133   "Granny Hayes": Reeves, *Gentleman Boss*, 142.

p. 133   "the Pet of the Petticoats": Ross, *Proud Kate*, 232.

p. 134   she and Conkling were a couple: Ross, *Proud Kate*, 241.

p. 134   When Sprague unexpectedly returned: Reeves, *Gentleman Boss*, 152–53.

p. 134   The affair ended abruptly: Ross, *Proud Kate*, 256.

p. 134   "no prejudices": Fogarty, *Desire and Duty*, 42.

p. 134   a huge bear trap: Hayes, *Diary and Letters*, 5:450, appendix C; Fogarty, *Desire and Duty*, 42.

p. 134   successful collective living: Klaw, *Without Sin*, 198.

p. 135   Noyes declared that Theodore: Wayland-Smith, *From Free Love Utopia*, 152.

p. 135   "The course Theodore has pursued": Fogarty, *Desire*, 106.

p. 135   "a crazy enthusiast": Fogarty, *Desire*, 163; Wayland-Smith, *Oneida*, 152.

p. 135   "were given little pads": Klaw, *Without Sin*, 224–25.

p. 136   Seventy-five percent of Oneidans: Roach, "The Loss of Religious Allegiance among the Youth of the Oneida Community," 787–806.

p. 136   a publicity-hungry academic named John Mears: Parker, *A Yankee Saint*, 268, 270.

p. 136   "free and licensed indulgence": Parker, *A Yankee Saint*, 268.

p. 136   "dark and slimy depths": Doyle, "Passionate Words," 6.

p. 136   The *Fulton Times*: Klaw, *Without Sin*, 244; Parker, *A Yankee Saint*, 271.

p. 137   "For the life of me": Parker, *A Yankee Saint*, 281.

p. 137   "Epicurean sty": Parker, *A Yankee Saint*, 270, 279.

p. 137   Although Mears banned reporters from the meeting: Doyle, "Passionate Words," 8–9.

p. 138   "Tonight!" they begged him: Noyes, *My Father's House*, 159; Parker, *A Yankee Saint*, 282.

10: Serpents in the Garden

p. 139   carrying his own spartan lunch: Peskin, *Garfield*, 433.

p. 140   a "general state of chaos": Peskin, *Garfield*, 433.

p. 140   "helpless as a child": Peskin, *Garfield*, 434.

p. 140   "considerably sprinkled with gray": Brown, *The Diary of James A. Garfield*, 4:326.

p. 140   "a suicidal policy": Peskin, *Garfield*, 430.

p. 141   Mississippi senator Blanche K. Bruce: "Senator Bruce and Grant," *New York Times*, December 7, 1878.

p. 141   "the whole contest": Reeves, *Gentleman Boss*, 150.

p. 141   When Grant arrived in San Francisco: Chernow, *Grant*, 886–88.

p. 142   "extremely anxious": Ackerman, *Dark Horse*, 41.

p. 142   "I like Blaine, always have": Reeves, *Gentleman Boss*, 163.

p. 142   "the Ohio Icicle": Peskin, *Garfield*, 453.

p. 142   The Republican showdown: Ackerman, *Dark Horse*, 78–79; Peskin, *Garfield*, 462.

p. 142   "boiling over with politics": Ackerman, *Dark Horse*, 27–28.

p. 142   "very fatiguing": Brown, *The Diary of James A. Garfield*, 4:424.

p. 143   "Many are fully of the belief": Shaw, *Crete and James*, 371.

p. 143   "I long ago made a resolution": Peskin, *Garfield*, 454.

p. 143   In the noisy chaos: Peskin, *Garfield*, 462.

p. 143   made Conkling "sea-sick": Jordan, *Roscoe Conkling*, 337.

p. 143   "We want Garfield!": Peskin, *Garfield*, 469.

p. 143   Three ballots later: Chidsey, *The Gentleman from New York*, 197.

p. 144   including Senator Blanche K. Bruce: Graham, *The Senator and the Socialite*, 128.

p. 144   "a greater honor": Reeves, *Gentleman Boss*, 180.

p. 144   At eleven o'clock that night: Ackerman, *Dark Horse*, 132.

p. 144   "his own eminent qualities": "James A. Garfield," *New York Times*, June 9, 1880.

pp. 144–45 And E. L. Godkin: Reeves, *Gentleman Boss*, 183.

p. 145 "the Little Giant from the West": *Report of the Proceedings*, 357–60, 565–81.

p. 145 the *Stonington*: "Fire and Flood," *Brooklyn Daily Eagle*, June 13, 1880; "Fire and Flood," *Brooklyn Daily Eagle*, June 14, 1880; "The Latest Horror," *Boston Post*, June 14, 1880; "Horrible Disaster," *Boston Weekly Globe*, June 16, 1880; *Report of the Proceedings*, 583–84.

p. 146 "felt sure," he said, "that I was on my way": Hayes, Hayes, Dunmire, and Bailey, *A Complete History*, 66.

p. 147 "to sit crosslegged and look wise": Peskin, *Garfield*, 482.

p. 147 trainloads of Americans: Brown, *The Diary of James A. Garfield*, 4:437, 470.

p. 147 the railroad built a special spur: Chidsey, *The Gentleman from New York*, 301–02.

p. 147 "a streak of sadness": "An Eerie Prescience: James Garfield Finds a 'Streak of Sadness' in His Nomination as President," Shapell Manuscript Foundation, https://www.shapell.org/manuscript /james-garfield-reflects-on-his-1880-presidential-nomination.

p. 147 so reluctant to campaign: Peskin, *Garfield*, 485.

p. 148 "If they shall now think": Brown, *The Diary of James A. Garfield*, 4:428.

p. 148 "an unreasonable demand": Brown, *The Diary of James A. Garfield*, 4:428.

p. 148 the "Northern Star": Ackerman, *Dark Horse*, 168.

p. 148 "the prince of good fellows": Brown, *The Diary of James A. Garfield*, 4:435.

p. 149 "zeal and enthusiasm": Brown, *The Diary of James A. Garfield*, 4:435.

p. 149 mounted and marching Republican veterans: "The Candidates Honored," *New York Times*, August 7, 1880; Ackerman, *Dark Horse*, 173–74; 179.

p. 149 it "didn't draw": Ackerman, *Dark Horse*, 179.

p. 150 "delightful and pleasant in every way": Ackerman, *Dark Horse*, 177.

p. 150 "I shall be nominated and elected": Hayes, Hayes, Dunmire, and Bailey, *A Complete History*, 66.

p. 150 "a cold-blooded, mousy, fidgeting little man": White, "Platt."

p. 150 "no trades, no shackles": Brown, *The Diary of James A. Garfield*, 4:438.

p. 150 "to concede anything and everything": Jordan, *Roscoe Conkling*, 354.

p. 151 a "competent" chief executive: Peskin, *Garfield*, 500.

p. 151 "a singular compound": Chidsey, *The Gentleman from New York*, 309.

p. 151   "Garfield is a grand, noble fellow": Ackerman, *Dark Horse*, 146.

p. 151   "a big good-natured man": Ackerman, *Dark Horse*, 231.

p. 151   "easily changed his mind": Jordan, *Roscoe Conkling*, 348.

p. 151   "The personal aspect of the presidency": Brown, *The Diary of James A. Garfield*, 4:505.

p. 152   "trying to survive the presidency": Brown, *The Diary of James A. Garfield*, 4:505.

p. 152   "all the desperate bad men of the party": Ackerman, *Dark Horse*, 237.

p. 152   "would act like strychnine": Reeves, *Gentleman Boss*, 212.

p. 153   "His next to the last sentence": Brown, *The Diary of James A. Garfield*, 4:512.

p. 153   "strangely disinclined": Brown, *The Diary of James A. Garfield*, 4:542.

p. 153   "the singular repugnance": Brown, *The Diary of James A. Garfield*, 4:545.

p. 154   "Morton broke down": Ackerman, *Dark Horse*, 256–57; Brown, *The Diary of James A. Garfield*, 4:552.

p. 154   To fill the now-vacant cabinet slot: Peskin, *Garfield*, 533–35; Ackerman, *Dark Horse*, 257–58.

p. 155   Roscoe Conkling, seated directly behind him: Peskin, *Garfield*, 539.

p. 155   including a hearse: Peskin, *Garfield*, 541.

p. 155   That night, invited revelers: Peskin, *Garfield*, 541; Ackerman, *Dark Horse*, 262; Brown, *The Diary of James A. Garfield*, 4:554.

p. 155   "a long series of happy years": Brown, *The Diary of James A. Garfield*, 4:519.

11: The Removal

p. 156   The drapes were ragged: Ackerman, *Dark Horse*, 270–78.

p. 157   Garfield had sometimes played hooky: Peskin, *Garfield*, 432.

p. 157   National Natatorium: Odlum, *The Life and Adventures*, 16.

p. 157   gray flannel swimming suits: Odlum, *The Life and Adventures*, 13–14.

p. 158   Half a million people: Wallace, *The Fabulous Showman*, 225–29; Wilson, *Barnum*, 258–60.

p. 158   Barnum wrote to the president: Saxon, *Selected Letters*, Barnum to James Garfield, March 12, 1881, 217.

p. 159   The Garfield children: Brown, *The Diary of James A. Garfield*, 4:578; Harrison Smith, "Step Right Up—and Fast—for this Famed Circus's Final Act," *Washington Post*, March 27, 2017.

p. 159   they opened the doors of the White House: Peskin, *Garfield*, 547; Ackerman, *Dark Horse*, 279.

p. 160   "I was one of the men": Ackerman, *Dark Horse*, 280–81.

p. 160   "the first shot": *Report of the Proceedings*, 124, 217.

p. 160   He had no socks on: *Report of the Proceedings*, 446.

p. 160   "at least ten": Ackerman, *Dark Horse*, 222.

p. 160   on the night of August 21: "Local Political Work," *New York Times*, August 22, 1880.

p. 160   "men of reputation": Ackerman, *Dark Horse*, 179, 223.

p. 160   "as a personal tribute": *Report of the Proceedings*, 128–29; Ackerman, *Dark Horse*, 223.

p. 161   he even lobbied ex-president Grant: *Report of the Proceedings*, 1155–56; Ackerman, *Dark Horse*, 406–07.

p. 161   "with dignity and grace": King, "The Stalking of the President," 3.

p. 161   "Mr. Guiteau's visits": *Report of the Proceedings*, 209.

p. 162   The office seeker was ushered: Ackerman, *Dark Horse*, 267–68, 407.

p. 162   "Assassination," he declared: Peskin, *Garfield*, 593.

p. 162   "It is said that no day in twelve years": Brown, *The Diary of James A. Garfield*, 4:554–59.

p. 163   "broken Blaine's heart": Ackerman, *Dark Horse*, 291.

p. 164   "a very lively bombshell": Ackerman, *Dark Horse*, 299.

p. 164   "a willing instrument": Reeves, *Gentleman Boss*, 224; Peskin, *Garfield*, 561.

p. 164   "a personal affront": Smith, *Life and Letters of James Abram Garfield*, 1112.

p. 164   "the crisis of his Fate": Reeves, *Gentleman Boss*, 225.

p. 164   "a deep damnation": Jordan, *Roscoe Conkling*, 385.

p. 164   "Conkling's abject slave": Ackerman, *Dark Horse*, 302.

p. 164   "I do not propose to be dictated to": Ackerman, *Dark Horse*, 326.

p. 165   Public sentiment: Peskin, *Garfield*, 569.

p. 166   a "great big baby boohooing": Peskin, *Garfield*, 569.

p. 166   From any point of view: "Comments of the Press," *New York Times*, May 17, 1881.

p. 166   According to the president's steward: Crump, William T., 1881–93, Box 54, Special Correspondence, Lucretia Garfield Papers, Manuscript Division, Library of Congress.

p. 167   He had "no heart": Brown, *The Diary of James A. Garfield*, 4:590.

p. 167   Lucretia's pain and headaches: William T. Crump, 1881–93, Box 54, Special Correspondence, Lucretia Garfield Papers, Manuscript Division, Library of Congress; Brown, *The Diary of James A. Garfield*, 4:590; Peskin, *Garfield*, 569.

p. 167   "measureless humiliation": Brown, *The Diary of James A. Garfield*, 4:608.

p. 168   "General Garfield: I wish to say": *Report of the Proceedings*, 210.

p. 168   "Mr. Blaine—the worst enemy": *Report of the Proceedings*, 588.

p. 168   "did not do it with any special harshness": Ackerman, *Dark Horse*, 338.

p. 169   "Blaine is 'a vindictive politician'": *Report of the Proceedings*, 212.

p. 169   The president, he believed, "was doing great wrong": *Report of the Proceedings*, 668.

p. 169   "the Blaine element": *Report of the Proceedings*, 211.

p. 169   "a deep strong current": Brown, *The Diary of James A. Garfield*, 4:601.

p. 169   "carry her about the house": William T. Crump, 1881–93, Box 54, Special Correspondence, Lucretia Garfield Papers, Manuscript Division, Library of Congress.

p. 169   It was a "very stupid sermon": Brown, *The Diary of James A. Garfield*, 4:609.

p. 171   "terrible strain": Brown, *The Diary of James A. Garfield*, 4:610.

p. 171   "Mrs. Garfield looked so thin": *Report of the Proceedings*, 216.

p. 172   "his old friend Jim": William T. Crump, 1881–93, Box 54, Special Correspondence, Lucretia Garfield Papers, Manuscript Division, Library of Congress.

p. 172   "his face beaming with anticipation": Harriet S. Blaine, memoir of assassination of James A. Garfield, Box 1, Diaries and Memoirs, 1871–1939, James Gillespie Blaine Papers, Library of Congress.

p. 173   "in the most delightful and cozy fellowship": Ackerman, *Dark Horse*, 373.

p. 173   it was an "excellent" facility: Ackerman, *Dark Horse*, 365.

p. 173   "I read the newspapers": Rosenberg, *Trial of the Assassin*, 40–41.

p. 174   "I have just shot the President": Rosenberg, *Trial of the Assassin*, 5.

p. 174   He was "unusually cheerful and jolly": William T. Crump, 1881–93, Box 54, Special Correspondence, Lucretia Garfield Papers, Manuscript Division, Library of Congress.

p. 174   "I am going out of this old prison for a month": William T. Crump, 1881–93, Box 54, Special Correspondence, Lucretia Garfield Papers, Manuscript Division, Library of Congress.

p. 175   "After the bedroom antics": William T. Crump, 1881–93, Box 54, Special Correspondence, Lucretia Garfield Papers, Manuscript Division, Library of Congress.

p. 175   Blaine was already there: William T. Crump, 1881–93, Box 54, Special Correspondence, Lucretia Garfield Papers, Manuscript Division, Library of Congress.

p. 175   Before he had left the house: Harriet S. Blaine, memoir of assassination of James A. Garfield, Box 1, Diaries and Memoirs, 1871–1939, James Gillespie Blaine Papers, Library of Congress.

12: End Times

p. 176   Harriet Blaine had finally sat down: Harriet Blaine to Margaret Blaine, Washington, July 3, 1881, in Beale, *Letters of Mrs. James G. Blaine*, 209–10.

p. 177   William Crump, meanwhile: William T. Crump, 1881–93, Box 54, Special Correspondence, Lucretia Garfield Papers, Manuscript Division, Library of Congress.

p. 177   When the ambulance arrived: Harriet Blaine to Margaret Blaine, Washington, July 3, 1881, in Beale, *Letters of Mrs. James G. Blaine*, 210–11.

p. 178   More than twenty doctors: William T. Crump, 1881–93, Box 54, Special Correspondence, Lucretia Garfield Papers, Manuscript Division, Library of Congress.

p. 178   The president could hear all the doctors: William T. Crump, 1881–93, Box 54, Special Correspondence, Lucretia Garfield Papers, Manuscript Division, Library of Congress.

p. 178   "What will this do for Crete?": Edson in Balch, *The Life of James Abram Garfield*, 612.

p. 179   "frail, fatigued, desperate": Harriet Blaine to Margaret Blaine, Washington, July 3, 1881, in Beale, *Letters of Mrs. James G. Blaine*, 211.

p. 179   they embraced each other silently: William T. Crump, 1881–93, Box 54, Special Correspondence, Lucretia Garfield Papers, Manuscript Division, Library of Congress.

p. 179   especially in his calves and feet: William T. Crump, 1881–93, Box 54, Special Correspondence, Lucretia Garfield Papers, Manuscript Division, Library of Congress.

p. 179   Harriet piled pillows: Harriet S. Blaine, memoir of assassination of James A. Garfield, Box 1, Diaries and Memoirs, 1871–1939, James Gillespie Blaine Papers, Library of Congress; Edson in Balch, *The Life of James Abram Garfield*, 614.

p. 179   For hours on end: William T. Crump, 1881–93, Box 54, Special Correspondence, Lucretia Garfield Papers, Manuscript Division, Library of Congress.

p. 179   four cabinet members: William T. Crump, 1881–93, Box 54, Special Correspondence, Lucretia Garfield Papers, Manuscript Division, Library of Congress.

p. 180   Despite the pain and prodding: Edson in Balch, *The Life of James Abram Garfield*, 618.

p. 180   "the death of the President at this time": Hayes, *Diary and Letters*, July 16, 1872.

p. 180   "with clenched teeth": Ackerman, *Dark Horse*, 385.

p. 180   A journalist who interviewed him: Reeves, *Gentleman Boss*, 242.

p. 181   Although he took only liquids: Ackerman, *Dark Horse*, 415–16; Edson in Balch, *The Life of James Abram Garfield*, 614.

p. 181   oatmeal, which he detested: William T. Crump, 1881–93, Box 54, Special Correspondence, Lucretia Garfield Papers, Manuscript Division, Library of Congress.

p. 181   James Wormley was enlisted: DeFerrari, "The Talented Mr. James Wormley."

p. 182   "At times," Crump recalled: William T. Crump, 1881–93, Box 54, Special Correspondence, Lucretia Garfield Papers, Manuscript Division, Library of Congress.

p. 182   "no danger now": Harriet Blaine to Margaret Blaine, July 6, 1881, Washington, in Beale, *Letters of Mrs. James G. Blaine*, 214.

p. 182   "He might as well be . . . a prisoner": Peskin, *Garfield*, 601.

p. 183   as despairing as "lost children": Harriet Blaine to Margaret Blaine, July 8, 1881, Washington, in Beale, *Letters of Mrs. James G. Blaine*, 222.

p. 183   "We are doing nothing but wait": Harriet Blaine to Margaret Blaine, July 8, 1881, Washington, in Beale, *Letters of Mrs. James G. Blaine*, 222.

pp. 183–84   "nutrient enemas": Bliss, "Feeding Per Rectum," 10.

p. 184   "very anxious now": Greenberger, *The Unexpected President*, 166.

p. 184   Every night when she went to bed: Harriet Blaine to Walker Blaine, August 25, 1881, Washington, in Beale, *Letters of Mrs. James G. Blaine*, 233.

p. 184   "We must get the President out of this": Ackerman, *Dark Horse*, 424.

p. 184   "poor dear Gaffy": Harriet Blaine to Margaret Blaine, September 1 and September 4, 1881, Washington, in Beale, *Letters of Mrs. James G. Blaine*, 235–37.

p. 185   four specially trained men: "A Busy Day at the White House," *New York Times*, September 6, 1881; "Taken from Washington," *New York Times*, September 7, 1881.

p. 185   he raised his right hand: "Taken from Washington," *New York Times*, September 7, 1881.

p. 185   He was then gently loaded: "A Busy Day at the White House," *New York Times*, September 6, 1881.

p. 185   the president opened his eyes: "Taken from Washington," *New York Times*, September 7, 1881.

p. 185   specially outfitted to circulate: "The President's Special Train," *New York Times*, September 5, 1881.

p. 185   a special Indian rubber waterbed: "The Patient's Proposed Removal," *New York Times*, September 5, 1881.

p. 185   Bliss and Crete were there to receive him: "Taken from Washington," *New York Times*, September 7, 1881.

p. 185   three hundred railroad workers: "Everything Ready at Elberon," *New York Times*, September 5, 1881.

p. 185   They had driven the last spike: "Final Preparations at Elberon," *New York Times*, September 7, 1881.

p. 186   pushed it by hand: "The Arrival at Elberon," *New York Times*, September 7, 1881; "Everything Ready at Elberon," *New York Times*, September 5, 1881.

p. 186   "All our journey through": Harriet Blaine to her children, September 8, 1881, Long Branch in Beale, *Letters of Mrs. James G. Blaine*, 239.

p. 187   Sitting alone: "The Nation's Dead Chief," *New York Times*, September 22, 1881.

p. 187   soldiers carried Garfield's coffin: "The Nation's Dead Chief," *New York Times*, September 22, 1881.

p. 187   Two days later: "On the Way to the Grave," *New York Times*, September 24, 1881.

p. 188   Guiteau dropped to his knees: Rosenberg, *Trial of the Assassin*, 48.

p. 188   Garfield was "a God send to you": Rosenberg, *Trial of the Assassin*, 49.

p. 188   "bitterly denouncing the President": *Report of the Proceedings*, 383, 1108.

p. 189   "the divine will": *Report of the Proceedings*, 600.

p. 189   "I did it, and will go to jail": Reeves, *Gentleman Boss*, 237.

p. 189   Guiteau said he was happier: Peskin, *Garfield*, 596.

p. 189   wheat bread, salted herring: Ackerman, *Dark Horse*, 406.

p. 189   he gained more than ten pounds: Rosenberg, *Trial of the Assassin*, 45.

p. 189   "I don't want to appear strained": Ackerman, *Dark Horse*, 406.

p. 190   as he was looking out his cell window: Rosenberg, *Trial of the Assassin*, 51–52.

p. 190   attorney George Scoville: Rosenberg, *Trial of the Assassin*, 79–86.

p. 190   The physicians killed him: Peskin, *Garfield*, 603.

p. 190   "Whatever the religious fanaticism": Rosenberg, *Trial of the Assassin*, 96–97.

p. 190   the *New York Herald* trumpeted: Rosenberg, *Trial of the Assassin*, 108.

p. 190   After escaping thirty miles: Parker, *A Yankee Saint*, 293; Klaw, *Without Sin*, 251.

p. 191   "the iron filings" flew apart: Huxley, *Adonis and the Alphabet*, 99.

p. 191   "awful state of disrespect": Wayland-Smith, *Oneida*, 164.

p. 191   The "sexual grab bag": Fogarty, *Desire and Duty*, 24.

p. 191   "like the explosion": Fogarty, *Desire and Duty*, 178.

p. 191   ten o'clock in the morning: Wayland-Smith, *Oneida*, 170.

p. 191   "They have abandoned": Fogarty, "Oneida," 202.

p. 192   more than two hundred Oneidans signed: Parker, *A Yankee Saint*, 287–90; Wayland-Smith, *Oneida*, 178.

p. 192   a house in Niagara, Canada: Parker, *A Yankee Saint*, 294.

p. 192   "exhibition of holy horror": John Humphrey Noyes, *Guiteau vs. Oneida Community*, 1, 12.

p. 193   another Oneidan was subpoenaed: "Moral Monstrosities," *Sunday Herald* (Syracuse), January 29, 1882; *Cazenovia Republican* (New York), July 27, 1882.

p. 193   "My sister told me": "Moral Monstrosities," *Sunday Herald* (Syracuse), January 29, 1882.

p. 194   a "racy, stirring" opening statement: Rosenberg, *Trial of the Assassin*, 110.

p. 194   a member of the Wormley clan: Rosenberg, *Trial of the Assassin*, 115.

p. 194   "pleasant and ingratiating": Rosenberg, *Trial of the Assassin*, 180.

p. 194   "like a half-tamed chimpanzee": Rosenberg, *Trial of the Assassin*, 187.

p. 195   a drunken farmer on horseback: Rosenberg, *Trial of the Assassin*, 121.

p. 195   "Guilty as indicted": Rosenberg, *Trial of the Assassin*, 22325.

p. 195   fried potatoes and steak: Rosenberg, *Trial of the Assassin*, 231.

p. 195   Guiteau lost his appeal: Rosenberg, *Trial of the Assassin*, 232.

p. 195   "instead of saying 'Guiteau the assassin'": *Report of the Proceedings*, 2207.

p. 196   As the warden of the jail mailed: Reeves, *Gentleman Boss*, 264; "Lot #573: Unique Printed Invitation to Assassin Guiteau's Execution," Raynors' Historical Collectible Auctions, http://www.hcaauctions .com/lot-31830.aspx.

p. 196   He planned to wear a white robe: Rosenberg, *Trial of the Assassin*, 235–37.

p. 196   quickly devoured a large meal: Rosenberg, *Trial of the Assassin*, 236.

p. 196   prison officials revived him: "Guiteau's Removal," *State* (Columbia, SC), March 21, 1892, in Woodyard, "Bring Me the Head."

p. 196   "I am going to the Lordy": Rosenberg, *Trial of the Assassin*, 237.

p. 196   Guiteau suddenly stopped speaking: Rosenberg, *Trial of the Assassin*, 237; "The Ends of Justice Met," *New York Tribune*, July 1, 1882.

p. 196   as flies swarmed: "The Ends of Justice Met," *New York Tribune*, July 1, 1882; Reeves, *Gentleman Boss*, 264.

p. 196   ghoulishly profitable souvenirs: "The Ends of Justice Met," *New York Tribune*, July 1, 1882.

13: Over the Falls

p. 197   Guiteau's corpse was quickly taken out: Woodyard, "Bring Me the Head"; "Official Report"; *New York Times*, September 16, 1893.

p. 197   George Scoville had hoped: "Scoville's Record," *Chicago Herald*, Oneida Community Collection, Box 45, Guiteau, Charles J., Syracuse University Special Collections.

p. 197   The doctors removed: "Brain of a Presidential Assassin."

p. 197   historical and educational collection: *New York Herald*, June 30, 1889, in Woodyard, "Bring Me the Head."

p. 197   "boil and bubble": "Guiteau's Removal," *State*, Columbia, SC, March 21, 1892, in Woodyard, "Bring Me the Head."

p. 197   "so skillfully": "Is It Guiteau's Head?" *Cleveland Leader*, June 22, 1887, in Woodyard, "Bring Me the Head."

p. 198   "on exhibition for the gratification": "Guiteau's Head," *New York Herald*, June 21, 1887, in Woodyard, "Bring Me the Head."

p. 198   "Professor" E. M. Worth: "Guiteau's Head," *Macon Telegraph*, June 24, 1887, in Woodyard, "Bring Me the Head."

p. 198   Worth took Guiteau's head on tour: *Fort Wayne News*, April 30, 1900, in Woodyard, "Bring Me the Head."

p. 198   In September 1916, however: "Head of Guiteau Burns Up," *Indiana Shoals News*, Sept. 29, 1916, in Woodyard, "Bring Me the Head."

p. 198   "nothing like it ever before": Rutherford B. Hayes, *Diary and Letters*, Vol. IV, October 30, 1888, 418.

p. 198   Work hours, too, were grueling: Miller, *The President's Kitchen Cabinet*, 43.

p. 198   Crump permanently left his post: Miller, *The President's Kitchen Cabinet*, 43–4.

p. 199   He then managed a touring museum: *Napa County Reporter*, July 31, 1885.

p. 199   he had dived from steamships: Odlum, *The Life and Adventures*, 174; John Kelly, "The Tragedy of Bob Odlum," *Washington Post*, February 22, 2020.

p. 200   Looking for his next triumph: Heather Thomas, "The Last Leap of Sam Patch"; Morton, "The Story of Sam Patch."

p. 200   Odlum chose May 19, 1885: Odlum, *The Life and Adventures*, 158–66.

p. 201   "an irresistible attraction": George E. Cragin, "On the Brink," Box 44, Cragin, George E., Oneida Community Collection, Syracuse University Special Collections.

p. 201   he could feel the torrent rattling: Parker, *A Yankee Saint*, 296; Pierrepont Noyes, *My Father's House*, 267.

NOTES

p. 201   It was a gabled home: Leonard, Stephen R. Recollections, Box 64, Oneida Community Collection Syracuse University Special Collections; Parker, *A Yankee Saint*, 295–98; Pierrepont Noyes, *My Father's House*, 272–73.

p. 202   Every day at supper: Pierrepont Noyes, *My Father's House*, 270; Leonard, Stephen R. Recollections, Box 64, Oneida Community Collection, Syracuse University Special Collections.

p. 202   Managers of those enterprises: Parker, *A Yankee Saint*, 295.

p. 202   Noyes would return to his room: Klaw, *Without Sin*, 278.

p. 202   Noyes would sit in his armchair: Pierrepont Noyes, *My Father's House*, 271–72.

p. 202   There were so many Community children: Parker, *A Yankee Saint*, 299; Pierrepont Noyes, *My Father's House*, 275–76.

p. 202   He "suffered dreadfully from fear": Klaw, *Without Sin*, 280–81.

p. 203   loving female spirit guides: Wayland-Smith, *From Free Love Utopia*, 181.

BIBLIOGRAPHY

Manuscript Sources

Oneida Community Collection, Syracuse University Special Collections

James Gillespie Blaine Family Papers, Library of Congress, Manuscript Division

Lucretia Garfield Rudolph Papers, Library of Congress, Manuscript Division

Abbott, Geoffrey. *Amazing True Stories of Execution Blunders*. Chichester, UK: Summersdale Publishers, 2006.

Ackerman, Kenneth D. *Dark Horse: The Surprise Election and Political Murder of President James A. Garfield*. New York: Carroll & Graf, 2003.

Balch, William Ralston. *The Life of James Abram Garfield*. Philadelphia: Hubbard Bros., 1881.

Barnard, Harry. *Rutherford B. Hayes and His America*. 1954; Newtown, CT: American Political Biography Press, 1992.

Barnum, P. T. *The Humbugs of the World*. Landisville, PA: Coachwhip, 1865.

Barnum, Phineas T. *The Life of P. T Barnum: Written by Himself*. 1855; Urbana: University of Chicago Press, 2000.

Beale, Harriet S. Blaine. *Letters of Mrs. James G. Blaine*, vol. I. New York: Duffield, 1908.

Benton, Joel, ed. *Greeley on Lincoln*. New York: The Baker and Taylor, 1893.

———. *Life of Hon. Phineas T. Barnum*. N.p.: Edgewood, 1891.

———. "Reminiscences of Horace Greeley," *The Cosmopolitan: A Monthly Illustrated Magazine* (1886–1907), July 1887.

Bestor, Arthur. *Backwoods Utopias: The Sectarian Origins and the Owenite Phase of Communitarian Socialism in America, 1663–1829*. Philadelphia: University of Pennsylvania Press, 1971.

Bliss, D. W. "Feeding Per Rectum: As Illustrated in the Case of the Late President Garfield." *The Medical Record*, July 15, 1882.

Bosworth, Amanda. "Barnum's Whales." *Perspectives on History*, April 2, 2018.

Boyd, David. *A History: Greeley and the Union Colony of Colorado*. Greeley, CO: Greeley Tribune Press, 1890.

"Brain of a Presidential Assassin: A Killer's Brain." *Memento Mütter*, http ://memento.muttermuseum.org/detail/brain-of-a-presidential-assassin.

Brands, H. W. *Andrew Jackson: His Life and Times*. New York: Anchor Books, 2006.

Braude, Ann. *Radical Spirits: Spiritualism and Women's Rights in Nineteenth-Century America*. Bloomington: Indiana University Press, 2001.

Brigham, Johnson. "Blaine, Conkling and Garfield: A Reminiscence and a Character Study." A paper read before the Prairie Club of Des Moines on Saturday, April 10, 1915.

Brown, Harry James, and Frederick D. Williams, ed. *The Diary of James A. Garfield*, vol. I and II. East Lansing: Michigan State University Press, 1967.

———, eds. *The Diary of James A. Garfield*, vol. III. East Lansing: Michigan State University Press, 1973.

———, eds. *The Diary of James A. Garfield*, vol. IV. East Lansing: Michigan State University Press, 1967.

Bunting, Josiah, III. *Ulysses S. Grant*. New York: Times Books, 2004.

Burrows, Edwin G., and Mike Wallace. *Gotham: A History of New York City to 1898*. New York: Oxford University Press, 1999.

Channing, William Ellery, ed. *Memoirs of Margaret Fuller Ossoli*, vol. II. Boston: Phillips, Sampson, 1852.

Chernow, Ron. *Grant*. New York: Penguin Press, 2017.

Chidsey, Donald Barr. *The Gentleman from New York: A Life of Roscoe Conkling*. New Haven, CT: Yale University Press, 1935.

Christen, William J. *Pauline Cushman: Spy of the Cumberland*. Roseville, MN: Edinborough Press, 2006.

Collins, Gail. *William Henry Harrison: The 9th President, 1841*. New York: Henry Holt, 2012.

Conkling, Alfred Ronald. *The Life and Letters of Roscoe Conkling: Orator, Statesman, Advocate*. New York: Charles L. Webster, 1889.

Cross, Whitney R. *The Burned-Over District: The Social and Intellectual History of Enthusiastic Religion in Western New York, 1800–1850*. New York: Harper Torchbooks, 1950.

Dana, Charles Anderson. *A Lecture on Association in Its Connection with Religion*. Boston: Benjamin H. Greene, 1844.

De Tocqueville, Alexis. *Democracy in America*. 1835; New York: Signet Classic, 1984.

DeFerrari, John D. "The Talented Mr. James Wormley." *Streets of Washington*, September 10, 2012, http://www.streetsofwashington.com/2012/09/the-talented-mr-james-wormley.html.

Delano, Sterling F. *Brook Farm: The Dark Side of Utopia*. Cambridge, MA: The Belknap Press of Harvard University Press, 2004.

"Diary and Letters of Rutherford B. Hayes." Rutherford B. Hayes Presidential Library and Museum Home, https://resources.ohiohistory.org/hayes.

Doyle, Arthur Conan. *The History of Spiritualism*, vol. I and II. N.p.: Adansonia, 1926.

Doyle, Michael. "Passionate Words: Rousing Rhetoric in the Ministers' Crusade against the Oneida Community." *April: Association for the Public Religion and Intellectual Life*, April 16, 2021, www.aprilonline.org/passionate-words.

Eastman, Hubbard. *Noyesism Unveiled: A History of the Sect Self-Styled Perfectionists: With a Summary View of Their Leading Doctrines*. Memphis: General Books, 2010.

Egerton, Douglas R. *The Wars of Reconstruction*. New York: Bloomsbury Press, 2014.

Eisenhower, John S. D. *Zachary Taylor: The 12th President, 1849–50*. New York: Times Book, 2008.

Emerson, Ralph Waldo. *Nature*. Boston: James Monroe and Company, 1849.

———. "Self-Reliance." *Essays*. Boston: James Monroe and Company, 1841.

———. *Lectures and Biographical Studies*, vol. 10 of *The Works of Ralph Waldo Emerson*. Boston: Houghton Mifflin, 1883.

Fogarty, Robert S., ed. *Desire and Duty at Oneida: Tirzah Miller's Intimate Memoir*. Bloomington: Indiana University Press, 2000.

———. "Oneida: A Utopian Search for Religious Security." *Labor History* 14, no. 2 (1973).

———, ed. *Special Love/Special Sex: An Oneida Community Diary*. Syracuse, NY: Syracuse University Press, 1994.

Fornell, Earl Wesley. *The Unhappy Medium: Spiritualism and the Life of Margaret Fox*. Austin: University of Texas Press, 1964.

Foster, Lawrence. *Religion and Sexuality: The Shakers, the Mormons, and the Oneida Community*. Urbana: University of Illinois Press, 1984.

Fuller, Corydon Eustathius. *Reminiscences of James A. Garfield: With Notes and Preliminary Collateral*. Cincinnati, OH: Standard Publishing, 1887.

Fuller, Margaret. *Memoirs of Margaret Fuller Ossoli*, vol. II. Boston: Phillips, Sampson: 1852.

———. *"These Sad but Glorious Days": Dispatches from Europe, 1846–1850*, ed. Larry J. Reynolds and Susan Belasco Smith. New Haven, CT: Yale University Press, 1991.

Gelderman, Carol. *A Free Man of Color and His Hotel*. Washington, D.C.: Potomac Books, 2012.

Gilmore, James Roberts. *Down in Tennessee, and Back by Way of Richmond*. New York: Carleton, 1864.

Goldsmith, Barbara. *Other Powers: The Age of Suffrage, Spiritualism, and the Scandalous Victoria Woodhull*. New York: Alfred A. Knopf, 1998.

Gornick, Vivian. "A Double Inheritance: On Margaret Fuller." *The Nation*, April 3, 2012.

Graham, Lawrence Otis. *The Senator and the Socialite: The True Story of America's First Black Dynasty*. New York: Harper Perennial, 2007.

Greeley, Horace. *Recollections of a Busy Life*. 1873; New York: Chelsea House, 1983.

Greenberger, Scott S. *The Unexpected President: The Life and Times of Chester Arthur*. New York: Da Capo Press, 2017.

Guarneri, Carl J. *The Utopian Alternative: Fourierism in Nineteenth-Century America*. Ithaca, NY: Cornell University Press, 1991.

Gunderson, Robert Gray. *The Log-Cabin Campaign*. Lexington: The University of Kentucky Press, 1957.

Habegger, Alfred. *The Father: A Life of Henry James, Sr.* New York: Farrar, Straus and Giroux, 1994.

Hale, William Harlan. *Horace Greeley: Voice of the People*. New York: Harper & Brothers, 1950.

———. "When Karl Marx Worked for Horace Greeley." *American Heritage* 8, no. 3 (April 1957).

Hall, A. Oakley. *Horace Greeley Decently Dissected*. New York: Ross & Tousey, 1862.

Handbook of the Oneida Community. Wallingford, CT: Office of the Circular, Wallingford Community, 1867.

Harris, Neil. *Humbug: The Art of P. T. Barnum*. Boston: Little, Brown, 1973.

Hawthorne, Nathaniel. *The Blithedale Romance*. Boston: Ticknor, Reed, and Fields, 1852.

Hayes, Henry G., Charles J. Hayes, Annie Dunmire, and Edmund A. Bailey. *A Complete History of the Life and Trial of Charles Julius Guiteau, Assassin of President Garfield*. Philadelphia: Hubbard Bros., 1882.

Hesseltine, William B. *Ulysses S. Grant, Politician*. New York: Dodd, Meade, 1935.

Higginson, Thomas Wentworth. *Margaret Fuller Ossoli*. New York: Chelsea House, 1981.

Holloway, Mark. *Heavens on Earth: Utopian Communities in America, 1680–1880*. New York: Dover, 1966.

Holzer, Harold, ed. *President Lincoln Assassinated!!: The Firsthand Story of the Murder, Manhunt, Trial, and Mourning*. New York: Literary Classics of the United States, 2014.

Hoogenboom, Ari. *Rutherford B. Hayes: Warrior and President*. Lawrence: University Press of Kansas, 1995.

Horner, Harlan Hoyt. *Lincoln and Greeley*. Champaign: University of Illinois Press, 1953.

How to See the New York Crystal Palace: Being a Concise Guide to the Principal Objects in the Exhibition as Remodeled, 1854. New York: G. P. Putnam, 1854.

Huxley, Aldous. *Adonis and the Alphabet*. London: Chatto & Windus, 1956.

Ingersoll, L. D. *The Life of Horace Greeley, Founder of the* New York Tribune. Chicago: Union Publishing, 1873.

James, Henry. *Henry James: Autobiography*, ed. Frederick Wilcox Dupee. 1983; Princeton, NJ: Princeton University Press, 2016.

Jennings, Chris. *Paradise Now: The Story of American Utopianism*. New York: Random House, 2016.

Johnson, Paul E., and Sean Wilentz. *The Kingdom of Matthias: A Story of Sex and Salvation in 19th-Century America*. New York: Oxford University Press, 1994.

Jordan, David M. *Roscoe Conkling of New York: Voice in the Senate*. Ithaca, NY: Cornell University Press, 1971.

Kephart, William M. "Experimental Family Organization: An Historico-Cultural Report on the Oneida Community." *Marriage and Family Living* 25, no. 3 (August 1963).

———, and William W. Zellner. *Extraordinary Groups: An Examination of Unconventional Life-Styles*. New York: St. Martin's Press, 1994.

Kern, Louis J. *An Ordered Love: Sex Roles and Sexuality in Victorian Utopias—the Shakers, the Mormons, and the Oneida Community*. Chapel Hill: University of North Carolina Press, 1981.

King, Gilbert. "The Stalking of the President." *Smithsonian Magazine*, January 17, 2012.

Klaw, Spencer. *Without Sin: The Life and Death of the Oneida Community*. New York: Penguin Books, 1993.

Knight, George R. *Millennial Fever and the End of the World*. Boise, ID: Pacific Press Publishing Association, 1993.

Kohl, Lawrence Frederick. *The Politics of Individualism: Parties and the American Character in the Jacksonian Era*. New York: Oxford University Press, 1989.

Landes, Richard. *Heaven on Earth: The Varieties of the Millennial Experience*. New York: Oxford University Press, 2011.

Leadon, Fran. *Broadway: A History of New York City in Thirteen Miles*. New York: W. W. Norton, 2018.

Lehman, Eric D. *Becoming Tom Thumb: Charles Stratton, P. T. Barnum, and the Dawn of American Celebrity*. Middletown, CT: Wesleyan University Press, 2013.

Linn, William Alexander. *Horace Greeley, Founder and Editor of the* New York Tribune. New York: D. Appleton and Company, 1903.

Lockwood, George. *The New Harmony Movement.* New York: D. Appleton, 1905.

Maihafer, Harry J. *The General and the Journalists: Ulysses S. Grant, Horace Greeley, and Charles Dana.* Washington: Brassey's, 1998.

Maizlish, Stephen E. "The Cholera Panic in Washington and the Compromise of 1850." *Washington History* 29, no. 1 (Spring 2017): 55–64.

Mandelker, Ira L. *Religion, Society, and Utopia in Nineteenth-Century America.* Amherst: The University of Massachusetts Press, 1984.

Marshall, Megan. *Margaret Fuller: A New American Life.* Boston: Houghton Mifflin Harcourt, 2013.

Martin, John H. "Saints, Sinners and Reformers: The Burned-Over District Re-Visited," Chapter 11: John Humphrey Noyes, *The Crooked Lake Review*, Fall 2005.

Miller, Adrian. *The President's Kitchen Cabinet: The Story of the African Americans Who Have Fed Our First Families, from the Washingtons to the Obamas.* Chapel Hill: University of North Carolina Press, 2017.

Morris, Roy, Jr. *Fraud of the Century: Rutherford B. Hayes, Samuel Tilden, and the Stolen Election of 1876.* New York: Simon & Schuster, 2003.

Morton, Ella. "The Story of Sam Patch, First Professional Waterfall Jumper." *Atlas Obscura*, June 7, 2016, https://www.atlasobscura.com/articles /sam-patch-the-great-waterfall-jumper-who-leapt-in-the-face-of-danger.

Murphy, Jan. *Mysteries and Legends of Colorado: True Stories of the Unsolved and Unexplained.* Helena, MT: Globe Pequot Press, 2007.

Murray, Meg McGavran. *Margaret Fuller: Wandering Pilgrim.* Athens: University of Georgia Press, 2008.

Nevins, Allan, and Milton Halsey Thomas, eds. *The Diary of George Templeton Strong.* Seattle: University of Washington Press, 1952.

Nissenbaum, Stephen. *Sex, Diet, and Debility in Jacksonian America: Sylvester Graham and Health Reform.* Westport, CT: Praeger, 1980.

Nordhoff, Charles. *The Communistic Societies of the United States.* 1875; New York: Schocken Books, 1965.

Northrop, Henry Davenport. *Life and Public Services of James G. Blaine, the Plumed Knight.* Richmond, VA: M. A. Winter, 1893.

Norton, Charles Eliot, ed. *The Correspondence of Thomas Carlyle and Ralph Waldo Emerson, 1834–1872*, vol. I. Boston: James R. Osgood, 1883.

Noyes, Corinna Ackley. *The Days of My Youth: A Childhood Memoir of Life in the Oneida Community.* 1960; Clinton, NY: Richard W. Couper Press, 2011.

Noyes, George Wallingford. *Free Love in Utopia: John Humphrey Noyes and the Origin of the Oneida Community.* Urbana: University of Illinois Press, 2001.

———. *Religious Experience of John Humphrey Noyes, Founder of the Oneida Community*, ed. Lawrence Foster. New York: Macmillan, 1923.

Noyes, John Humphrey. *Dixon and His Copyists: A Criticism of the Accounts of the Oneida Community in "New America," "Spiritual Wives" and Kindred Publications.* Oneida, NY: Oneida Community, 1871.

———. *Guiteau vs. Oneida Community.* 1882; Farmington Hills, MI: Gale, Making of Modern Law, 2012.

———. *History of American Socialisms.* 1870; New York: Hillary House, 1961.

———. *Male Continence.* New York: Gordon Press, 1975.

Noyes, Pierrepont. *My Father's House: An Oneida Boyhood.* 1937; Gloucester, MA: Holt, Rhinehart and Winston, 1966.

Odlum, Catherine. *The Life and Adventures of Prof. Robert Emmet Odlum.* Washington, D.C.: Gray and Clarkson Printers, 1885.

"Official Report of the Microscopical Examination of the Brain of Charles J. Guiteau." *The Medical News* 41 (September 9, 1882).

Olcott, Henry S. *People from the Other World.* Hartford, CT: American Publishing, 1875.

Packer, Barbara L. *The Transcendentalists.* Athens: University of Georgia Press, 2007.

Parker, Robert Allerton. *A Yankee Saint: John Humphrey Noyes and the Oneida Community.* New York: G. P. Putnam's Sons, 1935.

Parton, James. *The Life of Horace Greeley, Editor of The New York Tribune.* New York: Mason Brothers, 1855.

Parton, James. *The Life of Horace Greeley, Editor of "The New-York Tribune."* Boston: James R. Osgood, 1872.

Patler, Nicholas. "A Black Vice President in the Gilded Age? Senator Blanche Kelso Bruce and the National Republican Convention of 1880." *The Journal of Mississippi History* LXXI, no. 2 (2009): 105–38.

Peskin, Allan. *Garfield.* Kent, OH: Kent State University Press, 1978.

Pyle, G. F. "The Diffusion of Cholera in the United States in the Nineteenth Century." *Geographical Analysis* 1, no. 1 (1969): 59–75.

Reavis, L. U. *A Representative Life of Horace Greeley.* 1872; New York: G. W. Carleton, 2007.

Reeves, Thomas C. *Gentleman Boss: The Life and Times of Chester Alan Arthur.* 1975; Newtown, CT: American Political Biography Press, 1991.

A Report of the Mysterious Noises Heard in the House of Mr. John D. Fox, in Hydesville, Arcadia, Wayne County, N.Y., Authenticated by the Certificates, and Confirmed by the Statements of the Citizens of That Place and Vicinity. Canandaigua, NY: E. E. Lewis, 1848.

Report of the Proceedings in the Case of the United States vs. Charles J. Guiteau, Tried in the Supreme Court of the District of Columbia, Holding a Criminal Term, and Beginning November 14, 1881, 3 vols. Washington, D.C.: Government Printing Office, 1882.

Reynolds, David S. *Waking Giant: America in the Age of Jackson*. New York: HarperCollins, 2008.

Richardson, Robert D., Jr. *Emerson: The Mind on Fire*. Berkeley: University of California Press, 1995.

Ridpath, John Clark. *The Life and Work of James A. Garfield, Twentieth President of the United States*. Cincinnati, OH: Jones Brothers, 1881.

———. *The Life and Work of James G. Blaine*. Philadelphia: Historical Publishing Company, 1893.

Roach, Monique Patenaude. "The Loss of Religious Allegiance among the Youth of the Oneida Community," *The Historian* 63, no. 4 (Summer 2001): 787–806.

Robertson, Constance Noyes. *Oneida Community: An Autobiography, 1851–1876*. Syracuse, NY: Oneida Community Mansion House/Syracuse University Press, 1970.

———. *Oneida Community Profiles*. Syracuse, NY: Syracuse University Press, 1977.

———. *Oneida Community: The Breakup, 1876–1881*. Syracuse, NY: Syracuse University Press, 1972.

Rolde, Neil. *Continental Liar from the State of Maine: James G. Blaine*. Gardiner, ME: Tilbury House, 2007.

Root, Harvey W. *The Unknown Barnum*. New York: Harper & Brothers, 1927.

Rosenberg, Charles E. *The Trial of the Assassin Guiteau*. Chicago: The University of Chicago Press, 1968.

Ross, Ishbel. *Proud Kate: Portrait of an Ambitious Woman*. New York: Harper & Brothers, 1953.

Sarmiento, F. L. *Life of Pauline Cushman: The Celebrated Union Spy and Scout*. Philadelphia: John Potter, 1865.

Saxon, A. H. *P. T. Barnum: The Legend and the Man*. New York: Columbia University Press, 1989.

———, ed. *Selected Letters of P. T. Barnum*. New York: Columbia University Press, 1983.

Schudson, Michael. *Discovering the News: A Social History of American Newspapers*. New York: Basic Books, 1967.

Seitz, Don C. *Horace Greeley, Founder of* The New York Tribune. 1926; New York: AMS Press, 1970.

Shafer, Ronald G. *The Carnival Campaign: How the Rollicking 1840 Campaign of "Tippecanoe and Tyler Too" Changed Presidential Elections Forever*. Chicago: Chicago Review Press, 2016.

Shain, Barry Alan. *The Myth of American Individualism*. Princeton, NJ: Princeton University Press, 1994.

Shaw, John, ed. *Crete and James: Personal Letters of Lucretia and James Garfield*. East Lansing: Michigan State University Press, 1994.

Shusko, Christa. "Criticising the Dead: Spiritualism and the Oneida Community." In *Handbook of Spiritualism and Channeling*, ed. Cathy Gutierrez. Lake Forest, IL: Brill, 2015.

Slater, Abby. *In Search of Margaret Fuller: A Biography*. New York: Delacorte Press, 1978.

Smith, Jean Edward. *Grant*. New York: Simon & Schuster, 2002.

Smith, Theodore Clarke. *The Life and Letters of James Abram Garfield, Vol. I*. New Haven, CT: Yale University, 1925.

Snay, Mitchell. *Horace Greeley and the Politics of Reform in Nineteenth-Century America*. Lanham, MD: Rowman & Littlefield, 2011.

Sphrintzen, Adam D. *The Vegetarian Crusade: The Rise of an American Reform Movement, 1817–1921*. Chapel Hill: University of North Carolina Press, 2013.

Stoehr, Taylor. *Free Love in America*. New York: AMS Press, Inc., 1979.

Summer, Mark Wahlgren. *The Press Gang: Newspapers and Politics, 1865–1878*. Chapel Hill: University of North Carolina Press, 1994.

Swift, Lindsay. *Brook Farm: Its Members, Scholars, and Visitors*, vol. 3. New York: Macmillan, 1900.

The American Heritage History of the Presidency. New York: American Heritage, 1968.

The Jackson Health Resort: Health for All. 1916; Geneseo, NY: Genesee Valley Historical Reprints series, 2021.

Thomas, Heather. "The Last Leap of Sam Patch." The Library of Congress (blog), October 2, 2018, https://blogs.loc.gov/headlinesandheroes/2018/10/the-last-leap-of-sam-patch.

Thomas, Robert David. *The Man Who Would Be Perfect: John Humphrey Noyes and the Utopian Impulse*. Philadelphia: University of Pennsylvania Press, 1977.

Thurman, Judith. "The Desires of Margaret Fuller." *The New Yorker*, April 1, 2013.

Trefousse, Hans L. *Andrew Johnson: A Biography*. New York: W. W. Norton, 1989.

———. *Rutherford B. Hayes: The 19th President, 1877–1881*. New York: Times Books, 2002.

Tuchinsky, Adam. *Horace Greeley's New York Tribune: Civil War–Era Socialism and the Crisis of Free Labor*. Ithaca, NY: Cornell University Press, 2009.

Uchill, Ida Libert. *Howdy, Sucker!: What P. T. Barnum Did in Colorado*. Denver: Pioneer Peddler Press, 2001.

Van Deusen, Glyndon G. *Horace Greeley: Nineteenth-Century Crusader*. Philadelphia: University of Pennsylvania Press, 1953.

Vermilya, Daniel J. *James Garfield and the Civil War: For Ohio and the Union*. Charleston, SC: History Press, 2015.

Villard, Henry. *Memoirs of Henry Villard, Journalist and Financier, 1835–1900*, vol. II. New York: Houghton, Mifflin, 1904.

Von Mehren, Joan. *Minerva and the Muse: A Life of Margaret Fuller*. Amherst: University of Massachusetts Press, 1994.

Von Zeigesar, Peter. "Reinventing Sex." *Lapham's Quarterly*, vol. IX, no. 4 (fall 2016), https://www.laphamsquarterly.org/flesh/reinventing-sex.

Wallace, Irving. *The Fabulous Showman: The Life and Times of P. T. Barnum*. New York: Alfred A. Knopf, 1959.

Wayland-Smith, Ellen. *Oneida: From Free Love Utopia to the Well-Set Table*. New York: Picador, 2016.

Weisberg, Barbara. *Talking to the Dead: Kate and Maggie Fox and the Rise of Spiritualism*. San Francisco: Harper San Francisco, 2004.

Werner, M. R. *Barnum*. New York: Harcourt, Brace, 1923.

White, William Allen. "Platt." *McClure's Magazine*, December 1901.

Whorton, James. "The Solitary Vice." *Western Journal of Medicine*, 175, no. 1 (July 2001).

Williams, Frederick D., ed. *The Wild Life of the Army: Civil War Letters of James Garfield*. East Lansing: Michigan State University Press, 1964.

Williams, Robert C. *Horace Greeley: Champion of American Freedom*. New York: New York University Press, 2006.

Wilson, James Harrison. *The Life of Charles A. Dana*. New York: Harper & Brothers, 1907.

Wilson, Robert. *Barnum: An American Life*. New York: Simon & Schuster, 2019.

ACKNOWLEDGMENTS

During the more than twelve years that I spent researching and writing this book, I have been profoundly grateful to so many. I owe deep thanks to Professor Barbara Loomis, who first introduced me to the extraordinary story of the Oneida Community. Carole Bidnick encouraged my efforts from the start and graciously introduced me to Caroline Pincus, whose guidance was hugely helpful, and to my wonderful literary agent, Jacqueline Flynn of Joelle Delbourgo Associates Literary Agency.

I am extraordinarily grateful to the talented team at Pegasus Books, including Claiborne Hancock, Jessica Case, Victoria Wenzel, Maria Fernandez, Julia Romero, and Meghan Jusczak. Archivists and staff were unfailingly helpful on my visits to Syracuse University's Special Collections, the Oneida Community Mansion House, and the Manuscript Reading Room in the Library of Congress.

I owe special thanks to Georgia Montgomery, who generously read chapters as I wrote them, and to many friends and loved ones for their support over the last dozen years, including Nancy Padian, Kevin Padian, Gail Arnold, Liz Perle, Jude Lange, Joan O'Connor, Regina Marler, Robin Wolaner, Deborah Kirk, Richard Kay, Dave Bon, Parie Bon, Justine Bon, Martin Glickfeld, Allan Carlin, Diane

ACKNOWLEDGMENTS

Carlin, Susan Mackin, Jackie Cornell, Paul Cornell, Alanna Dittoe, Jack Dittoe, Lisa Monetta, David Monetta, Nick Hoppe, Linda Hoppe, Susanne Pari, Shahram Shirazi, Gail Jones, David Pettus, Craig Collins, Stephanie Collins, Jeanne Austrian, Bob Austrian, Jane Lindner, Sandy Gustafson, Jack Ripstein, Halsey Varady, Stuart Rosenberg, Toni Brayer, Lisa Sikes, David Sikes, Joy D'Ovidio, Gene D'Ovidio, Paula Sonenberg Bradman, Jesse Bradman, Patti Richards, Angie Byrd, Chip Mallari, Zeni Mallari, Jodi Brown Carter, Tim Carter, Debbie Fournier, Dudley Fournier, Carole Littleton, Vince Littleton, Leslie Jonath, Carolyn Baker, Jason Ekaireb, Emma Rosenbush, Kirstin Niver, Dylan Smith, Bradley Rabkin Golden, Jane Norcross, Amy Wels, and Michael Udelson. And most of all, I am thankful for the tireless encouragement of my husband, David Hagerman; my daughters, Emily Zadeh and Casey Hagerman; and my son-in-law, Joseph Zadeh.

INDEX